Credit and Debt in Medieval England

Credit and Debt in Medieval England *c*.1180–*c*.1350

Edited by
P. R. Schofield and N. J. Mayhew

Oxbow Books

First published in the United Kingdom in 2002. Reprinted in 2016 by
OXBOW BOOKS
10 Hythe Bridge Street, Oxford OX1 2EW

and in the United States by
OXBOW BOOKS
1950 Lawrence Road, Havertown, PA 19083

Paperback Edition: ISBN 978-1-84217-073-1
Digital Edition: ISBN 978-1-78570-402-4 (ePub)

A CIP record for this book is available from the British Library

For a complete list of Oxbow titles, please contact:

UNITED KINGDOM
Oxbow Books
Telephone (01865) 241249, Fax (01865) 794449
Email: oxbow@oxbowbooks.com
www.oxbowbooks.com

UNITED STATES OF AMERICA
Oxbow Books
Telephone (800) 791-9354, Fax (610) 853-9146
Email: queries@casemateacademic.com
www.casemateacademic.com/oxbow

Oxbow Books is part of the Casemate Group

Front cover: Exchequer of receipt (E/401), Jewish rolls n. 87. Hilary Term 17 Henry III. This image, which depicts a man holding scales, is reproduced in V. D. Lipman, *The Jews of Medueval Norwich* (London 1967), figure 1, with notes on p. 313.

Contents

Acknowledgements

The conference, Credit and Debt in Medieval and Early Modern England, held at St Cross College, Oxford, 14 and 15 September 2000, and from which this volume arises, was funded by the Heberden Coin Room at the Ashmolean Museum, through the generosity of the Carl and Eileen Subak Family Foundation. The editors would like to thank the Foundation for the support which was essential to the success of the conference. We would also like to extend our thanks to all those who attended the conference. Particular thanks also go to Roz Britton-Strong for sterling work in the organisation and running of the conference and to the Fellows and staff of St Cross College for their hospitality. We are also very grateful to David Brown and Julie Choppin of Oxbow Books for the care and commitment they have shown to this work. Phillipp Schofield would also like to thank Chris Briggs who read drafts of the introduction and chapter 5 and offered invaluable comment.

The work of the editors has divided principally between the establishment of the conference and its subsequent organisation (Nick Mayhew) and the editing of the volume (Phillipp Schofield).

PRS
NJM
April 2002

List of Contributors

Paul Brand is a Senior Research Fellow at All Souls College, Oxford

Chris Briggs is a Research Fellow at Trinity College, Cambridge

Christopher McNall is a Lecturer at Cardiff Law School

Robin R. Mundill is Head of History at Glenalmond College, Perth

Pamela Nightingale is E.S.R.C. Research Fellow at the Heberden Coin Room, The Ashmolean Museum, University of Oxford

Phillipp R. Schofield is Lecturer in Medieval History at the Department of History and Welsh History, University of Wales, Aberystwyth.

List of Figures

List of Tables

Credit and debt in medieval England: Introduction

Phillipp R. Schofield

Four of the six papers in this volume were given at a conference on 'Credit and debt in medieval and early modern England', held at St Cross College, Oxford in September 2000. The other two papers, by Briggs and McNall, both draw on important recent postgraduate theses, elements of which both authors kindly agreed to include here. The conference at St Cross included papers which covered a much longer time period than that represented by this volume, the period covered stretching from the late-twelfth through to the late-eighteenth century. A striking feature of the papers delivered at the conference was the fracture of agenda between studies beginning either before or after 1500. Whereas early modernists used exploration of credit and debt, typically either through probate record or litigation, to examine broader issues, such as those of gender or life-cycle, medievalists at the conference were as or more concerned with the mechanics of debt, the legal process, and its economics.

A signficant further feature of the early modern discussion of credit and debt was its breadth of approach, the sense that the study of credit and debt which, after all, has a long tradition amongst early modernists, has moved away from close preoccupation with process, institutions, and forms and, instead, has provided early modernists with a sounding board against which to test some of the grand themes of early modern studies, most notably, in the work of Muldrew, community and the wider sense of 'credit'.[1] This breadth was revealed at the conference in the variety of approaches by early modernists, which used credit agreements and disputes over debt as points of access to studies that had at their core themes which were one or two degrees removed from the direct study of indebtedness or the exchange of credit.[2] In apparent contrast, the themes of the medievalists were more obviously and closely integrated, which appears to reflect the persistence or, perhaps, resurrection, of established approaches to the study of credit and debt in the middle ages and a continued/revived preoccupation with process and structure, evident, unsurprisingly, from the earliest investigations. Given this apparent integration of theme and approach, as well as the nascent/reborn stage of such initiatives, the organisers thought it would be worthwhile to publish the medieval papers in a single volume. That they reflect such common themes is surely a measure of their response to the available sources, the methodologies involved in their exploitation, and this earlier historiography which established approaches and continues to exert a real influence on current practitioners, encouraging them to refine and to build upon a rich heritage.

Medieval credit and debt: sources

The tripartite distinction, outlined by Postan almost seventy-five years ago, of sources exhibiting the potential to supply researchers with insights into the nature of credit transactions, broadly, registers, pleas and non-specific/miscellaneous, continues to provide a useful organising principle for historians.[3] For Postan, the principal class of records of debt, were, broadly speaking, the registers of debt. Here he included records of recognizances entered on the registers of various official institutions. Most important amongst these were the registries established by the statutes Acton Burnell and *de Mercatoribus*, and which are discussed more fully by McNall, Nightingale, and Mundill in this volume.[4] As McNall reminds us, these were not the only 'modes for the recognition of debt'. In addition to Postan's original list, which includes mention of the Letter Books of the City of London, the Exchequer Memoranda Rolls, the Chancery Close Rolls and the rolls of King's court, McNall adds pleas enrolled before the Steward and Marshal.[5] We can also add here the registers of debts owed to Jewish creditors. These are discussed in some detail by Mundill in his chapter in this volume and include, as well as the signally important record of the Exchequer of the Jews, local registers of debt, notably the Norwich day book of the mid-thirteenth century.[6]

In addition to the registers of debts there are the legal records. In describing this category, Postan placed particular emphasis on pleas of debt. In the context of his main theme, credit in medieval trade, he confined his attention to the sources most likely to reveal mercantile pleas, especially the petitions of debt enrolled at the Chancery and the pleas enrolled by municipal authorities, such as are recorded in the Plea and Memoranda Rolls for London. He acknowledged also the potential, as then largely untapped, of the plea rolls (King's Bench and, especially, Common Pleas) and of local courts, by which he must have meant, in particular, hundred, borough and manor courts.[7] Further to the pleas and their sources outlined by Postan, we might be tempted here also to consider other sub-categories of source which fit under the broad umbrella not of 'pleas' but of 'law'. The law-books of *Glanvill* and of *Bracton*, as Brand discusses in his chapter, have a great deal to say on matters of debt, as do, hardly surprisingly, the contemporary law reports, the year-books.[8] We might also want to include the relevant statutes and parliamentary rolls, sources which Postan reserved for this third, less specific category. Finally, we would also need to add the records generated by the church and by canon law. Not only the records of ecclesiastical courts, where debt pleas were tyically entered as instance actions in perjury (*fidei lesionis et periurii*), but also the writings of canon lawyers who, in discussing, *inter alia*, usury, shed much light on attitudes to credit and to debt, at least in so far it is discussed in the *Corpus iuris Canonici*.[9]

In his third and final category, Postan included those sources which, although they had much to say on credit and debt, had not originated 'in their recording, enforcement or adjudication'.[10] He included here the private archives, the inventories and accounts, the transactions of merchants, as well as parliamentary rolls and statutes. Again, we might want to add further definition to Postan's general categorisation, and not solely because, unlike Postan, our eye is directed to more than just mercantile credit. To remain within one part of the world of mercantile credit, there is an abundance of source associated with the wool trade and the purchase through credit of wool clips.

The accounts of monastic wool producers have much to say on credit transactions, as do the muniments of those, including the Italian purchasers, who extended credit to them.[11] Monastic chroniclers also pass occasional comment on credit transactons, especially those involving the sale of wool.[12] Furthermore, beyond the wool trade, industrial England in the middle ages employed extensive credit mechanisms and recorded associated transactions as is, for instance, evident in the case of the tin industry.[13]

Aside from trade and industry, aspects of everday life in high and late medieval England were conducted through and supported by the extension of credit and some, at least, of this business has left its own record. Rents and leases, recorded in account rolls and books, could add up year after year, the arrears serving as *de facto* credit agreements; the same could also be said of long series of purchases, unpaid for by the consumer until his or her death. As a consequence, wills and probates, especially evident from the fifteenth century, contain a great deal of information on debts, including, most obviously, the sizes of debts and the names of creditors and debtors. As well as sale credits, probate inventories also record direct loans of cash.[14]

In their dealings with lordship and government also, medieval men and women encountered the instruments of credit as well, of course, as the associated concepts. Taxation, especially purveyance, was dependent for its collection on credit instruments, notably the tally; tallies were also employed by estate administrators and used by reeves and bailiffs as security for their actions, effectively as receipts. Sales of grain or livestock *per talliam* were legitimated by the credit instrument; unsupported sales were not.[15] As a consequence, mention of credit and credit instruments appears in associated documents, including eyres and inquiries into inequitable levies of taxation, manorial and household account rolls, texts on estate-management, as well as political songs and poems.[16]

Medieval credit and debt: Historiography

This wealth of material on credit and indebtedness has already been exploited in significant ways by historians. Whilst research into credit and debt in recent years has looked to employ evidence for either the extension of credit or indebtedness as an index of economic change, a point to which we will return later in this introduction, medieval historians, both current and past practitioners, have examined these issues for other reasons. In particular, they have sought to describe the institutions of credit and the manner in which credit was extended. Closely associated with this first research agenda is the second, the exploration of the law of credit and of indebtedness, the development of law, modes of proof, forms of recovery, and so on. Beyond the examination of the institutional nature of credit and debt lies discussion of creditors and debtors themselves: who borrows, who lends, and in what circumstances. Finally, and clearly less developed amongst medieval researchers in recent years than amongst their early modern counterparts, there is discussion of credit and debt as social indices, informants not solely of economic change but of shifts within social networks and communities. In following each of these strands within the historiography, it is immediately evident that historical discussion of credit and debt in recent years has been less a novel departure than a continuation, albeit sometimes a tacit one, of earlier investigations.

Credit and debt: law, forms and institutions

Despite, as Brand points out in his chapter on common law debt in this volume, the tendency for legal historians to offer general overviews of the law of debt more than closer temporal studies, some of the most significant work on credit and debt has emerged in the commentaries of legal historians, where discussion of the developing aspects of the law of debt in the middle ages has provided an important stimulus to socio-economic investigations of the high and late middle ages. Some of this early legal discussion concerning credit and debt is revealed simply in the publication with scholarly commentary of relevant court and register material. From the late nineteenth century, series of local and national record societies included court records which contain debt cases. Maitland's Selden Society volume of selected manorial court pleas, to refer to a particularly famous example, contains both transcriptions of pleas in debt as well as some commentary upon them.[17] Numerous editions of, *inter alia*, borough court rolls, county rolls, and manorial court rolls also include detailed pleas of debt and some limited editorial comment.[18] In terms of mercantile debt, some of the most extensive commentary has been offered by editors of the staple court books and statute merchant rolls of the fourteenth and fifteenth centuries; there is also discussion in the edition of the Memoranda Rolls.[19] As is the case with editions of national and local court records, the publication of church court material has also encouraged some comment on debt cases in this particular context.[20]

The variety of the source material is indicative of the various contexts in which legal historians have been able to approach aspects of the law of debt and of contracts. As has often been noted, medieval law did not develop at a uniform pace but responded to circumstance and to expectation.[21] The considerable variety of medieval courts offered a range of remedies which were chiefly tailored to meet the requirements of their clientele. There is, therefore, some distinction to be drawn between the processes of common law, revealed through the central and provincial courts of the king, and the law of more local courts which was specifically honed to meet the needs of certain interest groups, most obviously, the merchants. In the most general terms, however, legal historians have divided their discussion according to the legal processes associated with the creation and action upon contracts.[22] They have described the creation of the contract, the extension of credit according to agreed terms, and they have examined the ways in which the contract was formed and the security attached to its formation.[23] They have also explored the ways in which the contract could be enforced and the methods available to the parties either, in the case of the plaintiff, to recover the debt or, in the case of the defendant, to effect a full and secure repayment. Legal historians have also interested themselves in matters ancillary or additional to the essential contract between the parties: could, for instance, the debt be assigned and how could recovery be effected against a third party?[24] What interest was permissible on a debt and how could it be recovered by a plaintiff?

These preoccupations of legal historians have directed the research agendas and interests of economic and social historians, the early foundations and framework dominating, to a fair degree, subsequent reflections on the subject. Beyond a programme of publication of sources and associated commentary, historians, legal as well as social and economic, have also engaged directly with the law of debt and its related aspects. Thus, early general discussions of the medieval economy include, as well as consideration of the identity and role of creditors and debtors, some account of the instruments of credit and the formation of credit agreements. Cunningham, for example, makes some comment on the development of more sophisticated mechanisms for the registration of debt from the late thirteenth century, referring to the Edwardian statutes, *Acton Burnell* (1283) and *Merchants* (1285).[25] Hilary Jenkinson also offered precise and effective description and discussion of instruments of credit, especially of the tally.[26] Most importantly, M. M. Postan, in 1930, developed the discussion of the instruments of credit and posited a sophistication in the creation and transfer of private financial instruments of which his predecessors, notably Cunningham, had been insufficiently aware.[27] Postan, in debunking the assertions of an earlier generation of historians, described developments in the form of credit in the late fourteenth and fifteenth century and provided a valuable overview of financial instruments for the period, and one that has not been superceded.

Postan's work on the instruments of mercantile credit and debt formation has limited parallels in other research on medieval credit. Local trade conducted in borough courts produced its own modes of proof, some of which could ape the bonds or recognizances made under statute. But here, as was less likely in the world of long-distance trade and high finance, contracts could be protected by less formal and ultimately less secure devices. Oral contracts, witnessed by third parties and symbolised by the transfer of earnest money, for instance, have been noted and discussed by historians. In particular, there is an extensive literature on compurgation, its employment and its social setting.[28] Other proofs deemed to lack the force of specialties, such as the tally, have also been described, *en passant*, and the same is true of the enrolled recognizance in local and private courts.[29] More evidently, historians of towns, trade and merchants have followed Postan's early lead and it is in their work that the most sophisticated treatments of credit formation and credit instruments are to be found. It goes without saying, of course, that their fully articulated discussions of credit are the product of the sources that they employ, not least of which are the detailed enrollments of debts according to statute merchant and statute staple.[30]

An awareness of the relationship between credit and its concomitant security is evident in work on other certain aspects of the medieval economy. The extension of credit on future supplies of wool, supported by a bond, has been described in a number of discussions of monastic estate organisation.[31] Similarly, discussion of land held as a gage or beneficial lease has necessarily been couched in terms of credit agreements. Richardson's description of the securities in land extended to Jewish creditors is one such treatment of this issue; Bean also describes the mortgaging of land by the Earls of Northumberland in the mid-fifteenth century to meet debts arising from the demands of estate management.[32] Whilst historians of high status land sales and leases have been long aware of the latent effects of credit in the land market, as, for example, in their analysis of the purchase of encumbered estates by wealthier buyers in the twelfth century,[33] historians of the land market in other social contexts, especially the peasant land market, have, generally, been less aware of the potential underpinning of debt and credit relationships. As Hyams has argued, an awareness of the importance of loans as a vital element of the market in land, inevitably modifies our view of that market.[34] Instead of being simply a means of exchanging plots of land according to need, evidence of an aggressive employment of credit gives the impression that the *inter-vivos* transfer of small plots was a more truly commercial market than has always been allowed.[35] To date, however, most investigations of the inter-peasant lease market in late medieval England have overlooked the possibility of gages and, instead, have tended to see the lease as a temporary expedient intended to adjust the size of the holding.[36]

Whilst a good deal of historical attention has focussed, especially in a more recent historiography, on the employment of court records as sources for credit/creditors and debt/debtors, there is also a long-standing and persistent interest in the process of debt and associated cases in local courts. There is also a literature devoted to consideration of credit mechanisms and the recovery of debt, especially in local courts. In some cases, social and economic historians have attempted thorough studies of inter-personal litigation, including investigations of debt litigation. They have also offered descriptions of the initiation and process of pleas. Kowaleski's investigation of borough court and common plea debts relating to Exeter offers one especially detailed recent example of an examination of the processes of credit extension and debt recovery and the legal mechanisms which facilitated both acts.[37] Amongst recent commentators on medieval credit and debt, historians of the manor court have also made important contributions to discussion of process and development in pleas.[38] Finally, a few attempts have also been made to explore in any detail the background to debt litigation and to employ debt litigation alongside other material in order to explore such issues as the use and understanding of law, and the creation of social and cultural norms.[39]

Not infrequently, however, discussion of the process of the litigation has been secondary to the analysis of the debt material. It is not always easy, in such cases, to identify the stages of the legal process; evidence of litigation, at whatever stage of the process, tends to be employed as an index of social or economic change.[40] Further, since economic and social historians have been less eager to engage with the processes of litigation than they have to describe the quantity and frequency of debt pleas, there has been relatively little direct commentary on the processes of debt recovery. For the most part, close description in this respect has remained the realm of legal historians.[41]

Where, however, developments in the law of debt and in contractual dealings have had significant implications for economic analyses, then historians have given them serious, if not always sustained, attention. The assignment of debt in mercantile exchanges is one example. To cite the most obvious example, Postan, in his discussion of private financial instruments, divided his discussion between a description of the obligation, a consideration of the assignability of the obligation, and, finally, a further description of the bill of exchange. He suggests that those jurisdictions which came into contact with mercantile credit on a regular basis were inclined to avoid hard and fast rulings in favour of business efficacy and, in any respect, the common law had little or no contact with bills of exchange. Common law did, however, have a good deal to say about bonds and their assignability, and, as Postan acknowledged, the attitude of common lawyers was less than friendly.[42]

There have also been discussions of statute law and its consequences for the extension of credit in the middle ages.[43] The Statutes of *Acton Burnell* (1283) and *de Mercatoribus* (1285), both of which enhanced the mechanisms for the recording and recovery of mercantile debt, have been the subject of no little legal discussion. In particular, Plucknett has offered detailed commentary on the relationship between the recovery of debt and landholding in the context of Edwardian legislation in the late thirteenth and early fourteenth centuries.[44] However, as McNall reminds us in this volume, the material associated with this legislation has hardly been overused; both he and Nightingale explore approaches in their contributons here while McNall offers some additional insight regarding form and development in debt registration.[45] The consequences of governmental pronouncement on credit and indebtedness, especially mercantile debt, have also been examined for later in the middle ages. Most obviously, the Ordinances of Bullion and Partition (1429–30), by attempting to restrict a wool trade conducted through credit, had significant ramifications for North Sea trade and for the movement of capital.[46]

Further matters relevant to law and credit transactions are also to be found in the territory shared between common law and canon law. Most especially, historical discussion of interest-bearing contracts has touched on both sides of the secular-spiritual divide. Secular issues, such as business efficacy and damages arising from breach of contract, have their spiritual counterweights in usurious contracts and the necessity of distinguishing between legitimate and illegitimate dealings. Mercantile credit transactions and the interest arising have been the subject of considerable historical attention. The extent to which agreed interest was attached to credit agreements has been a central theme of historical discussions of, for instance, international trade in the middle ages.[47] Power's detailed discussion of interest on wool sales, cloaked under exchange rates or the term of the loan, is an early attempt to characterise interest-bearing transactions amongst merchant traders.[48] In the records of church courts, historians have also found much to say on the subject of debt. There is, as is well known, plenty of indication that pleas of debt were heard in church courts.[49] Helmholz, in particular, has discussed links between church court and common law debt and contract, and the jurisdictional limits of debt cases relating both to usury and to testamentary dispositions.[50]

In considering the historiography of developments in the record and process of credit and debt, we also need to mention commentary, including that of Rigg in the early years of the last century, upon the establishment and refinement of Jewish registers of debt, notably the Exchequer of the Jews, as well as description and discussion of the establishment of *archae* from the close of the twelfth century and the regulation of bonds and starrs by Jewish and Christian chirographers. Mundill makes some return to this topic in his chapter and describes the early development of institutions that would, within a century, come to be mirrored and quickly replaced by their Christian equivalents.[51]

Creditors/credit and debtors/debts

Aside from observations directly pertinent to the history of the legal developments of indebtedness and the extension of credit, research within and beyond legal records has also encouraged observation of the size and frequency of credit agreements, the extent to which these dominated exchanges and the variety of social and economic levels at which they operated. Credit in the medieval countryside has been discussed both in terms of piecemeal and everyday exchange but also in terms of larger individual agreements.[52] There is also some historical discussion of credit between countryside and town, principally in the context of urban-based creditors and rural debtors.[53] By comparison, rather more historical endeavour has been directed at the extent of credit in medieval trade and also amongst the social, economic and political elites. The size and frequency of credit arrangements have particular resonance in discussions of loans to and otherwise involving royalty, nobility and the church in this period. The sheer scale of some loans, such as the repeated loans to Henry III by his brother, Richard earl of Cornwall or the large sums, amounting to £120,000, lent by Italian bankers in the first decade of the fourteenth century, and the implications for the autonomy of, above all, royal government, have, not unsurprisingly, attracted the attention of political historians as much as or more than they have social and economic historians.[54] That said, the workings of governmental loans in this period, especially the close association of lenders to the crown with woollen exports and the developing system of customs, have also been matters of study, principally by those who have sought to describe the history of the medieval trade in wool.[55] Whilst the immediacy of the relationship between high politics and credit linked to international trade has certainly not been lost on social and economic historians, their own particular intention has been to describe the extent and nature of the discernible credit arrangements, often with a view to illustrating their sophistication and pervasiveness.[56]

The range of sources has also permitted historians to attempt identification and categorisation of creditors and debtors. At various points in the development of English medieval historiography, the focus, in shifting from one social or political group to another, has also revealed different credit relationships and, hence, very different creditors and debtors. A late ninteenth-century emphasis on high politics and constitutional development, persistent in muted form throughout the last century, has found room for discussion of the major creditors and debtors of the realm. In so far as, for instance, the great Italian merchants or the wealthier denizens, through their financial relations with the Crown, provided a challenge to the controlling authority of the community of the realm and an emergent Commons, discussion of loans and their constitutional importance has remained central to the debates of political historians.[57] This has encouraged historians to explore the identity and aspirations of both lenders and borrowers. Investigations of alien merchants, especially Italians such as the Frescobaldi, the Peruzzi, and the Bardi, of the great native wool merchants of the fourteenth century, of the leading figures of church and state, and of the Jewish financiers of the late twelfth and thirteenth centuries, have shed a good deal of light on their methods and the context in which they operated.[58] The consequences of their lending for borrowers, of which more below, but also for themselves has also been described, especially the disastrous extensions of capital to the English crown which brought ruin to some of the great merchant lenders of the late thirteenth and early fourteenth centuries.[59] It has also revealed the opportunities which financiers offered to other investors, the latter supporting the former with capital in return for the resultant benefits of banking and the ease of transfer of their resources.[60] It is not, however, only the great lenders that have come under scrutiny through this route; political historians have, for example, also identified relatively minor lenders as central to the aspirations of the Crown.[61] Beyond these lenders, amongst which were counted the county gentry and some villagers, there was a still greater number of indirect lenders, the tax-payers, especially those payers of lay subsidies levied, at least in part, to meet the demands of the Crown's creditors.[62] Tax paid was, after all, not a gift but a loan with the expectation of future benefits, preferably with returned interest.

As well as the lenders within the world of high politics there were, of course, the borrowers. Principal amongst these was the Crown. That the Crown sought financial support through forced and unforced loans during the middle ages is, as already noted, a central plank of political and constitutional historiography. The extent to which loans to the Crown effected opportunities for royal spending and royal policy, and weakened the position of other powerful influences has been examined in a variety of particular circumstances. The borrowings of other significant political figures has also been noted by a number of historians, their use of creditors explored in the context of their political circumstance. For instance, Aymer de Valence, earl of Pembroke was obliged to raise crippling loans to meet a ransom payment of £10, 400, the result of his capture in France in 1317. Valence turned to the king, Italian lenders and other magnates in order to gather the funds; though he managed to repay substantial amounts of this money, it left him ruined and had the added consequence that he was left owing wages to his own retainers.[63]

Beneath the elevated plane of high politics and international finance, lurk huge numbers of credit and debt transactions. Some of these, the transactions and those who conducted them, moved between social and economic worlds, merchants and traders, clerics and Jews, extending and receiving credit to and from their social superiors, equals and inferiors. Again, research into the changing financial role of Jews in twelfth- and thirteenth-century England has been especially revealing of the social and economic fluidity of the debtors of particular groups of creditors. Mundill addresses this theme in his chapter in this volume, describing the lack of social and economic standing of Jewish debtors in the final quarter of the thirteenth century, a situation which was in marked contrast to that pertaining in the previous century.[64] Mundill revisits here, as well as in his own earlier work, issues discussed by a number of historians of Jewish creditors and their debtors.[65] The altered experience of Jewish creditors, the product of governmental intervention as Mundill describes below, has also been used as an explanation for the changing opportunities presented to other creditors, especially alien and denizen merchants.[66]

The discussion of the extension of credit between various social, economic, national, and religious sectors has also manifested itself in other areas of historical enquiry. The identification of those individuals or groups with surplus capital has proceeded beyond the more obvious categories of Jews, merchants and wealthy landowners. Minor clerics, prosperous peasants, local officers and petty administrators, and smaller landlords had, it is recognised, the potential to act as lenders of money and other resources.[67] Whilst calling, office and business acumen could furnish an individual with surplus capital, so also could life-cycle and the accidents of birth and death. Widows, in particular, may have enjoyed the advantages of excess capital which they could redistribute to their own advantage but the same might also apply to single heirs.[68]

Further to this, in the strict and limited sense that credit is generally applied, creditors become men and women who extend credit from a position of relative advantage. It is clear that to chose to identify creditors and debtors according to a single criteria, typically economic strength, creates its own problems of interpretation. Of course, the meanest peasant could be a creditor to a wealthier debtor in that he or she might be owed, for example, wages or simply a good turn. That they were in the credit of another is also reflected in the medieval sources, where we find that, for instance, servants do bring pleas against masters for arrears and communities demand what they are due.[69] Whilst the studies that follow do not, for the greater part, attempt to engage with these wider and, perhaps, more nuanced categorisations of credit and debt, they do offer firm foundation for such future study.

Credit, debt and society

The social value and the social cost of credit have also been given some attention by medieval historians. In certain measure aspects of this particular work have a developed historiography whilst in other respects they remain a relatively novel departure. Thus research into usury and the social consequences of excessive interest is well-established. Some of its roots are to be found in studies of the Jews and their role as money-lenders, others in the appropriation of Jewish lending techniques by Christians. While historians have identified the social and religious obloquy directed at usurious contracts and those who created them, they have also been mindful of ways in which lay and religious society sought a solution between moral stricture and everyday living.[70] Attempts by canonists to rationalise the need for interest-bearing contracts and to accommodate that need within appropriate norms of secular and religious life evidence this social concern.[71] In turn, that altering attitude to commercial transactions, their appropriateness and their limits, has fuelled discussion of the changing nature of medieval economy and society. Rosenwein and Little's discussion of the social salve that was mendicant teaching in this area has found elaboration and extension in later studies.[72]

Historians have also discussed the deleterious and socially divisive consequences of the extension of credit in other contexts. The combination of moral indignation, an absorption of Christian teaching on usury, and the everyday experience of disadvantageous credit arrangements, prompted distrust and opposition to certain forms of credit arrangment, as Maddicott's discussion of purveyance has shown.[73] That social and moral distaste is revealed especially in contemporary literature where 'creaunce' generally gets a particularly bad press, and 'dette' draws the 'communes...to the devyll'.[74] It is also revealed in attitudes to credit arrangements and those who extend credit to the loss of others. Local courts contain plentiful references to a variety of modes of opposition levelled at creditors. These include counter-claims in litigation but also the collective stirrings of a subaltern culture which, by employing the weapons of gossip, defamation and small-scale physical acts of resistance against the creditor, look to have reinforced moral norms. Medieval historians, here following the lead of early modernists, have, in recent years, begun to extract and to discuss this type of material from their sources.[75] Contemporary concern over aspects of credit and indebtedness is also revealed in hostility to the wealthiest creditors, especially those lending to the Crown, where the extension of loans offered direct challenge to the developing concept of government by counsel.[76]

Discussion of credit and indebtedness, as well as creditors and debtors, in this social context has tended to employ a fairly rigid economic and legal categorisation. This will clearly not satisfy all interpretations or scenarios. As the work of Muldrew has especially emphasised, 'credit' is extended from a variety of sources and achieved in a number of ways.[77] Late medievalists and early modernists have turned their attention, in recent years, to discussion of social capital and the extent to which individuals construct their own social credit within communities.[78] In her introduction to a collection of essays on credit and debt in the medieval and early modern countryside in Europe, Fontaine has also stressed the need to explore the wider implications of 'credit'.[79] Linked to this, there has been some work by medievalists aimed at illustrating the perceived social benefits of material credit, especially in times of particular need.[80] The social and economic benefits of capital within the manorial economy, for both tenants and lords, have also recently been investigated by Raftis.[81] The ambivalence with which credit relationships were perceived in the middle ages is also suggested by the employment of the language of business in other social contexts. Loans as metaphor, as social credit and debt gained and owed, is, for instance, briefly discussed by Kermode, who notes that Thomas Gra, a York merchant in the second half of the fourteenth century, referred in his will to 'the souls for which I am bound or am debtor'.[82]

In this treatment of credit and debt as social indices, medieval historians have shared agendas with early modernists, where work on the, widely construed, 'political' contextualisation of 'credit' and 'capital' has taken a central place in recent discussions.[83] If, however, we were to categorise in the most general terms recent work on credit and debt by medievalists we would tend to not think of socio-political commentaries.

Conclusion

The study of credit and indebtedness in medieval England has, in recent years, gained a certain momentum through the writings of historians whose main research agendas might best be described as 'economic'. Research on the extension of credit and its employment is especially evident in the work of historians of trade and of towns. Nightingale's work on the relationship between monetary contraction and mercantile credit helped foster a renewed interest in credit as an index of economic change, which is also evident in the work of Kermode.[84] While both Nightingale and Kermode concentrated their attention on the fifteenth century, others, notably historians of towns, have discussed credit in an urban context for earlier periods. Kowaleski's investigation of credit relationships in fourteenth-century Exeter and Britnell's similar and earlier analysis for fourteenth- and fifteenth-century Colchester were also pioneering attempts to employ borough court records to investigate fluctuations in the supply of credit and the extent of urban and mercantile indebtedness.[85] Mayhew also, in attempting thorough analyses of movements in money supply and domestic product in the middle ages, has had a good deal to say on the extension and withdrawal of credit, as well as the relationship between credit and money.[86] Alongside investigation of urban and mercantile credit there have been investigations of rural credit, especially the availability of credit and the extent of indebtedness amongst the peasantry.[87] This research into rural credit has also, at least in part, sought to consider fluctuations in credit markets.[88] A decade and more before urban and mercantile historians, as well as historians of the peasantry, had begun their explorations into credit and credit movements, historians of medieval industry, notably Hatcher in his work on the English tin industry and trade in the middle ages, had also mined seams rich in credit.[89]

In that sense, the study of credit and indebtedness in medieval society has looked to describe a dynamic, change in supply, and has also searched for explanations of that change. Fluctuating patterns of trade, governmental expectations, demographic and climatic shifts, the consequences of shifts in the money supply, have all been employed as causative agents in this respect. The sifting of exogenous and endogenous influences on fluctuations in the credit supply and of indebtedness continues, as the studies in the present volume illustrate. The chapters by McNall, Nightingale and Briggs, in particular, offer insight into changing opportunities for credit extension and for variation in levels of indebtedness. While not employing data series in the same way, Mundill and Schofield also explore ways in which the supply of credit could be controlled while Brand presents a view of development in the law of debt which should be highly germane to studies of long- and short-term shifts in the availability of credit. While each of the following chapters offers a particular view of credit and/or debt in the long thirteenth century, their partial messages cannot easily be disassociated one from the other. Credit and indebtedness in the countryside of the mid- to late-thirteenth century cannot be studied without some regard for external systems of credit, including Jewish urban financiers. Developments at common law had their echoes in local and private jurisdiction while the business dealings of merchants and urban traders had consequences for their rural counterparts. Fluctuations in international trade or shifts in the policies of the Crown also had the most fundamental and far-reaching implications for networks of credit. In the inter-connectedness of institutions, trade networks, demographic regimes, polities, lie challenges for future research into credit and debt in this period, and a closer understanding of shared conceptions of both credit and debt.

Notes

1 C. Muldrew, *The economy of obligation* (Basingstoke, 1998).

2 Early modern papers at the conference included studies of life-cycle indebtedness (C. Frances; M.

Overton and D. Dean), the relationship of the poor to the credit economy (C. Muldrew), women and credit (M. Hunt), credit in particular legal and institutional contexts (M. Finn; B. Lemire), and public and private credit at moments of crisis (J. Hoppit).

3 M. M. Postan, 'Credit in medieval trade', *Economic history review* 1 (1928), reprinted in Postan, *Medieval trade and finance* (from which subsequent references are taken), pp. 3–4.

4 See below, cc. 2–4.

5 Below, p. 69. Other Chancery rolls recorded debts arising in different contexts, see, for example, E. A. Bond, 'Extracts from the Liberate Rolls relative to loans', *Archaeologia* 1st ser., xxviii (1840).

6 Below, pp. 45–8. See also, *Select pleas, starrs and other records from the rolls of the Exchequer of the Jews A.D. 1220–1284*, ed. J. M. Rigg (Seldon Society, London, 1902; S. Levy, 'The Norwich Day-Book', *Transactions of the Jewish Historical Society of England* 5 (1902).

7 Postan, 'Credit in medieval trade', p. 3.

8 Below, pp. 22–33.

9 B. L. Woodcock, *Medieval ecclesiastical courts in the diocese of Canterbury* (Oxford, 1952), p. 89; T.P. McLaughlin, 'The teaching of the canonists on usury (XII, XIII, and XIV centuries)', *Medieval Studies* 1 (1939); R. H. Helmholz, 'Assumpsit and fidei laesio', *Law Quarterly Review* 91 (1976).

10 Postan, 'Credit in medieval trade', p. 3.

11 For example, E. B. Fryde, *Peasants and landlords in later medieval England* (Stroud, 1996), c. 6.

12 For example, *Chronica monasterii de Melsa*, ed. E. A Bond (Rolls series, 3 vols., 1866–68), iii, pp. 104, 144.

13 See, for instance, the source references in J. Hatcher, *The English tin industry and trade before 1550* (Oxford, 1973), pp. 51–9.

14 For one such early example, see *Court rolls of Walsham-le-Willows, 1303–1350*, ed. R. Lock (Suffolk Records Society, xli, 1998), p. 135; for similar references to debts in thirteenth- and fourteenth-century London and its environs, see *Calendar of wills proved and enrolled in the court of Husting, London. Part I. A.D. 1258–A.D. 1358*, ed. R. R. Sharpe (London, 1889), pp. 3, 170 and *passim.*

15 J. R. Maddicott, *The English peasantry and the demands of the crown, 1294–1341, Past and Present Supplement 1* (1975), repr. in T. H. Aston, ed., *Landlords, peasants and politics in medieval England* (Cambridge, 1987), pp. 296, 310 (from which this and subsequent references are taken); D. Oschinsky, *Walter of Henley and other treatises on estate management and accounting* (Oxford, 1971), pp. 222–4.

16 For examples of each: *A Lincolnshire Assize Roll for 1298 (P.R.O. Assize Roll No. 505)*, ed. W.S. Thomson (Lincolnshire Record Society, 36, 1944); *Manorial records of Cuxham, c. 1200–1349*, ed. P. D. A. Harvey (Oxfordshire Record Society, 50, 1976); Oschinsky, *Walter of Henley and other treatises*; I. S. T. Aspin, *Anglo-Norman Political Songs* (Anglo-Norman Text Society, 1953).

17 *Select pleas in manorial and other seignorial courts*, ed. F. W. Maitland (Selden Society, 2, 1888).

18 For county and manorial rolls, and editorial work associated with them, see also below, pp. 108–14, 117–19. See, also, for litigation in the borough court, M. Bateson, *Borough customs* (Selden Society, 21, 1906).

19 *The statute merchant roll of Coventry, 1392–1416*, ed. A. Beardwood (Dugdale Society, 17, 1939); *The staple court book of Bristol*, ed. E. E. Rich (Bristol Record Society, 5, 1934); *Calendar of plea and memoranda rolls, 1381–1412*, ed. A. H. Thomas (London, 1926); *Calendar of plea and memoranda rolls, 1413–1437*, ed. A. H. Thomas (London, 1943).

20 For example, *Select cases from the ecclesiastical courts of the province of Canterbury c. 1200–1301*, eds, N. Adams and Donahue jr (Selden Society, London, 1981).

21 A. Harding, *The law courts of medieval England* (London, 1973).

22 For early general discussion of common law developments, see Sir F. Pollock and F. W. Maitland, *The history of English law before the time of Edward I* (2 vols., Cambridge, 2nd ed., 1968), ii, pp. 203–216. See also, below, pp. 19–41.

23 See, for example, R. L. Henry, *Contracts in the local courts of medieval England* (London, 1926); R.C. Palmer, *The county courts of medieval England, 1150–1350* (Princeton, 1982); J.S. Beckerman, 'Procedural innovation and institutional change in medieval English manorial courts', *Law and History Review*, 10 (1992).

24 For instance, S. Bailey, 'Assignment of debts in England from the twelfth to the twentieth century. II', *Law Quarterly Review* 48 (1932).

25 W. Cunningham, *The growth of English industry and commerce during the early and middle ages* (Cambridge, 5th ed., 1910), p. 249; see also, E. Lipson, *An introduction to the economic history of England. I. The middle ages* (London, 1915), pp. 528–31; L. F. Salzman, *English trade in the middle ages* (Oxford, 1931), cc. 2, 9.

26 H. Jenkinson, 'Exchequer tallies' *Archaeologia* lxii (1911); *idem*, 'Medieval tallies, public and private', *Archaeologia* lxxiv (1925); for a recent contribution, see, for example, L. Kuchenbuch, 'Kerbhölzer in Alteuropa – Zwischen dorfschmiede und schatzamt' in B. Nagy and M. Sebök, eds, ...*The man of many devices who wandered full many ways.... Festschrift in Honor of János M. Bak* (Budapest, 1999), pp. 312–15.

27 M. M. Postan, 'Private financial instruments in medieval England', *Vierteljahrschrift fur Social- und Wirtschaftsgeschicte* xxiii (1930), reprinted in idem, *Medieval trade and finance* (Cambridge, 1973), from which subsequent references are taken.

28 See, for example, P. R. Schofield, 'Peasants and the manor court: gossip and litigation in a Suffolk village at the close of the thirteenth century', *Past and Present* 159 (1998), 35–6 and references threin.

29 *Manorial records of Cuxham*, ed. Harvey, p. 628 for an example of the latter.

30 For example, M. Kowaleski, *Local markets and regional trade in medieval Exeter* (Cambridge, 1995), pp. 212–3.

31 See, for instance, I. Kershaw, *Bolton Priory. The economy of a northern monastery, 1286–1325* (Oxford, 1973), p. 91; N. Denholm-Young, *Seignorial administration in England* (London, 1937), pp. 54–6; D.D. Knowles, *The religious orders in England. 3 vols* (Cambridge, 1956–9), i, p. 68.

32 H. G. Richardson, *The English Jewry under Angevin kings* (London, 1960), c. v; J. M. W. Bean, *The estates of the Percy family, 1416–1537* (Oxford, 1958), pp. 102–3.

33 Richardson, *English Jewry under Angevin kings*, pp. 91–2.

34 P. R. Hyams, 'The origins of a peasant land market in England', *Economic History Review*, xxiii (1970), 20; see also, M. Spufford, 'Peasant inheritance customs and land distribution in Cambridgeshire from the sixteenth to the eighteenth centuries', in J. Goody, J. Thirsk and E. P. Thompson, eds, *Family and Inheritance. Rural society in Western Europe, 1200–1800*, (Cambridge, 1976), pp. 162–3.

35 M. M. Postan, 'Medieval agrarian society in its prime: England', in M. M. Postan, ed., *The Cambridge Economic History of Europe, I, The Agrarian Life of the Middle Ages* (2nd ed., Cambridge, 1966), pp. 626–8.

36 Discussion of the land market has been heavily influenced by the work of M. M. Postan, in particular his application of the thesis of A.V. Chayanov that changes in family size created a market in short-term buying and selling of small parcles of land, intended to adjust the size of the family holding, [cf.] *The theory of peasant economy*, eds, D. Thorner, B. Kerblay, and R. E. F. Smith (Homewood, 1966); M. M. Postan, 'The charters of the villeins' in M. M. Postan, *Essays in medieval agriculture and general problems of the medieval economy* (Cambridge, 1973), pp. 114–7; see also, R. H. Hilton, *The English peasantry in the later middle ages* (Oxford, 1975), pp. 6–7; R. M. Smith, 'Some issues concerning families and their property in rural England 1250–1800' in *idem*, ed., *Land, kinship and life-cycle* (Cambridge, 1984), pp. 6–38; C. Dyer, 'Changes in the size of peasant holdings in some west midland villages, 1400–1540', *ibidem*, pp. 277–8; P. D. A. Harvey, 'Conclusion' in *idem*, ed., *The peasant land market in medieval England* (Oxford, 1984), pp. 349–53; Postan felt that mortgages were not easily accommodated within this thesis, whilst 'husbandry leases' those simply intended to be cultivated by the lessee, were, but as Paul Hyams has shown, both can be happily assimilated, Hyams, 'Origins of a peasant land market', 28–31. For examples of the interpretation of all leases as 'husbandry leases', J. Williamson, 'Norfolk: thirteenth century' in Harvey, ed., *The peasant land market*, pp. 53–4, 59, 77; R. J. Faith, 'Berkshire: fourteenth and fifteenth centuries', *ibidem*, pp. 125–6; A. C. Jones, 'Bedfordshire: fifteenth century', *ibidem*, p. 243; T. Lomas, 'Durham: late fourteenth and fifteenth centuries', *ibidem*, pp. 293–4. The mortgaging of peasant land is well-evidenced in the early modern period: see, for example, B. A. Holderness, 'Widows in pre-industrial society: an essay upon their economic functions', in Smith, ed., *Land, kinship and life-cycle*, pp. 437–9; Lord Leconfield, *Petworth manor in the seventeenth century* (Oxford, 1954), pp. 11–13, and *passim*. For the late middle ages, B. F. Harvey, *Westminster Abbey and its estates in the middle ages* (Oxford, 1977), pp. 317, 318; C. Dyer, *Standards of living in the later middle ages. Social change in England, c. 1200–1520* (Cambridge, 1989), p. 180; M.

Mate, 'The East Sussex land market and the agrarian class structure in the late middle ages', *Past & Present* 139 (1993), 60.

37 Kowleski, *Medieval Exeter*, pp. 214–21.

38 M. K. McIntosh, *Autonomy and community. The royal manor of Havering, 1200–1500* (Cambridge, 1986), pp. 166–70; E. Clark, 'Debt litigation in a late medieval English vill' in J. A. Raftis, ed., *Pathways to medieval peasants* (Toronto, 1981); P. R. Schofield, 'L'endettement et le crédit dans la campagne anglaise au moyen âge', in M. Berthe, ed., *Endettement paysan et crédit rural dans l'Europe médiévale et moderne. Actes des XVIIes journées internationales d'histoire de l'abbaye de Flaran, Septembre 1995* (Toulouse, 1998), pp. 74–6; *idem*, 'Dearth, debt and the local land market in a late thirteenth century village community', *Agricultural History Review* 45 (1997), 12–14; N. J. Mayhew, unpublished paper on Gussage All Saints, Dorset; C. D. Briggs, 'Credit and debt in medieval Cambridgeshire: Oakington, Cottenham and Dry Drayton, 1291–1348' (unpublished M.Phil thesis, University of Cambridge, 1998), c. 1.

39 Schofield, 'Peasants and the manor court'.

40 E. B. Dewindt, *Land and people in Holywell-cum-Needingworth. Structures of tenure and patterns of social organization in an east midlands village, 1252–1457* (Toronto, 1971), pp. 250–4; E. Britton, *The community of the vill* (Toronto, 1977); Z. Razi, *Life, marriage and death in a medieval parish: economy, society and demography in Halesowen (1270–1400)* (Cambridge, 1980), p. 37; R. H. Britnell, *Growth and decline in Colchester, 1300–1525* (Cambridge, 1986), pp. 19–20, 102–3, 206–8.

41 For some observations here, however, see Britnell, *Colchester*, pp. 105–6; Kowaleski, *Medieval Exeter*, pp. 214 ff. and references therein for legal commentaries.

42 Postan, 'Private financial instruments', pp. 43, 46–9, 61.

43 See especially, T. F. T. Plucknett, *Legislation of Edward I* (Oxford, 1949).

44 *ibid.*, pp. 138ff.

45 See below, cc. 3, 4.

46 E. E. Power, 'The wool trade in the fifteenth century', in E. E. Power and M. M. Postan, eds, *Studies in English trade in the fifteenth century* (London, 1933), pp. 83–4.

47 For instance, G. A. Holmes, 'The "Libel of English policy"', *English Historical Review*, ccxcix (1961), 201; *The Libelle of Englyshe Polcyce. A poem on the use of sea-power, 1436*, ed. Sir G. Warner (Oxford, 1926), pp. 21–3.

48 Power, 'Wool trade in the fifteenth century', p. 65.

49 For example, Woodcock, *Medieval ecclesiastical courts*, pp. 90, 102, 106–7; C. Morris, 'A consistory court in the middle ages', *Journal of Ecclesiastical History* 14 (1963), p. 157,

50 R. H. Helmholz, 'Assumpsit and *fidei laesio*', *Law Quarterly Review* 91 (1976); *idem*, 'Debt claims and probate jurisdiction in historical perspective', *American Journal of Legal History* 23 (1979); *idem*, 'Usury and the medieval English church courts', *Speculum* 61 (1986). These articles are also published in R.H. Helmholz, *Canon law and the law of England* (London, 1987) from which any subsequent reforms are taken. On links between secular and ecclesiastical court developments in debt cases see also, Woodcock, *Medieval ecclesiastical courts*, p. 91. On jurisdictional clashes over debt, see also, for example, P. R. Hyams, 'Deans and their doings: the Norwich inquiry of 1286', *Proceedings of the Berkeley Congress of Medieval Canon Law, 1980* (Monumenta Iuris Canonici, Series C, Subsidia, 7, Vatican City, 1985), pp. 619–46, especially, p. 622.

51 Below, c. 2. For an early description of Jewish archae, chirographs and starrs, see *Select pleas, starrs and other records*, ed. Rigg, pp. xviii–xx.

52 See, for example, Hilton, *English peasantry*, pp. 46–7, which offers a brief and early statement regarding the range of inter-peasant credit arrangements. See also, Clark, 'Debt litigation', pp. 253–68; McIntosh, *Autonomy and community*, pp. 166–70; Schofield, 'L'endettement et le crédit', pp. 85–8. See also, below, c. 5.

53 See, for example, discussion of Jewish dealings with poorer rural debtors in the thirteenth century, as discussed by R. R. Mundill, *England's Jewish solution. Experiment and expulsion, 1262–1290* (Cambridge, 1998), pp. 11–12 and references therein.

54 E. B. and M. M. Fryde, 'Public credit, with special reference to North-western Europe', in M. M. Postan, E. E. Rich and E. Miller, eds, *The Cambridge Economic History of Europe. iii. Economic organization and policies in the middle ages* (Cambridge, 1963), pp. 453, 457–8.

55 T. H. Lloyd, *The English wool trade in the middle ages* (Cambridge, 1977).

56 See, for example, Power, 'Wool trade', pp. 64–5 where she describes the credit agreements made between English and Flemish wool merchants in the fifteenth century.

57 See, for various aspects of an ongoing discussion, R. J. Whitwell, 'Italian bankers and the English crown', *Transactions of the Royal Historical Society* New series, 17 (1903); T. F. Tout, *The political history of England from the accession of Henry III to the death of Edward III (1216–1377)* (London, 1905), p. 176; J. F. Willard, 'The crown and its creditors, 1327–33', *English History Review*, 42 (1927); G.L. Harris, 'Aids, loans and benevolences', *Historical Journal* vi (1963), ; idem, *King, parliament and public finance in medieval England to 1369* (Oxford, 1975); E. B. Fryde, *Studies in medieval trade and finance* (London, 1983), especially cc. 3, 4; *idem*, 'Materials for the study of Edward III's credit operations, 1327–48', *Bull. Inst. Hist. Res.* xii (1949).

58 R. W. Kaeuper, *Bankers to the crown* (Princeton, N. J., 1973); *idem*, 'The Frescobaldi of Florence and the English crown', *Studies in medieval and renaissance history* 1 (1973); E. Re, 'La compagnia dei Riccardi in Inghilterra e il suo fallimento all fino del secolo XIII', *Archivio della Societa Romana di Storia Patria* 37 (1914); E. Russell, 'The societies of the Bardi and the Peruzzi and their dealings with Edward III, 1327–45', in G. Unwin, ed., *Finance and trade under Edward III* (Manchester, 1918); A. Beardwood, *Alien merchants in England, 1350 to 1377* (Cambridge, Mass., 1931); N. Fryde, 'Antonio Pessagno of Genoa, king's merchant of Edward II of England', *Studi in memoria di Frederigo Melis*, ii (1978); H. Jenkinson, 'William Cade a financier of the twelfth century', *English Historical Review* 26 (1913); E. B. Fryde, *William de la Pole, merchant and king's banker* (London, 1988); J. Jacobs, 'Aaron of Lincoln', *Transactions of the Jewish Historical Society of England* 3 (1899); R. R. Mundill, 'Anglo-Jewry under Edward I – credit agents and their clients', *Jewish Historical Studies* 31 (1990). See also below, pp. 42–5.

59 See, for instance, E. B. Fryde, 'Loans to the English crown, 1328–31', *English Historical Review* lxx (1955), reprinted with same page numbering in idem, *Studies in medieval trade and finance*, pp. 198–9; also, T. H. Lloyd, *Alien merchants in England in the high middle ages* (Brighton, 1982), pp. 176–83; Kaeuper, *Bankers to the crown*, c.v.

60 E. B. Fryde, 'The deposits of Hugh Despenser the younger with Italian bankers', *Economic History Reviews:* second ser., iii (1951), reprinted with same page numbering in idem, *Studies in medieval trade and finance*, pp. 344–62, espec. pp. 354–9.

61 Harris, 'Aids, loans and benevolences', 2–3; also, K. B. McFarlane, 'Loans to the Lancastrian kings: the problem of inducement', *Cambridge Historical Journal* ix (1947), reprinted in idem, *England in the fifteenth century. Collected essays* (London, 1981).

62 For instance, Fryde, 'Loans to the English crown', pp. 208–9; Willard, 'The Crown and its creditors'.

63 J. R. S. Phillips, *Aymer de Valence, earl of Pembroke, 1307–1324. Baronial politics in the reign of Edward II* (Oxford, 1972), pp. 194–7.

64 Below, pp. 48–63.

65 Mundill, 'Anglo-Jewry under Edward I'; *idem*, 'Lumbard and son: the business and debtors of two Jewish moneylenders in late thirteenth-century England', *The Jewish Quarterly Review* lxxxii (1991); 'Rabbi Elias Menahem: a late-thirteenth-century English entrepreneur', *Transactions of the Jewish Historical Society of England* xxxiv (1994–6). See also, R. C. Stacey, 'Jewish lending and the medieval English economy' in R. H. Britnell and B. M. S. Campbell, eds, *A commercialising economy. England, 1086–c.1300* (Manchester, 1995), pp. 95–6. For earlier discussions, see, for example, Richardson, *English Jewry under Angevin kings*, c. iv; P. Elman, 'Jewish finance in thirteenth-century England', *Transactions of the Jewish Historical Society of England* xvi (1945–51), 93–4.

66 Stacey, 'Jewish lending and the medieval English economy', p. 98.

67 J. A. Raftis, *Peasant economic development within the English manorial system* (Stroud, 1997). See also, below, pp. 90–106.

68 Hilton, *English peasantry*, pp. 103–4; Schofield, 'L'endettement et le crédit', p. 91; Holderness, 'Widows in pre-industrial society'. See also, J. M. Bennett, *Women in the medieval English countryside. Gender and household in Brigstock before the plague* (Oxford, 1987), p. 160.

69 See, for example, M. J. Hettinger, 'Defining the servant: legal and extra-legal terms of employment in fifteenth-century England', in A. J. Frantzen and D. Moffat, *The work of work. Servitude, slavery, and labor in medieval England* (Skelmorlie, 1994).

70 For a short summary of vehement comment directed at usurers, see, for example, M. Rubin, *Charity and community in medieval Cambridge* (Cambridge, 1987), pp. 66–7.

71 B. H. Rosenwein and L. K. Little, 'Social meaning in the monastic and mendicant spiritualities', *Past and Present* 63 (1974), 29–30 and references n. 89; L. K. Little, 'Pride goes before avarice: social change and the vices in Latin Christendom', *American Historical Review* lxxvi (1971).

72 See, for example, Helmholz, 'Usury and the medieval English church courts', pp. 333–5; Rubin, *Charity and community*, pp. 88–9. See also, J. Gilchrist, *The church and economic activity in the middle ages* (New York, 1969).

73 J. R. Maddicott, 'English peasantry and the demands of the crown', p. 310 and n. 87, citing Aspin, *Anglo-Norman Political Songs*, p. 186.

74 Richard the Redeless, Passus iv, ll. 17–19, in W. W. Skeat, *The vision of William concerning Piers the Plowman in three parallel texts together with Richard the Redeless by William Langland* (Oxford, 2 vols., 1886), i, p. 626; see also *ibid.*, p. 606, l. 12. For later examples revealing similar attitudes, see R. Carew, *Survey of Cornwall* (1769 ed.), pp. 15–16, quoted in Hatcher, *English tin industry and trade*, p. 55; also T. Wilson, *A discourse upon usury by way of dialogue and orations, for the better variety and more delight of all those that shall read this treatise [1572]* (with an historical introduction by R. H. Tawney, London, 1925).

75 See, for instance, for a broad attempt to investigate the transmission and maintenance of shared cultural norms, and one that crosses the medieval/early modern divide, M. K. McIntosh, *Controlling misbehavior in England, 1370–1600* (Cambridge, 1998). On particular aspects of the moral discourse surrounding the extension of credit at the local level, see, for example, Schofield, 'Peasants and the manor court'; also, *idem*, 'The social economy of the medieval village' (forthcoming). Contributions by early modernists, include an important essay by J. Walter, 'The social economy of dearth in early modern England', in J. Walter and R. Schofield, eds, *Famine, disease and the social order in early modern society* (Cambridge, 1989).

76 As also above, pp. 8–9. Indebtedness of the Crown and the advantage of foreign merchants are both important themes of the Ordinances of 1311, *English Historical Documents, 1189–1327*, ed. H. Rothwell (London, 1975), pp. 527–539. See also, J. C. Davies, *The baronial opposition to Edward II, its character and policyex:* (Cambridge, 1918), pp. 379–80.

77 Muldrew, *Economy of obligation*.

78 McIntosh, *Controlling misbehavior*.

79 L. Fontaine, 'Introduction', in Berthe, ed., *Endettement et crédit*, pp. 11–12.

80 W. C. Jordan, *The great famine. Northern Europe in the early fourteenth century* (Princeton, 1996), pp. 110–11.

81 Raftis, *Peasant economic development*.

82 J. Kermode, *Medieval merchants. York, Beverley and Hull in the later middle ages* (Cambridge, 1998), p. 71.

83 Muldrew, *Economy of obligation*; *idem*, 'The culture of reconciliation: community and the settlement of economic disputes in early moderrn England', *The Historical Journal* 39 (1996).

84 P. Nightingale, 'Monetary contraction and mercantile credit in later medieval England', *Economic History Review*, 2nd ser., xliii (1990); J. I. Kermode, 'Money and credit in the fiftenth century: some lessons form Yorkshire', *Business History Review* 65 (1991); *idem*, 'Medieval indebtedness: the regions versus London', in N. Rogers, ed., *England in the fifteenth century* (Stamford, 1994).

85 Britnell, *Colchester*; Kowaleski, *Medieval Exeter*. See also, Kermode, *Medieval merchants*; also, D. Keene, 'Changes in London's economic hinterland as indicated by debt cases in the Court of Common Pleas', in J. A. Galloway, ed., *Trade, urban hinterlands and market integration, c. 1300–1600* (London, 2000).

86 N. J. Mayhew, 'Population, money supply, and the velocity of circulation in England, 1300–1700', *Economic History Review*, 2nd ser., xlviii (1995), 253–4. Martin Allen, 'The volume of the English currency, 1158–1470', *Economic History Review*, 54 (2001), and *idem*, 'The volume and composition of the English silver currency, 1279–1351', *British Numismatic Journal*, 2000, forthcoming, suggest alternative money supply figures. Paul Latimer, 'The English Inflation of 1180–1220 Reconsidered', *Past and Present*, 171 (2001), 3–29, discusses Velocity. It needs always to be remembered that money supply and credit moved together. Greater availability of coin permitted the further extension of

credit; a dearth of coin would squeeze credit too. See R. H. Britnell, *The Commercialisation of English Society, 1000–1500* (Cambridge, 1993) p.181; Nicholas Mayhew, *Sterling: The Rise and Fall of a Currency* (1999), p.37; Peter Spufford, *Money and its Use in Medieval Europe* (Cambridge, 1988), p. 261, notes that interest rates were lowest where the money supply was most plentiful.

87 Clark, 'Debt litigation'; Schofield, 'L'endettement et le crédit'.

88 Schofield, 'Dearth, debt and the local land market'.

89 Hatcher, *English tin industry and trade.*

Chapter 1

Aspects of the Law of Debt, 1189–1307

Paul Brand

There is no modern general overview of the development of the law of debt in England during the period of just over a century between the final years of the reign of Henry II and the end of the reign of Edward I.[1] What follows is an initial, preliminary attempt to sketch some of the main outlines of that law and its development during that period. It does not claim to be a comprehensive account and further research in the surviving original sources of the period may well modify some of its conclusions. Its main concentration is on the law of the king's courts and so it deliberately ignores the rather different rules applicable in the many important local urban and rural jurisdictions. Nor does it have anything to say about the rather different legal rules that governed credit transactions and debt litigation involving Jews. The focus of the discussion (in keeping with the overall theme of this volume) is primarily on loans and measures to ensure their repayment; the discussion therefore largely ignores debts created by other kinds of transaction. One other major omission is the law and practice relating to debts recorded in the various kinds of official record (including the statute merchants registries created by legislation of 1283 and 1285) where very different mechanisms were used to enforce payment of the debt.

In Glanvill

'Pleas concerning the debts of laymen also belong to the Crown and the dignity of the lord king. So when anyone complains to the court in respect of a debt which is owed him, if he can bring that plea in the court of the lord king, he will have a writ of first summons of the following kind ...'.[2] Thus begins book X of *Glanvill*, the first text-book devoted to the nascent English common law, thought to have been completed between 1187 and 1189, which is virtually our only source on the law of the final years of the reign of Henry II. Fortunately book X provides us with what seems to be a fairly comprehensive overview of the law relating to debt as it then existed. The following is a brief summary of what it has to tell us.

Jurisdiction

At first sight, the words just quoted seem to be staking out a broad territory for the king's jurisdiction and (by apparent implication) for the jurisdiction of the royal courts: *all* litigation about the debts of 'laymen', excluding only litigation about the debts of 'clerics' which is conceded, at least by implication, to the church courts. But is the author really trying to claim all other debt litigation for the king's courts, to the exclusion of county, hundred, seignorial (honorial and manorial) courts as well as church courts? This hardly seems plausible, for we know that most such litigation was in fact heard at this time, indeed was to be heard for some centuries to come, in these lower-level local courts. There are, moreover, signs in *Glanvill* itself that the author knew that debt litigation was in fact quite rare in the king's courts. What he seems to be doing (as had the draftsmen of c. 15 of the Constitutions of Clarendon in 1164) is to use 'royal jurisdiction' as a kind of shorthand for the lay courts in general.[3] His primary concern was to assert lay jurisdiction over debt litigation involving laymen, more particularly where the church courts asserted a rival jurisdiction to hear such litigation on the basis of breach of faith or perjury.[4] What he does not mention, however, are any mechanisms for enforcement of this exclusive jurisdiction.

Credit transactions

The author seems to envisage that an enforceable debt obligation can be created in one of two different ways. One is by a purely oral transaction for which there was no written evidence. The creditor had only to be able to produce a 'suitable witness' of the transaction in court and in the context this means one who, if his testimony was challenged, was willing to fight battle to prove that his testimony was not perjured and that the debt had been contracted.[5] The king's court would not act on the basis of the mere assertion (*solam fidem*) of the supposed creditor alone.[6] The second way is by means of a (sealed) charter or what would later be described as a bond.

The author has disappointingly little to say about possible defences to claims based on either of these two forms of debt creation. In the case of the oral transaction, the only possibility apparently envisaged is total denial, with this then leading to battle, presumably by a similar mechanism to that mentioned elsewhere in the book: through the defendant embarking on the preliminary stages to formal denial on oath but being prevented from doing this by the plaintiff's witness, or rather champion, challenging this as perjury.[7] In the case of a transaction for which there was written charter evidence, only two possibilities are mentioned. If the debtor denied the genuineness of the charter but admitted that the attached seal was genuine this would not excuse him. Only if he denied both charter and seal would the genuineness of the bond be tested, either by comparison of the seal with with that attached to other charters admitted to be genuine or by battle fought by a suitable witness, especially one mentioned in the charter.

Nothing is said about claims by the debtor to have paid all or part of what was claimed;[8] nor of the parties having agreed to some form of alternative satisfaction of the claim (what was later known as 'accord and satisfaction')[9] nor of other kinds of attack on the validity of the charter or orally contracted debt, for example, that the debtor was incapable in law of contracting the debt because a minor or a married woman or for like reasons.

The provision of additional sureties for debts

The most detailed and the most interesting section of what *Glanvill* has to say on debt is concerned with the various forms of additional security which the debtor may be compelled to provide. These are of three different kinds.

The first is the finding of personal sureties for the repayment of the loan.[10] The account in *Glanvill* suggests that it was normal for all the sureties to be liable severally for the whole of the debt, though possible for some, or even all, of them to be liable only for shares in the total; that their liability was normally contracted without writing (the account says nothing of any charter being required to establish their liability and envisages compurgation and possibly battle as ways of resolving disputes about liability); that they would only become liable to pay when it became clear that the principal debtor was unable to do so; that their liability was enforced through a specially modified form of the action of debt; and that they could bring the standard form of the action of debt once they had paid, if the original debtor subsequently acquired sufficient assets to reimburse them.

The second way is by the pawning of a movable chattel.[11] The account in *Glanvill* suggests that in his day a pawned chattel might either be handed over for a definite, fixed period of time or for an unspecific and unfixed period. In the latter case the creditor could call for repayment of his debt whenever he wished but there seems to have been no provision allowing him to treat the gage as forfeit after the expiration of any specific period of time. When the gage had been handed over for a fixed period, the parties might agree that, if the debt was not paid at the expiry of that period, the gage was to be forfeit to the creditor; if they did not, the creditor would need to bring a special action to force the creditor to pay the debt within a specified period or lose ownership of the pawned object.

The third form of additional security is by the gaging of immovable, real property (lands, tenements and/or rents).[12] *Glanvill* mentions two forms of gage of real property: the mortgage (*mortuum vadium*) and what he might have called (but did not call) the 'vifgage' (*vivum vadium*). Under both types of arrangement the creditor took possession of the property gaged while the debt was outstanding. If it was a 'vifgage', any income he received went towards paying off the outstanding debt; under the mortgage, such income went to the creditor but as profit, without reducing the amount owed (as in effect a form of interest). *Glanvill* was clear that such an arrangement was both 'unjust and dishonourable' (*injusta est et inhonesta*) and that it was to be considered a species of usury; but he was equally clear that it was not a form of arrangement which the king's courts actually prohibited. From his account it is reasonably clear that the debtor and his heirs were fully protected (by a special writ) against a creditor who attempted to retain his gage after the end of the agreed period when the debt had been paid off or payment offered; the creditor was much less well protected (indeed not protected at all) against the possibility that he might be ejected from the land by the debtor himself or by some third party (in the latter case only the debtor could bring action to recover the land).

The post-mortem transmission of liability for debt and of the benefit of debts

There is no specific discussion in book X of what happens to a debt on the death of either debtor or creditor. From what is said elsewhere (in book VII), however, we can deduce that the primary responsibility for payment of the debts of a deceased debtor lay with the estate of the deceased and with his executors, but that if his assets did not suffice his heir was liable for them. There seems to be no suggestion that this is only the case if the debtor has specifically made his heirs liable by a written deed specifically stating their liability.[13] Nowhere is there any discussion of the transmission of the benefit of debts, though elsewhere (in chapter VII) the author seems to give primary responsibility to the executors for taking control of the chattels of the deceased (perhaps including some of his debts), though possibly only of the one-third share left to his free disposal.[14]

The assignability of debts

There is no discussion anywhere in *Glanvill* of the possibility of the creditor assigning the benefit of the debt to a third party or even simply assigning an agent to receive a debt on his behalf.

Judgment

Another obvious gap in the coverage of the action for debt in *Glanvill* is any mention of whether the successful creditor was entitled to damages and, if so, what the measure of those damages was to be.

Subsequent developments down to *c.* 1307

In the remainder of this paper I want to look at the development of the law of debt during the period of rather over a century that lay between the composition of *Glanvill* and the end of the reign of Edward I, using the evidence primarily of plea-roll enrolments and (for the later part of this period) of various published and unpublished contemporary law reports.

Jurisdiction

There is no writ of prohibition in *Glanvill* to allow someone impleaded for a lay debt in an ecclesiastical court to attempt to halt the proceedings and no writ of attachment to follow up the prohibition if it was breached, although the treatise does contain writs of prohibition to prevent litigation in court christian in two other contested areas. Such a writ was, however, in use in England from the early years of the reign of Henry III.[15] From the beginning it allowed two major exceptions: pleas relating to wills (but, as will be seen later, this did not mean that the king's courts did not also claim jurisdiction over certain types of plea relating to wills) and pleas relating to marriages (primarily, in respect of moneys or chattels promised in connexion with marriage). What the writ does not mention is any exception in respect of litigation solely between clerks, as *Glanvill* suggests would have been allowed in his day. One passage in *Bracton* would also have allowed litigation of this kind as an exception to the general rule;[16] and a similar general exception is mentioned in the side-note of the annotator to a case of 1225 in *Bracton's Note-Book*.[17] Two other passages in *Bracton*, however, reject this and they seem to state the general view of the king's courts for the remainder of the thirteenth century (and beyond).[18]

Lesser local lay courts (hundred and seignorial courts) heard debt litigation throughout the thirteenth century and beyond. As Bob Palmer has shown, there was no attempt to impose a limit on the amount which could be claimed in such courts prior to the final decade of the thirteenth century. However, from the early 1290s it was being asserted that any litigation for a debt of forty shillings or more (other than in cases involving merchants) had to be initiated by writ and from 1295 onwards defendants impleaded without a writ for sums amounting to forty shillings or more could obtain royal prohibitions to stop the litigation.[19] Since there were no royal writs to initiate litigation in these courts, they were effectively prevented from hearing cases involving debts of forty shillings or over. There were, moreover, other limitations that were older than this on the jurisdiction of such lower courts. Measures to ensure the attendance of the defendant or (after judgment) to levy any debt adjudged due from him could only be taken in the case of a seignorial court within the lands held of the lord of the court; in the case of a hundred court within the lands that formed part of the hundred and only on chattels that belonged to the defendant concerned.

From the very early years of the thirteenth century, litigants bringing debt suits in the county court had a choice between initiating their litigation by royal writ (the writ *justicies*) or by oral complaint (plaint).[20] Bob Palmer has discussed the various possible reasons for litigants to choose the less convenient and more expensive option of the royal writ.[21] His preferred explanation is that purchase of the writ gained for the plaintiff a right to procedural advantages if he had a written proof of his claim. In the last decade of the thirteenth century, however, with the emergence of the new forty shilling rule, the use of the writ became essential in *any* debt case where the debt being claimed was forty shillings or more.

During the course of the thirteenth century the king's courts (the Common Bench and also the Eyre) seem to have heard an increasing amount of debt litigation. Such litigation generally had to be initiated by writ but from 1278 onwards it was also possible to bring an action of debt without limit in the Eyre by written, informal complaint (bill). Defendants who objected to answering claims for £20 and ten marks in the 1292 Shropshire and 1299 Cambridgeshire eyre without writ had their objections firmly overruled.[22]

Credit transactions

i) making and recording debts

It continued to be possible to create an enforceable obligation to repay a debt (whether a straight loan of money or a sale on credit) through a purely oral transaction between the two parties (or indeed between the debtor and an agent of the creditor).[23] A plaintiff suing on such a transaction had to be able to produce 'suit' in support of his claim, apparently here meaning supposed witnesses to the transaction on which the creditor was suing;[24] and plaintiffs who failed to produce suit (when challenged) would have their cases dismissed.[25] There are at last two cases of the 1220s which show the plaintiff's suit also being 'examined'. In a case of 1226 (*William le Veil v. Warin of Bassingbourne*) the plaintiff's claim was rejected when the suit admitted not knowing anything about the matter (*nichil inde sciunt in omnibus rebus*),[26] while in the second case (of 1223) (*Robert de Cloville v. abbot of Westminster*), when the suit had been examined and they had attested the transaction the defendant was still allowed to wage his law in denial of the alleged transaction with the defendant's predecessor and of the debt.[27] By the late thirteenth century, however, there was some doubt as to whether the defendant was still entitled to have the suit 'examined' by the justices. The point is known to have been argued at some length in a case brought in the 1293–4 Yorkshire eyre by two merchants (John and Walter Musard) who had a written bond for six marks of the debt they were claiming from John de Hanton but only suit to prove they were owed an additional two and half marks.[28] The plea roll records the production of two individuals as 'suit' (John of Doncaster and Peter de Fayceby); the defendant's request that they be examined and the plaintiffs' assertion that the law and custom of the realm only required them to produce suit, not to submit to its examination, in order to put the defendant to his answer.[29] The two reports both mention the suggestion of an individual (perhaps a clerk) identified only as 'Bek' that the examination of suit was a novelty and that it was better to stick to the existing law,[30] while a serjeant suggested that the examination of suit was the practice of the church courts and should not be followed in this lay court.[31] However, one of the reports records the leading serjeant, William Inge, telling the justices that it was the practice of the justices of the Common Bench to examine suit if the defendant asked for it;[32] the same report notes Chief Justice Cressingham as saying that he had sometimes seen suit examined and sometimes not.[33] Eventually the court held that the refusal of the plaintiffs to submit their suit to examination deprived that suit of its effect and dismissed their claim.[34] Bereford, J. in an unidentified Common Bench case of the 1290s had similarly held that the defendant was entitled to defend himself either by compurgation or by wager of law or by the examination of the plaintiff's suit.[35] Although the late thirteenth century lawbook *Fleta* suggests that after the examination of suit a defendant could still deny owing the debt by compurgation (wager of law) provided he produced twice the number of compurgators as there were witnesses,[36] the terms on which the defendant asks for examination (it is said to be *suo periculo* in the 1293–4 Yorkshire eyre case) and the terms in which the procedure is discussed in the reports suggest that it would be conclusive by itself.[37] A report of an early fourteenth century case where a London merchant (Peter Burhard) was suing the earl of Norfolk for £35 12s for robes purchased from him on credit shows that by then a clever serjeant would ensure that he had his witnesses well-instructed against the possibility of their being examined. The report tells us that when the earl's serjeant asked for examination of the suit, Laver, the serjeant acting for Peter Burhard, had four witnesses present who were each instructed by a written note as to the day, year and place of the individual sales and the days when payment was due[38] but that when the earl's serjeant (Mutford) saw this he managed to switch at the very last moment to asking for jury trial instead.[39]

The second way of creating a debt (recording the debt in a sealed charter or bond) continued to be a common way of doing this, but these two methods of recording a debt mentioned by *Glanvill* were joined in the thirteenth century by a third method, the tally stick. This might either be sealed by the debtor or left unsealed.[40] A sealed tally stick might apparently contain many of the same kind of details as a bond: the amount of the debt and where and when it was to be paid and the names of witnesses to the transaction.[41]

ii) defences

There were various possible answers to a debt claimed in the king's courts on the basis of one of these different ways of establishing the creditor's entitlement and how the king's court handled them often depended on the type of proof offered of the debt's existence. But this was not true of all types of answer. One exception, for example, was the pleading of contractual incapacity on the part of the supposed debtor at the time the loan was contracted: a woman who was married at the time of contracting the loan and thus unable to do so;[42] or a debtor who was under age when the supposed loan was contracted.[43]

iia) payment of the debt in part or in whole

To start with perhaps the most obvious answer to a claim: that part or all of the debt was no longer owing because it had already been paid. If the debt had been created by the kind of oral agreement of which 'suit' was the only proof, then wager of law and then compurgation (an oath of denial by the defendant that the money was owed supported by the oaths of eleven other oath-helpers) was a perfectly proper and adequate response, whether the defendant's underlying claim was that he had never owed the money or that he had once owed the money but paid it in full. Even by the time of the earliest surviving plea-rolls it seems to have ceased to be possible for the plaintiff's 'witness' to prevent the compurgation from proceeding by offering battle. If the debt was attested by a bond, the standard later medieval rule (already clearly stated in a case of 1303) was that only a written acknowledgment was admissible as proof of payment 'especially as a debt ought to be dissolved in the same way as it was created' (*maxime cum debitum habeat dissolvi eo genere quo ligatum est*).[44] It seems clear, however, that this rule was only just becoming firmly established. It was still permissible as late as 1278 for defendants in a debt case where the debt was attested by a bond and who alleged payment of the debt simply to produce suit of having paid what they owed. The plaintiff was then, however, allowed simply to wage his law to deny receiving payment.[45] No later case is found where suit alone was produced to prove payment in this type of case and the practice probably disappeared in the king's courts, at least. No objection was recorded by the defendant to the use of tallies to prove partial payment of a debt attested in writing in a case of 1285,[46] and in a case of 1295 the plaintiff accepted the evidence of all the tallies produced to prove payment other than one, whose genuineness went to a jury.[47] Objections were, however, made in two unconnected cases of 1294 to the use of tallies,[48] and in a 1299 case judgment was given against a defendant who produced a tally to prove payment (though a small door at least was left ajar because the tally concerned was specifically stated to be an 'unsealed' one).[49] However, the judgment already quoted from the 1303 case which talked of a requirement that obligations be dissolved in the same way that they were created (given specifically in the context of an attempt to plead tallies attesting payment and disallowing them) suggests that the courts had probably now set their faces against the attempt to plead tallies attesting payment as an answer to claims to debts based on bonds.[50]

A series of cases raise the question of whether a defendant could plead a prior recovery of the debt in some other court and, if he did, whether he could get to jury trial on that allegation. In a case of 1301 (*Alice daughter of William Grant of Huckote v. Walter of Cranford)* where the defendant pleaded a prior recovery in the court of Walter fitzJohn of Aylesbury the defendant was denied jury trial on the grounds that the plaintiff's possession of an undamaged bond rendered it unlikely that the recovery had taken place and, according to a report of the same case, the grounds that if the plaintiff had indeed recovered the debt there the defendant would have an action of false judgment against the court.[51] However, in two other cases of the early 1290s when it was a county court involved and the plaintiff admitting bringing debt litigation there but denied that the sheriff had then levied the judgment debt, the defendant was allowed a jury on his claim that the debt had in fact been levied.[52]

If the defendant wished to rely on letters of acquittance he had to produce them in court. This rule was evidently felt to be harsh in cases where such letters had been destroyed by accident in a fire, but the king's court took a firm decision in 1294 that jury trial was not be allowed in such cases since the jury could not conceivably have full knowledge of the wording of the acquittance,[53] and because 'it would be harsh in this case, because of like cases that might occur, to admit jury trial on the basis of assertion alone against his deed which is fully acknowledged, since deeds are more believable than words and to be preferred and the king's court can give judgment on their basis.'[54]

iib) denial of the bond or tally

A second form of defence in the case of both bonds and tallies was to attack the validity of the bond or tally itself. There were several possible lines of attack in the case of bonds. A straight denial that the bond concerned was the defendant's deed was the commonest response and would go to a jury. More legally interesting were claims that the bond concerned had been materially altered in significant places (which was in principle a matter for the court itself to decide on inspection of the bond),[55] or that the bond mentioned a sum that differed materially from that which was mentioned in the plaintiff's count (his formal claim in court)[56] or that the bond had only been made under duress, generally while the defendant was in prison.[57]

In a series of cases recorded on the plea rolls from the early thirteenth century onward the defendant was simply allowed to wage his law in denial of the underlying transaction giving rise to the debt, the making of the tally and owing the debt. These cases may (but do not necessarily) all involve unsealed tallies. Certainly an early fourteenth century case (*Robert of Migham v. John de Thuddene*) suggests that wager was available only where the tally was unsealed, jury trial if it was sealed.[58] There is also some late-thirteenth-century evidence of a special rule applicable to merchants, particularly where both parties were merchants, which denied the defendant the possibility of wager of law against a tally and instead allowed the plaintiff to 'prove' that the defendant had made the tally by wager of law. This rule is mentioned in a case in the 1285 Essex eyre (*Stephen of Cornhill v. John of Roding*) in which the parties reached agreement before the law was made;[59] and can be seen in action in a case in the 1286 Norfolk eyre (*John Alayn senior v. John of Brampton*) where the plaintiff proved his debt three-handed (with just two compurgators) in accordance with mercantile law and custom *(lex et consuetudo mercatoria)*.[60]

iic) accord and satisfaction

A third kind of defence that seems (so far as I have noted) to arise directly and explicitly only in the case of debts evidenced by bonds is what was later to be called 'accord and satisfaction': the defendant's claim that he (or more rarely a third party acting in his interest)[61] had satisfied the creditor for all or part of the sum claimed not by direct payment but in some alternative fashion: by a permanent grant,[62] or by the lease of lands for a fixed period of time,[63] or until the debt was paid off;[64] the granting of permission to reap and carry off the crops on the defendant's land in one particular year[65] or the delivery of corn belonging to the defendant's church in a particular year;[66] the lease of the tithes belonging to churches that belonged to the defendant;[67] or by the delivery of a valuable horse[68] or of silver vessels.[69] Alternative forms of 'accord and satisfaction' were to plead (in effect) that the debt had been set off against another debt owed by the plaintiff to the defendant,[70] or that the plaintiff had subsequently agreed to accept a lesser sum (but had then deliberately avoided being paid).[71] Such allegations did sometimes lead to a jury trial on the alleged 'accord and satisfaction'[72] and in a case in the 1293–4 Yorkshire eyre where jury trial was admitted to prove the lease of tithes in payment of a debt it was even said that the lease of a manor or of tithes in payment of a debt was so much a matter within the knowledge of 'the country' that jury trial on such a claim was both admissible and customarily allowed.[73] Yet there were difficulties even about matters as public as this, since, as counsel pointed out in a case in the 1286 Cambridgeshire eyre, even if a jury could be expected to know of the delivery of a manor they could not be expected to know whether it was for the reason alleged or under some other agreement.[74] During 1291 and 1292 a series of such cases were adjourned for judgment on the general point of principle involved;[75] the court then made up its mind and gave judgment in 1294 against defendants being allowed to plead such arrangements when they were unattested by any written documentation on the grounds (as one of the judgments put it) that 'works are more believable than words and to be preferred (*credibiliora sunt opera sermonibus et preferenda*)'.[76]

iid) failure of consideration

A further type of defence regularly leading to jury trial found in the later thirteenth and early fourteenth century sources can perhaps best be described as a 'failure of consideration': a claim that the debt was contracted only for some matching advantage (specified in the bond which provided evidence of the debt) that the defendant was supposed to enjoy and that in the event he had not enjoyed it, whether by the default or the positive action of either the plaintiff or some third party. In the 1272 Warwickshire eyre Nicholas of Lunderthorpe claimed a debt of £25 against William Tuk of Leake on the basis of a deed which specified that the money was due in two instalments for the sale of grain belonging to Nicholas at Leake. William admitted the deed but denied that he had ever taken possession of the crop. He explained that immediately after the agreement men of Hugh Despenser had come to the manor and threshed and consumed the crop and Nicholas had failed to secure any remedy. The case was repleaded at Michaelmas term 1275 in the Common Bench when William added that Nicholas had brought an action of trespass claiming damages for this crop in the eyre at Lincoln and since Nicholas was unable to deny this William was freed of his claim.[77] Other defendants can be found simply denying that they had ever received the income of a church they had supposedly purchased for a year;[78] or that a three year lease of a church, a manor and leasehold land and a rent had ever been carried into effect.[79] Action by a third party which deprived the defendant of the benefit he had expected was pleaded in other cases, but with the addition of allegations that the plaintiff had been asked but failed to warrant what he had sold: for example, the purchaser of tithe corn who had lost all gain from his purchase when the bishop of Norwich had levied a debt owed by the plaintiff by virtue of the king's writ from the grain purchased.[80] In what seems to be a teaching note (rather than a record of a real case), however, we find it being suggested that when money was borrowed it was not possible for the borrower to deny receiving the money because he had specifically admitted this in advance in the bond itself.[81]

The provision of additional sureties for debts

i) personal sureties

Even in *Glanvill's* day, as we have seen, it was the normal practice for sureties to be severally liable for the whole of the debt for which they were standing surety. Although there is a case in the Common Bench as late as 1249 (*Ralph of Leicester v. Anketin of Wickwane and others*) in which the individual sureties had evidently agreed to stand surety for individual portions of a debt of 100 marks and were separately sued for five or ten marks each,[82] such evidence as I have noted from the second half of the thirteenth century and early years of the fourteenth suggests that by then it had become the invariable practice for each surety to be liable for the whole amount.[83] The largest number of sureties found in any case is the twelve mentioned in the reports of a case of 1294 who had stood surety for the 210 marks due on a sale of grain made on credit in 1291.[84] The special writ given in *Glanvill* for the creditor's action against the sureties seems to have disappeared fairly rapidly, for it does not appear in even the earliest surviving registers of writs.[85] It was replaced in practice by the standard writ of debt and it is only the creditor's count in actions of debt brought against sureties that reveals that his claim is against the defendant(s) as sureties rather than as the principal debtor. Something else that changed, but not till the last quarter of the thirteenth century, was the establishment of a requirement that the liability of sureties be stipulated in writing. A case of 1286 (*Henry Chapman of Downton v.. Executors of William Aubyn*) shows a creditor establishing the liability of a surety for a sale of wool on credit through a tally made by the surety,[86] but in a case of 1288 (*William Lok of Acton Burnel v. Ralph of Chadworth and Gilbert de Cranemere*) where a creditor was only able to produce tallies to show two sureties becoming liable for a debt contracted in 1278, the case was dismissed, apparently on the grounds that a bond was necessary to establish their liability.[87] Another important change (and one which had already happened by the time of the production of 'Glanvill Revised' at the end of the 1220s) allowed the creditor to sue the sureties for the debt, even where the main debtor was not insolvent.[88] All the sureties could do was obtain a writ from chancery that ordered the sheriff not to distrain the surety or allow him to be distrained as long as the chief debtor was able to acquit the debt himself.[89] By the reign of Edward I it had even become permissible, though not mandatory, for the creditor to sue both the principal debtor and his sureties for the debt at one and the same time. This is clearly what happened in cases both of 1298 (*Walter of Rothbury v. Thomas of Richmond and six others*)[90] and 1302 (*prior of Coventry v. John of Coleshill and Alan Talbot*).[91] What seems then to have happened was that the judgment authorised the sheriff to levy the money due (and the damages) from the debtor and his sureties collectively (not in equal shares, but from whomsoever could be made to pay). There might indeed be problems if the sureties were sued without the main debtor, for the latter might possess a deed of acquittance showing that he had paid all or part of the debt being claimed. It was then up to the sureties to ensure that they warned the main debtor to come to court with them or to hand over the acquittances for them to produce in court.[92] If the sureties did find themselves being sued or paying in place of the main debtor, their remedy ceased not long after the writing of *Glanvill* to be the standard writ of debt and became instead a special action.[93] If they were to succeed in their action they would, however, either have to show the original bond for the debt with a clause specifically stating that the debtor had made them his sureties or a clause obliging him to acquit them or perhaps a separate bond creating an obligation of the latter kind.[94] A different kind of personal surety is mentioned in a Common Bench case of 1220 brought by Faukes de Breaute, a hostage given to him by a debtor, who was the daughter of that debtor: he was seeking repayment not just of the original debt but also of twelve pence a day for her custody.[95] This is, however, the only reference so far noted to the giving of a hostage for the payment of a debt.

ii) the pawning of movables

There is comparatively little evidence on the plea-rolls of the royal courts of what was clearly a common practice in the thirteenth as in later centuries, the pawning of movables as surety for the repayment of a loan. Most litigation arising in connexion with this kind of arrangement probably continued to be dealt with in the various kinds of local court. But even from the small quantity of relevant cases it is possible to see the considerable variation in the arrangements adopted. One creditor (in a case of 1278) apparently accepted wheat barley, oats, horses, tables and utensils to the value of only £12 in pawn for a debt of 30 marks;[96] while at the opposite extreme another creditor (in a case of 1300) allegedly received a cart plus eight vats and other utensils to the supposed value of forty shillings in pawn for a debt of only three shillings (more than thirteen times the value of the debt).[97] Some cases specifically mention periods for the intended duration of the loan. In all cases where this is specified this is under a year.[98] Most of the cases are actions of detinue of chattels brought for the return of the pawned chattels, on the grounds the debt has already been paid,[99] or that the creditor was allegedly refusing to accept repayment;[100] but there is also at least one action of debt where the defendant refused to pay until the chattels he had pawned were returned to him.[101] It is only from the jury verdict in a debt and detinue of chattels case of 1306 (*executors of Laurence of Bootham v. John Sampson of York*) that we learn of some fascinating details relating to money-lending in York in 1288.[102] John Sampson had apparently agreed to pay Queen Eleanor 20 marks to expedite certain (unspecified) business in London but was still in London when the sheriff of Yorkshire began to distrain his manor of Acaster for payment (seizing all his animals and driving them to York castle prior to selling them). John's nephew and local agent (Alan Baldwin) approached Laurence of Bootham for a loan till John's return to York. Laurence did not have the money handy but went to the merchant Thomas de Luk (whom I take to be a Lucchese merchant) to ask for a loan and handed over eight linen cloths and one silver cup as surety for this. He then handed the money over to Alan who was able to secure the release of his uncle's animals. Laurence was unable to repay the money on the date it was due and so Thomas, with the assent of his debtor, transferred the loan and the pawned security to one or more members of the local Jewry. When John returned to York he ratified Alan's action and promised Laurence he would profit from it, but failed to repay the debt. Eventually Laurence repaid it but in the course of doing so forfeited one of the cloths (worth 5 marks) and the cup (worth 2 marks) because the period of the loan had expired and 'by way of usury'. After his death Laurence's executors sued both for the money originally lent (twenty marks) and for the cloth and cup (valued by the jury at five and two marks respectively) paid for the loan and recovered them plus damages.

iii) using land as a security

The standard form of mortgage of the later twelfth century gave the creditor possession of the land which was security for payment of the debt until the debt itself was paid off,[103] but this was not a freehold interest in the land, merely a 'gage' and, in the absence of any further agreement between the parties, would never pass definitively to the creditor.[104] New mortgages of this kind seem to have become relatively rare during the course of the thirteenth century (perhaps because the creditor's interest in the land was so badly protected at law) but there are at least three cases from the years around 1300 showing that they were still then being created and that even then the form was not wholly obsolete.[105]

What seems to have taken its place as the normal form of mortgage was a rather different type of arrangement (also known as a mortgage)[106] which was even more favourable to creditors. Under this the creditor initially took possession of the land as a 'gage' for a limited period of of time, but with provision that if the loan was not repaid at the end of that period the land was to pass to the creditor in perpetuity.[107] If the creditor was being careful the arrangement was recorded in two separate documents: a bipartite chirograph for both of the parties recording the acknowledgment of the debt and the date for payment and the initial term for holding the land and the agreement about what was to happen at the end of the term, and a separate, and unconditional, permanent grant of the land or other property by the debtor to the creditor.[108] Debtors were sometimes content to let the creditor have immediate possession of the charter of feoffment;[109] more commonly it went in escrow to a neutral third party (*in equali manu*) until the day for payment had passed. Sometimes the only security which the debtor had to offer (or which the creditor wanted to accept) was the reversion to land already in possession of the creditor, but under a limited interest: here nothing more was handed over to the creditor when the debt was contracted but a quitclaim was drawn up which was to pass to the creditor if the debt was not repaid.[110] The classic mortgage of the later English common law was a conditional grant in fee, which put the creditor in immediate possession of a freehold interest in the land, but subject to a condition for reconveyance of the land to the debtor if he repaid the money on or before the day of payment. Arrangements of this kind are occasionally encountered from 1230 onwards but seem to have been much less common than the kind of mortgage of which I have just been speaking.[111]

The 'vifgage' is rather more difficult to find in the surviving evidence since it can be rather difficult to distinguish from an ordinary lease, particularly if creditor and debtor agreed in advance as to the value of the land the debtor was handing over and so handed it over for a determinate period. Our main clue to the existence of the 'vifgage' is normally only the fact that the creditor paid over a relatively large sum at the beginning of the 'lease' and thereafter made only nominal payments during the term of the lease or that there is other collateral evidence indicating that the debtor was in financial difficulties and granted his lands away for a period for this reason.[112] In a case in the 1293–4 Yorkshire eyre (*Robert son of Thomas Ughtred v. Arnold de Percy*) we discover a vifgager protecting his interest in the land during the fifteen years he was holding the land by ensuring that he was enfeoffed for the nominal service of a grain of pepper for the fifteen years of the gage with a subsequent rent of £34 a year (in excess of the value of the manor which was worth only £24 a year).[113]

Post-mortem transmission of liability and benefit of debts

The primary responsibility for payment of the debts of a deceased debtor in the later years of Henry II's reign, seems (to judge from *Glanvill*) to have rested with his executors, and with his heir only being liable if the executors did not possess sufficient assets, and his silence may be interpreted as implying that the executors could only be sued in respect of those debts in the ecclesiastical courts. The dividing-line between the responsibilities of executors and heirs seems not, however, to have been a firm one. A passage in *Bracton* seems to imply that executors can only be sued (in the ecclesiastical court) in respect of debts that their testator had acknowledged owing or which had been established (by legal process) as being owed by him during his lifetime.[114] Two cases of 1219 and 1222, however, suggest a rather different rule: that the executors are liable only if the debtor had mentioned the debt in his will.[115] Otherwise, the heir was liable. Things changed around the middle of the century. In 1253 we find the first debt suit being brought against executors in the king's court (*William de Ferrers earl of Derby v. executors of cecily widow of Savary de Bohun*) and the pleading in this case suggests that the only criterion which needed to be satisfied when suing them was that they should possess enough of the assets of the deceased to pay the debt, and that it was no longer necessary to establish either that the debt was one which had been acknowledged or proved in the debtor's lifetime or one that was mentioned in the debtor's will.[116] The increased responsibility of the executors for the debts of the deceased removed most of the responsibility from the heir's shoulders. Not long afterwards, the residual responsibility of the heir for paying the debts of the deceased if the latter did not leave sufficient assets partially disappeared: the heir remaining liable only if the debtor had specifically stipulated (in a bond) that his heirs should also be liable (this was the rule by 1275 at latest);[117] and then only if the heir had inherited assets (in the form of land or other real property) from the debtor (this was the rule by 1281 at latest).[118] Special rules of proof might be applicable when executors were sued for their testator's debt.

Creditors also died without collecting debts. As we have seen, the position in *Glanvill* seems to be that it is the executors who have the primary responsibility for doing this. If so, the position seems to changed by the early 1230s, if not before. The rule enunciated in two prohibition cases of 1231 and 1233 (and echoed in *Bracton*) is that the executors can only bring suit (in the ecclesiastical court) and collect those debts acknowledged or proved in the lifetime of the creditor;[119] other debts went to the heir, who could sue for them in the king's court.[120] By around 1260, however, executors were being allowed to bring suits for debts in the lay courts;[121] and actions brought by executors soon become common on the plea-rolls. These cases show no restriction of the executors' right to sue to debts acknowledged or proven during the creditor's own lifetime. Somewhat puzzlingly, there continue to be occasional suits for debts brought by heirs through to the end of the thirteenth century and beyond, even on occasion where there seem to have been executors living, and it is not clear on what basis the heir (rather than the executors) was bringing such suits.[122] Suits brought by executors raised some of the same problems about proof as suits brought against them.

Assignability of debts

It was clearly not uncommon for creditors to assign agents to receive payment of debts on their behalf, and there are examples of actions of debt brought by such creditors against their agents when they failed to pay over the money they had received,[123] and by the debtors against the agents when they failed to procure the necessary acquittance from the creditor or repay the sum received.[124] There is also clear evidence in cases enrolled on the plea-rolls of debtors being able to plead payment to third parties by the assignment of their creditors, though the cases from the years around 1300 suggest that by then it was normal (and perhaps necessary) for the debtor to have to produce written evidence of the assignment from the creditor.[125] What one does not find at all, however, are actions in which the plaintiff sues on the basis of an assignment from the original creditor, except in a case of 1260 (*John de Gisors v. Hugh Liun and Richard Fader of Ipswich*) where a plaintiff succeeded in an action of debt in a claim based on a bond to a third party or anyone bearing his bond, though there is no recorded argument on any specific objection to the assignment.[126] From the absence of other cases it seems reasonable to assume that the normal rule was that debts were not assignable, and that generally the only way this could be done was by getting the debtor to agree to a new bond in favour of the assignee (which would make him look like the original creditor) in return for a cancellation of the original bond.

Damages

Damages were regularly awarded in actions of debt from the early thirteenth century onwards, as assessed by the jury (if there had been jury trial) or by the court (if there had been wager of law or judgment given on the basis of the pleading). In the last decade of the thirteenth century the court adopted a rule calculated to discourage defendants from waging law in the action. If they failed, for whatever reason, to make their law, whatever damages had been assigned by the plaintiff in his count would be awarded against them, without any 'taxation'.[127] A case of 1288 (*Richard de Meteburn v. William Murdak*) makes plain that normally the amount of damages was related to the period of time the defendant had withheld payment of the debt. Here a brother and heir sued for 48 marks was adjudged liable for damages only in respect of the period of four years since his brother's death, which were assessed at 100 shillings (about 4 per cent per annum).[128] An as yet unidentified report from the period Hengham was chief justice of the court considered it relevant that the deceased creditor had been a merchant. His executors were awarded 100 shillings for six years of non-payment of a debt of £11 (around 7 per cent) since that was what he could have earned with the money (*ceo pout aver esprouve solom lor descrecion de c souz en les vj auns*).[129] Damages were indeed English law's version of lawful interest as Lotero de Boneguyde was told when he sued the prior of Lewes for 700 marks in the 1279 Sussex eyre on the basis of a loan by himself and his partner of 500 marks in 1273 repayable in 1274 with an additional payment of one in every ten marks every two months thereafter for recompense of damage, interest and expenses and the expenses of one merchant with a horse wherever he was (*pro recompensacione dampni, interesse et expensarum et expense unius mercatoris cum uno equo ubicumque fuerit*). He was awarded the 500 marks but was told he would not get the remainder other than damages assessed by the justices at 100 marks as such matters were allowed in the assessment of damages.[130]

Some conclusions

What general conclusions is it possible to draw from all this? The jurisdictional (and some of the substantive) changes examined (allowing executors to sue and be sued in lay courts; excluding clerics from suing on lay debts in church courts) had the effect, in theory at least, of redefining the boundaries between lay and ecclesiastical court jurisdiction in a way that favoured the former as against the latter and the introduction of an action of prohibition to police this boundary introduced a reasonably effective way of policing the boundary which depended only on the self-interest of litigants. Within the lay sector the late thirteenth century jurisdictional changes noted squeezed out the lower courts from jurisdiction over the more valuable types of debt litigation and reserved them for hearing in the county court and the king's court.

Debt litigation was an area where certain types of procedure that had once been used in a variety of actions but had gradually been superseded or rendered mere formalities lasted longest: the examination of the plaintiff's suit; the use of wager of law by defendants on a regular basis for debts unattested by bonds or tallies (though, as we have seen, the rules introduced at the very end of the thirteenth century denying the defendant who failed to make his law the benefit of taxation may have been intended to discourage its use). Distrust of the 'country', jury trial, also emerges as a fairly clear theme (perhaps because so many transactions giving rise to debt were conducted in private) though only in the very late thirteenth century, with the denial of jury trial to debtors who alleged that they had possessed acquittances which had been destroyed by fire or who pleaded accord and satisfaction not attested by any written agreement or who pleaded payment to a third party without specific written authority to do so.

A third more general theme that seems to run through the material is a general movement in the law and in legal practice in favour of creditors: allowing them to sue sureties even before it had emerged that the main debtor as unable to pay; introduction of a new kind of mortgage providing for land to pass to the creditor in perpetuity if money was not repaid on the day fixed.

Notes

1 But see the more general account of the development of the medieval law of debt in chapter II of A. W. B. Simpson, *A History of the Common Law of Contract: The Rise of Assumpsit* (Oxford, 1975).

2 *Glanvill*, X, 1, ed. G. D. G. Hall (London, 1965), p. 116. I have amended Hall's translation. All subsequent references are to Hall's edition [hereafter *Glanvill*].

3 *Stubbs' Select Charters* C9th, edition revised, Oxford, 1921), p. 167.

4 *Glanvill*, X, 12, p. 126. He does, however, allow the church court to enjoin either penance or satisfaction and the latter might amount to enforcing payment of the underlying debt.

5 *Glanvill*, X, 12, p. 126: *per testem siquidem idoneum potest fieri disracionacio et per duellum.* Hall's translation mistakenly treats these as two separate modes of proof rather than just one.

6 *Glanvill*, X, 12, p. 126: *creditor ipse si non habeat inde ... aliquam disracionacionem nisi solam fidem nulla hec est probacio in curia domini regis.* The author then, however, goes on to treat jurisdiction over *fidei lesione* where the *fides* involved is that of the debtor.

7 For the procedural mechanisms involved see *Glanvill*, X, 5, p. 120.

8 But note that this is discussed as a possible answer by sureties for a debt to a claim made against them, *si confiteantur, tunc autem tenentur ad terminos competentes ei in curia ad id assignatos vel se ab illa plegiacione per solucionem vel alio modo acquietasse tenentur probare legitime: Glanvill*, X, 5, p. 118.

9 But note that this may be envisaged as possible answer to a debt claim against sureties: see above note 8 and the reference to acquittal of the debt *alio modo*.

10 Discussed in *Glanvill*, X, 3–5, pp. 118–20.

11 *Glanvill*, X, 6–8, pp. 120–4.
12 *Glanvill*, X, 6, 8–11, pp. 120–1, 124–6.
13 *Glanvill*, VII, 8, p. 81. Note also the mention in Book X, 12, p. 127 of the charter of either the debtor or his ancestor as a means of establishing liability for the debt.
14 *Glanvill*, VII, 6, pp. 80–1.
15 The earliest example seems to come from Michaelmas term 1219: *Ralph de Limesy v. Philip of Hertford*: *Curia Regis Rolls*, viii, 22.
16 *Bracton*, ed. G. E. Woodbine and revised and translated by S. E. Thorne (four vols, Cambridge, Mass., 1968–77) [hereafter *Bracton*], iv, pp. 283–4.
17 *Bracton's Note-Book*, ed. F. W. Maitland (three vols, London, 1877) [hereafter *BNB*], pl. 719.
18 *Bracton*, iv, pp. 249 and 264–6. But see Public Record Office [hereafter PRO] JUST 1/874, m. 14 (*Hugh de la Penne v. Thomas de Swynebrok*) for a case from the 1262–3 Surrey eyre in which the defendant pleaded the clerical status of both parties and the clause in the agreement binding both parties to the jurisdiction of the archdeacon of Surrey (within whose jurisdiction both were beneficed and who had never failed to act) as a defence to an action of debt and judgment was adjourned.
19 Palmer, *County Courts of Medieval England*, pp. 252–8.
20 For the date of the origin of the writ *justicies* for debt see Palmer, *County Courts of Medieval England*, pp. 185–7.
21 Palmer, *County Courts of Medieval England*, pp. 187–218.
22 *Year Books 20 & 21 Edward I*, ed. A. J. Horwood (Rolls Series, 1866), p. 223; British Library [hereafter BL] MSS. Stowe 386, f. 107v and Harley 25, f. 182v (reports of *prior of Barnwell v. John son and heir of Richard Fraunceys*: PRO, JUST 1/96, m. 34).
23 For an action of debt brought in Hilary term 1294 on the basis of a credit sale made by a servant of the creditor see *Benedict of Utterby v. William de Holm* (PRO, CP 40/103, m. 101d).
24 For the theory of the suit as witnesses present at the transaction see *Fleta*, ed. H. G. Richardson and G. O. Sayles (Selden Society, vols. 72 (1953), 89 (1972), 99 (1983)) book 2, c. 63 (I, 211–2) and the early fourteenth century case of *Peter Burhard of London v. Roger Bigot earl of Norfolk* as reported in BL MS. Additional 35116, f. 380r.
25 For cases dismissed when no suit was forthcoming (though promised) see the 1260 case of *Walter of Detling v. William of Stafford* (PRO, KB 26/169, m. 66); the 1293 case of *Walter de Urtiaco and wife Maud v. John of Acton* (PRO, CP 40/102, m. 239) and the early fourteenth century case reported in Lincoln's Inn [hereafter LI] MS. Miscellaneous 738, ff. 40v–41r.
26 *Curia Regis Rolls*, xii, no. 1609.
27 *Curia Regis Rolls*, xi, no. 1120.
28 PRO, JUST 1/1085, m. 36d. The reports are in BL MS. Additional 31826, ff. 380r–v and Harvard Law School MS. 206, ff. 52v–53r.
29 *'Et Walterus et Johannes Musard dicunt quod secundum legem et consuetudinem hactenus usitatam sufficit eis producere sectam tantum ad ponendum predictum Johannem de Hanton' in responsionem etc.'*, PRO, JUST 1/1085, m. 36d.
30 *'...mes de examiner syute si est ley meyns use e novele, par quai bon est prendre a la ley aunciene'* (BL MS. Additional 31826, f. 380v); *'...e qe la sute ad este examine cest la plus novele voie e meyns use e pur ceo il est bon qe nous tenoms launciene lei'* (Harvard Law School MS. 206, f. 52v).
31 *'Haveryng. Nous ne sumes pas ceinz a foer de chapistre destre examine ..'.* (BL MS. Additional 31826, f. 380r); *'Hampt'. Ceo nest pas ordre de plee en court de examiner suite einz est ordre de chapitre ...'* (Harvard Law School MS. 206, f. 52v).
32 *'Inge. Devaunt voz compaynouns en Baunk si est la sute examine si le defendant le prie ...'* (Harvard Law School MS. 206, f. 52v).
33 *'Crec'. Nous avoms veu qe la sute ad este examine e nous avoms veu qe noun...'* (Harvard Law School MS. 206, f. 52v).
34 The Musards had earlier resisted the examination of their suit in an unrelated debt case in the Common Bench for which no judgment is recorded: *Walter and John Musard v. Norman d'Arcy* (PRO, CP 40/86, m. 36d: Michaelmas term 1290). There is a similar, but briefer, argument about the same point in the unidentified Common Bench case of the 1290s reported in BL MSS. Additional 31826, f. 91r, Stowe 386, f. 124r, Harley 835, f. 28r and Additional 37657, f. 162v.

35 See BL MSS. Additional 31826, f. 91r, Stowe 386, f. 124r, Harley 835, f. 28r and Additional 37657, f. 162v.

36 *Fleta*, book 2, c. 63 (ed. Richardson and Sayles: I, pp. 211–2).

37 *'Ille. ... e jeo pri qe ele soit examine a mon peril – cest adire qe si voz tesmoines ne sacordent mie qe jeo soie assoutz de la dette. Et dautrepart qe vous recoverissez sils provassent la dette.'*

38 *'Lauf' habuit iiij testes presentes quorum quilibet per bilettum inde scriptum erat instructus de die, anno et loco et re per se particulariter vendita et de diebus solucionum.'*

39 BL MS. Additional 31826, f. 380r.

40 The distinction between the probative value of the two different kinds of tally is made by counsel and accepted by chief justice Hengham in a report of a case of Easter term 1304 in BL MS. Additional 31826, f. 360v (report of *Robert of Migham v. John de Thuddene*, enrolled in PRO, CP 40/151, m. 56d). The earliest mention of a tally as a proof of a debt is in a case of 1203: *Curia Regis Rolls*, ii, 206.

41 The enrolment in *Robert of Migham v. John de Thuddene* (see preceding note) mentions the production of a 'tally to which is attached the seal of the same John and whose circumscription attests the said debt payable in the said form' (*'quandam talliam cui appensum est sigillum ejusdem Johannis et cujus circumscripcio testatur predictum debitum solvendum in forma predicta'*) and the sheriff was told to produce for jury trial two named men who were 'the witnesses named in the circumscription of the said tally' (*'testes nominatos in circumscripcione predicte tallie'*).

42 For an example see the 1280 case of *John son of Rannulph of Bedford v. Christine widow of Richard of Hereford* (PRO, CP 40/33, m. 18).

43 For examples (both pleaded in response to sealed bonds): see the 1291 case of *John le Breton v. Alexander of Clavering* (PRO, CP 40/90, m. 29d) and the 1300 case of *master Henry of Nassington v. William de Sprouton* (PRO, CP 40/134, m. 108).

44 *Nicholas son of Godfrey and his wife Margery v. Richard of Cornard*: PRO, CP 40/145, m. 323.

45 *Walter of Binetre v. Simon Bonet and his wife Cecilia*: PRO, CP 40/27, m. 99. A similar process is mentioned in what seems to be a teaching note in Cambridge University Library [hereafter CUL] MS. Dd.7.14, ff. 403r–v. But in the debt plea in *Brevia Placitata* on similar facts the defendant is apparently allowed to wage his law instead: *Brevia Placitata*, ed. G. J. Turner and T. F. T. Plucknett (Selden Society, 66, 1947), pp. 103–5.

46 *Joan daughter of Robert Rofot v. Nicholas Durdent*: PRO, CP 40/60, m. 59d (only the amount thus paid was in dispute).

47 *William of Shepeye parson of Haddenham v. Robert son of Constance of Swavesey and others*: PRO, CP 40/107, m. 91d.

48 The two cases heard in Michaelmas term 1294 were *Walter of Kesteven v. John of Lynn* and *Robert of Benhall v. abbess of Romsey*: PRO, CP 40/106, mm. 95, 139d. In the latter the eventual concord constituted an admission that the money was still owed.

49 *William parson of Bolehuth v. Robert son of Thomas of Beanfield*: PRO, CP 40/127, m. 82d.

50 Above, p. 000.

51 PRO, CP 40/138, m. 147; reported in BL MS. Harley 25, ff. 173v and 178r–v.

52 The Easter 1292 case of *Richard of Bingham v. Rannulph of Friskney* (PRO, CP 40/93, m. 77: reported in *Year Books 21 & 22 Edward I*, ed. A. J. Horwood (Rolls Series, 1873), pp. 63–5, 79–81); the Easter 1294 case of *John of Northgate v. James of Astley* (PRO, CP 40/104, m. 62d).

53 *'de quo patria plenam noticiam habere non potest ...'*

54 *'durum esset in casu isto pro casibus consimilibus contingentibus verificacionem patrie admittere super dicto suo simplici contra factum suum quod plane congnovit, cum credibiliora sint opera sermonibus et preferenda, de quibus operibus curia regis mere potest dijudicare'*: PRO, CP 40/103, m. 47: *master William of Essex v. master Adam of Hales* (Hilary 1294). A similar judgment was given in the same term in very similar terms in *Ralph of Chategrave v. Henry of Sirlingham rector of Uggethale* (PRO, CP 40/103, m. 139) and (but without reasons) in Trinity 1294 in a case originally heard in Michaelmas 1293: *William Gerberge the Vintner v. Hugh de Bussey and John Christmas* (PRO, CP 40/102, m. 78d).

55 For an example of a bond being challenged on such grounds see *Richard Brinyng executor of William Brinyng v. William Wynck of Framlingham* (Michaelmas term 1293: PRO, CP 40/102, m. 90) (though no judgment is recorded). In another case of the same term (*Simon Sandford chaplain v. Henry of Walworth rector of St George Southwark*: PRO, CP 40/102, m. 148) a bond was challenged as *cancellatum et viciosum* and the case then dismissed.

56 See *Richard of Cateby v. Philip de Chauncy of Swynehop* (PRO, CP 40/100, m. 91: Easter 1293) where the count specified a debt of sixteen marks, but the bond specified payment of £10 13s 8d. Although there was only four pence difference and the plaintiff was claiming less than the amount in the bond, the defendant asked for judgment of the variation and the plaintiff asked for (and received) permission to withdraw from his action.

57 For cases where it was alleged that it was the plaintiff or one of his agents who was also responsible for the imprisonment of the defendant see the Easter 1286 case of *Lawrence of Ludlow v. Geoffrey Goldsmith of Ludlow* (PRO, CP 40/62, m. 37); the Michaelmas 1294 case of *William de Fyenles v. Simon of Fordington* (PRO, CP 40/106, m. 281d) and the Trinity 1307 case of *Thomas of Moulton of Copeland v. Stephen son of Peter of Hawkdon* (PRO, CP 40/164, m. 121). For cases where it was not alleged that the plaintiff had been responsible for the imprisonment see the Easter 1291 case of *Thomas of Timworth v. Robert of Rimpton parson of Langton* (PRO, CP 40/89, m. 127d) and the Trinity 1306 case of *Hugh Armourer of London v. master John de St Valery* (PRO, CP 40/160, m. 197d).

58 PRO, CP 40/151, m. 56d reported in *Year Books 32 & 33 Edward I*, ed. A. J. Horwood (Rolls Series, 1864), p. 185 and more fully in BL MS. Additional 31826, f. 360v. It is the second of these two reports that makes the distinction between the two kinds of tally. In another reported case of the following year (*Ralph of Fuldon merchant v. Richard of Shirford of Yaxley merchant*: PRO, CP 40/156, m. 51 and reported in BL MS. Hargrave 375, f. 118r and LI Misc. 738, f. 37r) the senior clerk Henry Hales refused to allow wager of law against a sealed tally, according to the report, because it was the equivalent of a writing (*qe contrevaut un escrit*).

59 PRO, JUST 1/246, m. 23.

60 PRO, JUST 1/578, m. 30d. The rule is also mentioned in *Casus Placitorum*, ed. W. H. Dunham jr. (Selden Society, 69, 1950), p. 25/58 and in *Year Books 20 & 21 Edward I*, ed. Horwood, p. 69.

61 A strong argument against this is recorded in the report of the 1286 Cambridgeshire eyre case of *Richard Poterel of London v. Warin of Hereford* in CUL MS. Dd.7.14, ff. 396v–397r and Bereford, J. is reported as disallowing it in a case of 1299 (*Michael de Farndon v. master Henry de Bray*; reported in CUL MS. Ee.6.18, f. 28v and in Harvard Law School MS. 206, f. 135v).

62 For examples see the Trinity 1291 case of *the executors of master Henry of Brandeston late bishop of Salisbury v. John fitzPeter* (PRO, CP 40/90, m. 8d) and the Michaelmas 1293 case of *the executors of Josep of Pontefract v. Ralph son of John de Rocheford* (PRO, CP 40/102, m. 157).

63 For examples see the 1286 Cambridgeshire eyre case of *Richard Poterel of London v. Warin of Hereford* (PRO, JUST 1/91, m. 17: reported in CUL MS. Dd.7.14, ff. 396v–397r); the Michaelmas 1291 case of *Nicholas of Langton v. John of Milford* (PRO, CP 40/91, m. 218d); the reports of the Michaelmas 1299 case of *Michael de Farndon v. master Henry de Bray* (enrolled on PRO, CP 40/130, m. 117) in CUL MS. Ee.6.18, f. 28v and Harvard Law School MS. 206, f. 135v.

64 For examples see the Michaelmas 1292 case of *the executors of Philip le Poer v. Robert of Tattershall* (PRO, CP 40/96, m. 6d); the Trinity 1294 case of *the executors of Roger le Blund of Iwerne v. Oliver de Dynham* (PRO, CP 40/105, m. 83).

65 For an example see the Trinity 1292 case of *Geoffrey son of John Reeve of Ampleforth v. William of London* (PRO, CP 40/95, m. 138d).

66 For an example see the Trinity 1292 case of *Thomas Belsire v. William de Percy* (PRO, CP 40/95, m. 80).

67 For examples see the 1293–4 Yorkshire eyre case of *the executors of master Robert Ughtred of Scarborough v. prior of Holy Trinity, York* (PRO, JUST 1/1085, m. 26); the Hilary 1303 case of *Walter of Kelk v. Robert Constable parson of Foston* (PRO, CP 40/146, m. 24d: reported in LI MS. Miscellaneous 738, f. 19r).

68 For an example see *Richard Poterel of London v. Warin of Hereford* as in footnote 63 above.

69 For an example see the Trinity 1297 case of *master Luke of St Leonard v. Thomas de Cruce* (PRO, CP 40/119, m. 133d).

70 For examples see the Easter 1294 case of *Ralph le Bret v. Robert of Helpeston rector of Stanham Gernegan* (PRO, CP 40/104, m. 97d) and the Michaelmas 1294 case of *the executors of Cecily Lovel v. John Barri* (PRO, CP 40/106, m. 221d). See also the argument about set-off in a case where the debt is apparently only attested by suit in *Brevia Placitata*, pp. 28, 101, 181.

71 For an example see the Easter 1294 case of *William Fossard v. Peter de Evercy* (PRO, CP 40/104, m. 14d).

72 For examples see the Michaelmas 1291 case of *Nicholas of Langton v. John of Milford* (PRO, CP 40/91,

m. 218d) and the Michaelmas 1293 case of *the executors of Josep of Pontefract v. Ralph son of John of Rocheford* (PRO, CP 40/102, m. 157).

73 PRO, JUST 1/1085, m. 26: *the executors of master Robert Ughtred of Scarborough v. prior of Holy Trinity York*.

74 CUL MS. Dd.7.14, ff. 396v–397r (report of *Richard Poterel of London v. Warin of Hereford*: PRO, JUST 1/91, m. 17).

75 For examples see the Trinity 1291 case of *the executors of master Henry of Brandeston late bishop of Salisbury v. John fitzPeter* (PRO, CP 40/90, m. 8d); the Trinity 1292 cases of *Thomas Belsire v. William de Percy* (PRO, CP 40/95, m. 80) and *Geoffrey son of John Reeve of Ampleforth v. William of London* (PRO, CP 40/95, m. 138d); and the Michaelmas 1292 case of *the executors of Philip le Poer v. Robert of Tattershall* (PRO, CP 40/96, m. 6d).

76 In the Michaelmas 1294 case of *the executors of Cecily Lovel v. John Barri* (PRO, CP 40/106, m. 221d).

77 PRO, CP 40/11, m. 30d.

78 *John de Marisco chaplain v. William of Bramber rector of Carlton*: PRO, CP 40/91, m. 94d (Michaelmas 1291): the jury found a third party had received them but with the permission of the defendant.

79 *The executors of master John of Melton parson of Kettleby v. William of Caldwell and others*: PRO, CP 40/105, m. 60 (Trinity 1294).

80 *Master Andrew Avenel rector of Gunthorpe v. Richard Bonde of Brunstead and others*: PRO, CP 40/98, m. 32 (Hilary 1293).

81 CUL MS. Dd.7.14, f. 397r.

82 PRO, KB 26/136, m. 5. For earlier cases of 1217 and 1221 in which the sureties were sued for the different sums for which they had stood surety see *Robert Maudut v. William de Wirmecote and others* and *Michael del Brud v. James de Mountsorrel and others*: *BNB*, pll. 1324 [mesne process stage only], 1543.

83 The only real evidence to the contrary comes from a case of Michaelmas 1293 where it was that part of the deed which contained the relevant words establishing this several liability for the whole of the debt which were alleged to have been altered: *Richard Brinyng executor of William Brinyng v. William Wynck of Framlingham*: PRO, CP 40/102, m. 90. But see also the rejected argument of counsel in the Common Bench case of 1289 (*Earliest English Law Reports, vol. II*, ed. Paul Brand (Selden Society, 112, 1996), pp. 322–3) who argued that the particular form of words used in the bond on which the plaintiff was relying made his client jointly responsible for the debt with the other surety, rather than individually liable for the whole.

84 *Richard fitzJohn v. Simon of Kent of Bricklesworth and others*: BL MSS. Harley 835, f. 28v, Stowe 386, ff. 133r–v; Additional 5925, f. 62r and Harvard Law School MS. 162, ff. 191v–192r; the enrolment is PRO, CP 40/106, m. 77.

85 But for possible evidence of its use in 1204 see *Roger le Waleys v. Roger de Cramaville* (*Curia Regis Rolls*, iii, 170) and in 1217 see *Robert Mauduit v. William de Wirmcote* (*BNB*, pl. 1324).

86 PRO, CP 40/64, m. 121.

87 PRO, CP 40/70, m. 2d.

88 'Glanvill revised' in F.W. Maitland, *Collected Papers* (three volumes, Cambridge, 1911), ii, 283; on the date of this revision see Hall, *Glanvill*, p. lviii The possibility of the pledges being distrained to pay not only if the debtor was unable to pay but also if he was unwilling to do so is one envisaged in the revised chapter 9 of the reissued Magna Carta of 1216: *Stubbs' Select Charters*, p. 337.

89 *Early Registers of Writs*, ed. E. de Haas and G. D. G. Hall (Selden Society, 87, 1970) Hib. 46, CA 32a and CC 144 (modified form).

90 PRO, CP 40/125, m. 72d; reported in BL MSS. Additional 31826, f. 153r and Stowe 386, f. 124r; CUL MSS. Ee.6.18, f. 10r and Mm.5.23, f. 8r.

91 PRO, CP 40/144, m. 222d: reported in BL MSS. Stowe 386, f. 168r and Additional 31826, f. 177v.

92 See *Richard fitzJohn v. Simon of Kent of Bricklesworth*: above, n. 000 where it is in the reports that Bereford, J. explains the procedure which the sureties have to adopt in these circumstances.

93 *Early Registers of Writs*, Hib. 43; CA 32; CC 145 and 145a

94 See the Michaelmas 1278 case of *Philip of Paunton v. master John Hok* (PRO, CP 40/27, m. 42d) and the 1293–4 Kent eyre case of *Simon le Saltweller and Henry Attebregge v. Henry de Sholeford and Richard of Westgate* (PRO, JUST 1/375, m. 62: reported in BL MSS. Harley 25, ff. 208r and 209r–v, Egerton 2811,

f. 98v and Harley 493B, ff. 141v–142r). Hence the decision at the end of the 1302 case of *the prior of Coventry v. John of Coleshill and Alan of Talbot* [above, note 91] that the bond be handed over to Alan for his suit against John.

95 *Faukes de Breaute v. Roger le Manaunt*: *Curia Regis Rolls*, ix, 226.

96 *Christine widow of John Malemeyns v. Peter of Huntingfield*: PRO, CP 40/27, m. 117d (but note that the creditor here denied having taken these chattels as surety for the debt).

97 *John Yol v. Lyotus de Brakenholm*: PRO, CP 40/134, m. 150 (but the defendant claimed the chattels had been sold to him and not pawned and the forty shillings may have been inflated to ensure the case reached the Common Bench).

98 From Thursday after Hoketide till Michaelmas in a case in the 1279 Sussex eyre (PRO, JUST 1/914, m. 10: *executors of Walter Greygrom v. John de Bohun*); from the Wednesday before St John the Baptist till Michaelmas in a case in the 1292 Herefordshire eyre (PRO, JUST 1/303, m. 24: *Peter of Brumpton v. John son of Roger of Burghull*); from the Sunday before Christmas till Easter in a Trinity 1300 case (PRO, CP 40/134, m. 150: *John Yol v. Lyotus de Brakenholm*); from the Monday after the octave of Easter till Ascensiontide in a Michaelmas 1304 case (PRO, CP 40/149, m. 338: *William son of William of Redness v. Walter of Bubwith*). Even where the facts of the case are contested the duration seems likely to have been one regarded as plausible by contemporaries.

99 The Michaelmas 1278 case of *Christine widow of John Malemeyns v. Peter of Huntingfield* (PRO, CP 40/27, m. 117d); the Michaelmas 1304 case of *William son of William Redness v. Walter of Bubwith* (PRO, CP 40/149, m. 338).

100 The Trinity 1290 case of *Albreda Parmynhod v. John le Eveke and wife Milla* (PRO, CP 40/83, m. 148); the 1292 Herefordshire eyre case of *Peter of Brumpton v. John son of Roger of Burghull* (PRO, JUST 1/303, m. 24); the Trinity 1300 case of *John Yol v. Lyotus de Brakenholm* (PRO, CP 40/134, m. 150); the Michaelmas 1306 case of *John de Totynges of St Ives v. William of Deeping merchant of Stamford* (PRO, CP 40/161, m. 315d).

101 *Executors of Walter Greygrom v. John de Bohun* (1279 Sussex eyre: PRO, JUST 1/914, m. 10).

102 PRO, CP 40/151, m. 199.

103 But for a 1199 case where the land that was the gage for the debt seems still to have been in the hand of the debtor when debt litigation was brought see *Maud daughter of Ralph Vintner v. Richard de Umfraville*: *Curia Regis Rolls*, i, 107.

104 Maitland's account of the law of this period (Pollock and Maitland, *History of English Law*, ii, pp. 119–120) seems to be wrong in suggesting that the kinds of provision for the forfeiture of gages of movables for non-payment (whether by agreement or by judgment in the absence of specific agreement) also applied to non-movables. There seems to be no trace in the cases of the period of around 1200 of such agreements or judgments being pleaded or given.

105 A case from the 1292 Westmorland eyre (*Thomas son of master William of Goldington and wife Avice v. William of Hastings*: PRO, JUST 1/987, m. 3); an unidentified case reported from the 1293 Staffordshire eyre (*YB 20 & 21 Edward I*, p. 423); a case from Hilary term 1300 (*Katherine daughter of Alexander Osewold v. Nicholas son of Hugh de la Chambre*: PRO, CP 40/132, m. 213d; reported in BL MS. Additional 31826, f. 164r).

106 For the application of this term to such an arrangement see, e.g., the pleading in the 1279–81 Yorkshire eyre case of *Emma daughter of William White and others v. John son of William of Beningborough* (PRO, JUST 1/1065, m. 47).

107 For an early example of such an arrangement but where the creditor was not entitled to possession until the day for payment had passed see the 1220 case of *Hamon Brand v. John Pim* (*Curia Regis Rolls*, ix, 76–7), though note that the creditor was amerced for usury apparently on the basis of these arrangements.

108 For the problems of a litigant who attempted to rely on an agreement for a mortgage and a subsequent quitclaim but did not have a charter of feoffment see the case cited in the preceding note.

109 E.g. the Easter 1293 case of *Thomas Chamberlain v. John son of JohnfitzJuliana* (PRO CP 40/101, m. 70d) reported in *Year Books 21 & 22 Edward I*, pp. 17–19.

110 For examples see two cases from the 1293–4 Yorkshire eyre: *Maud the daughter of Alan of Kneton of Middleton v. Roger Mynyot* (PRO, JUST 1/1085, m. 31) and *Robert son of Thomas Ughtred v. Arnold de Percy* (PRO, JUST 1/1085, m. 39).

111 See the enrolled deed of 1230 in *BNB*, pl. 458. Similar arrangements seem to be envisaged in an assize of novel disseisin of Michaelmas 1260 (*Hugh Peverel v. William de la Forde and Richard of Anstey*: PRO, KB 26/169, m. 24) and in assize of Easter 1281 (*Bartholomew de Castello v. Adam de Creting and his wife Nicholaa and others*: PRO, CP 40/38, m. 78d).

112 For what are clearly vifgages mentioned in a case of 1204 see *William de St Michael v. William Albus* (*Curia Regis Rolls*, iii, 165–6) and in a case in the 1241 Surrey eyre see *Gilbert chaplain of Sandon v. John de Fay* (PRO, JUST 1/867, m. 11d). For a vifgage arrangement agreed in 1220 in settlement of debt suit see *Curia Regis Rolls*, ix, 318 (*Andrew Bukerel v. Robert de Pinkeny*). Here the gage can be seen to come into operation only if the money was not repaid on time.

113 *Robert son of Thomas Ughtred v. Arnold de Percy*: PRO, JUST 1/1085, m. 39.

114 *Bracton*, iv, pp. 267–8.

115 *Curia Regis Rolls* , viii, 62 [=*BNB*, pl. 52] (*Philip of Hertford and wife Beatrice v. Gilbert de Clare*) and *BNB*, pl. 162 (*John of Wiggenhall and others v. Ralph parson of Irthlingborough*).

116 PRO, KB 26/149, m. 21d.

117 See *Nicholas of Lunderthorp v. Philip of Paunton*: PRO, CP 40/11, m. 10. See also the 1279 Sussex eyre case of *Henry de la Croys of Lewes v. Geoffrey Maungefer* (PRO, JUST 1/914, m. 5) and the 1284 Leicestershire eyre case of *William le Mazon v. Geoffrey de Camville* (PRO, JUST 1/460, m. 14d). As early as 1251 a suit against an heir was explicitly based on a deed obliging the debtor and her heirs, but the genuineness of the deed was denied: *Hugh de Dunstorp v. Roger of Staunton* (PRO, KB 26/145, m. 49).

118 See *William Walter de Peleville v. Geoffrey Ode*: PRO, CP 40/38, m. 11. For an earlier case which suggests the same rule heard in the 1262–3 Surrey eyre see *William le Vyneter v. William son of Richard Chatre* (PRO, JUST 1/874, m. 12d).

119 *Hamon de Valoines v. Gervase of Aldermanbury*: *BNB*, pl. 550; *Peter de Maulay v. abbot of Tupholme and Baldwin of Paunton*: *BNB*, pl. 810; *Bracton*, iv, pp. 267–8.

120 For early examples see the 1203 case of *Eustace the clerk v. Henry Sumer: Curia Regis Rolls*, ii, 206 and *Richard de Plessey, son and heir of William de Plessey v. William Luvel*: *Curia Regis Rolls*, vii, 207–8.

121 The earliest suit I have found is one in Michaelmas term 1258 (*executors of Stephen Baustan v. Laurence of Birdingbury and others*): PRO, KB 26/160, m. 12 [though the plaintiffs then had licence to withdraw from their suit]. For other early examples from Michaelmas term 1261 see PRO, KB 26/171, mm. 20 and 25d.

122 For examples see the 1272 Cambridgeshire eyre case of *Gilbert earl of Gloucester v. John Walerand* (PRO, JUST 1/84, m. 15); the 1272 Lincolnshire eyre case of *Roger son of Roger Champneys v. Henry Wyrmod* (PRO, JUST 1/483, m. 65) in which the defendant specifically objects that Roger's father has living executors with a greater entitlement than he to bring the suit, but then waives this; the Michaelmas 1291 case of *John son of Thomas of Goldington v. Thomas of Helbeck and his wife Avice* (PRO, CP 40/91, m. 226d and reported in *Year Books 21 & 22 Edward I*, pp. 515–9) and the Easter 1292 case of *Robert son of Nicholas of Boothby and wife Juliana v. John de Gaunt* (PRO, CP 40/93, m. 77d).

123 For examples see the case in the 1281–4 Lincolnshire eyre of *Christine Mouhardi v. John de Chartres* (PRO, JUST 1/492, m. 58d); the Trinity 1284 case of *Andrew de Merck v. Gilbert of Stanford* (PRO, CP 40/54, m. 14); the Trinity 1285 case of *Roger Miniot v. Thomas de Byrston*: (PRO, CP 40/59, m. 10). For an action of trespass brought by writ of *audita querela* in similar circumstances before assize justices in 1288 see *master William de Coudrey v. Alan of Wallingford*: PRO, JUST 1/1280, m. 9d.

124 For examples see the Easter 1293 cases of *Gerard de Vylers v. Benedict Renward* (PRO, CP 40/100, m. 15) and *William de Blumville v. John del Hagge* (PRO, CP 40/100, m. 31d).

125 For evidence of cases where written evidence of the assignment was not apparently required see the 1272 Lincolnshire eyre case of *Roger son of Roger le Champeneys v. Henry Wyrmod* (PRO, JUST 1/483, m. 65) and the Michaelmas 1275 case of *Robert of Stokes v. Hugh Wake* (PRO, CP 40/11, m. 114) where the assigns are legatees of Robert's late wife and Robert's deed of assignment is said to have been burnt. For cases in which letters of assignment were produced in court see the Michaelmas 1294 case of *Walter of Kesteven v. John of Lynn* (PRO, CP 40/106, m. 95) and the Michaelmas 1305 case of *executors of William Faukes of Felstead v. Reginald Wade and two others* (PRO, CP 40/153, m. 404). For the requirement of a deed of assignment see the unidentified case of *c.* 1300 reported in BL MS. Additional 5925, f. 60v.

126 PRO, KB 26/169, m. 19.

127 The rule was evidently not in force in 1286 when a plaintiff was awarded less than the damages he had claimed (*Walter of Bocking v. John de Belecombe*: PRO, CP 40/61, m. 66d) but was apparently in force by 1291 (*Robert of Rochewelle v. Joan widow of Adam de Neufmarche*: PRO, CP 40/91, m. 276d). For a good legal argument on the point in an unidentified case of c. 1300 see BL MSS. Harley 25, f. 183v and Additional 31826, f. 325r.

128 CP 40/72, m. 48d.

129 BL MS. Harley 25, ff. 174r–v.

130 '*et quo ad residuum predicti debiti dictum est predicto Lotero quod expectet hic versus predictum priorem eo quod hujusmodi placitum hic non audietur nec terminetur set allocetur ei in taxacione dampnorum*'': PRO, JUST 1/914, m. 3.

Chapter 2

Christian and Jewish lending patterns and financial dealings during the twelfth and thirteenth centuries

Robin R. Mundill

It is right that any history of indebtedness, commerce and credit should give some consideration to the Jewish presence in medieval England. Historians and others have portrayed the medieval Jew as the archetypal professional money-lender and they are nearly always mentioned in association with the provision of medieval credit.[1] Economic histories have often included a fleeting reference to them, nearly always quickly passing onto their replacement by Italian lenders after the expulsion of the Jews in 1290.[2] Other wider ranging histories have also tended to make the general assumption that the Jews were moneylenders because usury was forbidden by canon law.[3] It is certainly the case that over the two centuries of their presence in England from 1066–1290 at various times Jewish finance included pawn broking, mortgaging, granting of fee debts, annuities, and the sale of debts.[4] Indeed Jacob Rabinowitz was convinced that it was the Jews who had shown the way in commerce and this chapter will highlight how their dealings in some ways broke new ground in the provision of credit.[5] In order to do so, this chapter will examine the evolution of credit in the twelfth and thirteenth centuries with particular reference to money-lending and trade. It will consider the development of lending agreements by both Christians and Jews alike. It will demonstrate the complicated nature of such agreements and will consider the degree of profit margin contained in them as well as the development of non-usurious mercantile loans in the form of the recognisance. It will also examine the effect of Edward I 's Statute of the Jewry of 1275 and the demise of the Jewish contribution to the development of credit facilities in the light of the new system provided by the Statute of Acton Burnell in 1283 for Christian merchants to register their loans. It seems, however, appropriate to be begin with two well-known Jewish and Christian financiers at the outset of our period.

Lenders: Jews and Christians in the late twelfth century

Aaron of Lincoln, has, recently, been identified as the ninth richest man in British history, with, according to a modern conversion, an estimated £21.6 billion pounds.[6] Aaron has always been viewed as one of the the most successful money-lenders of all time. It is of course well known that he was a lender to the rich. His debtors included the kings of England and Scotland, various earls, abbots, priors, towns, sheriffs and even the Archbishop of Canterbury.[7] Between 1140–52, Aaron even made massive loans totaling well over £4374 13s 4d to the Cistercian foundations of Rievaulx, New Minster, Kirkstead, Louth Park, Revesby, Rufford, Kirkstall, Roche and Biddlesden. Later Richard the Lionheart, in need of cash, wrote these off for £666 13s. 4d. (1000 marks).[8] But Aaron was of course more than just a moneylender. His financial activities included buying the debts of other Jews, lending both large and small sums, securing rent charges, property development, pawnbroking and even speculating in grain.

He was not just a lender to the rich but also risked loans to comparatively poor people and other Jews. The details in the *Scaccarium Aaronis* (Exchequer of Aaron), set up after his death in 1187 to aid the collection of his debts, show that he was owed in excess of £15,000 (22,500 marks).[9] Some of the finer details have survived for his dealings in Rutlandshire. (Table 2.1) These show that he was owed for eleven different agreements which range from the debts of Count Aubrey of Dammartin who owed £115, to a lady named True who was in debt for as little as 13s. 4d. Other debtors included William Mauduit, one of the King's chamberlains and many of the local clergy: the Prior and Convent of Brooke, and the parsons of Bisbrook, Luffenham, Morcot and Whissendine. Amongst these debts there was also an agreement between Aaron and Robert, the parson of Bisbrook, who owed a debt for 125 soams of oats at Stamford measure.[10] This agreement for cereal amply demonstrates the fact that to be a successful credit agent there is a need to be flexible in the medium of repayment.[11]

Flexibility in the medium of repayment can also be seen by the arrangements of the Christian moneylender, William Cade. Cade also operated as a financier in the 1160s and was described by Sir Hilary Jenkinson as, ' a Christian usurer......on a large scale'.[12] His debts, which amounted to over £5000 (7500 marks), show that his debtors include the king, Richard fitz Neal (the author of the *Dialogus de Scaccario*) and his uncle the bishop of Ely (a former justiciar and treasurer), the two chamberlains – William Mauduit and Henry fitz Gerald, the steward, Manasser Bisset; three justices, and the constable of Lincoln castle, Richard de la Haye.[13] To these it is possible to add Gilbert Foliot, Geoffrey the archdeacon of Canterbury, Ralph of Diss, archdeacon of London and several monasteries such as the prior and convent of Merton, the monks of Louth park and the abbot of St Augustine's Canterbury. There were also the earls of Clare, Gloucester, Alba Mara, Leicester, Geoffrey de Mandeville and the Count of Eu.[14]

Amongst Cade's debts were also some repayments for commodities. In Yorkshire, the abbot and monks of Roche owed 22 weys of wool (44 sacks) '*cum saccis*' and 2200 fleeces '*cum saccis*' (7 1/3 sacks), '*in Everwicscira, Abbas et monachi de Rocha .xxii. pensa lane sum saccis, et Idem .mm. et.cc. vellera cum saccis in Everwicscira*'.[15] In Kent, Marsilius, monk of St Bertino, owed 100 soams of corn, 100 soams of barley, 60 soams of oats and 30 '*pisarum de trallea et per taliam de xv marcis*' (£10 0s 0d).[16] The monks of Louth Park , in Lincolnshire, owed £46 13s 4d (70 marks) 'which they had received from their wool which William ought to have six shillings'.[17] In Yorkshire, William de Vesci owed 4 weys (eight sacks) of wool; in Essex, Muricius filius Gaufridi owed 400 soams of corn, 30 pigs and one runt in respect of debts to the king; in Northumberland, Folbold , the moneyer, owed one last of wool 'by the weight of Berwick or Newcastle on Tyne'.[18] Cade, was therefore a lender on a large scale who was also flexible in being prepared to receive repayments in different commodities; this was part of being a creditor.

Table 2.1 The Rutlandshire debtors of Aaron of Lincoln, 1179–1185

Debtor (plus original creditor)	No. of debts	Details (debts other than money)	£	s	d
Count Alberic of Dammartin (Benedict fil Isaac Jew of Lincoln)	1		115	0	0
Herbert, Parson of Whissendine (Aaron of Lincoln)	1		93	6	8
Hubert, Parson of Whissendine Church (Deulesaut Jew of Stamford)	1		61	6	8
Robert, Parson of Bisbrooke (Aaron of Lincoln)	1	125 qtrs of wheat – Stamford measure = Approx. £31 5s 0d (5s per qtr)	31	5	0
Richard of Bisbrooke (Aaron of Lincoln)	1		10	0	0
William Mauduit, King's chamberlain (Vives fil Aaron)	1		32	0	0
Henry Parson of Morcott Church (Samuel the Jew son of Solomon of London)	1		30	0	0
Randulph Prior of Brooke and the convent of Brooke (Aaron of Lincoln)	1		13	0	0
Hugh, Parson of Luffenham Church (Deulesaut Jew of Stamford)	1		6	13	4
Simon the son of Paganus of Ryhall (Aaron of Lincoln)	1		1	0	0
True (Aaron of Lincoln)	1			13	4
Total	11		361	0	0

Source: H.G. Richardson, *The English Jewry under Angevin Kings*, (London, 1960), pp. 247–53. Public Record Office (hereafter P.R.O.) E/101/249/1

Thus in the late twelfth century we have a Christian and a Jew acting as financiers at about the same time. There is little dispute that their debtors are on the whole of high social status. Certainly they even share some of the same clients like William Mauduit, the King's chamberlains and the monks of Louth Park. Both are occasionally involved in demanding repayments, which are secured on or are to be paid in commodities. The lists of their debts present the same problems, which confront anyone engaged in studying the provision of credit – namely economy of detail. Such records only tend to record the amount of debt, the debtor's name, an indication of where the debtor might be found if the debts needed to be collected and a possible hint of interest to be paid. Clearly to the practising financier who knew his debtor the risk would be measured at an actual meeting when the loan was made and the whereabouts of a debtor who was known to the creditor might not even be required on any documentation. Thus mere lists of details of debts can only be taken as indicators and the descriptions of the debtors might well be shortened on them if the debtor was known to the creditor.[19]

Jews and Christians: lending patterns, *c*.1170–*c*.1270

Exchequer of the Jews

What distinguishes Jewish lending from Christian lending in the late twelfth century is the maintenance of more detailed records for Jewish lending. The experience of the collection of Aaron of Lincoln's estate through the *Scaccarium Aaronis* led to further developments in recording Jewish debts. The foundation of the *Scaccarium Judaeorum* (Exchequer of the Jews) was in part a response to the loss of Jewish financial records and royal revenue which had been destroyed in the massacre of *Shabbat ha Gadol* in 1190.[20] Certainly at both York and Lincoln the houses of moneylenders and the bonds were the targets of some of the rioters. In the case of York, Richard I (always in need of cash) was quick to act. Not only was an inquiry held and arrests made but a safer system to protect the Jewish credit market was quickly instituted. As a direct result of the loss of Jewish debts Hubert Walter set up one of the earliest archive systems in England.[21] Jewish lending was systematised and legalised almost a century before similar attempts were made to control Christian lending. The Ordinances of the Jewry of 1194 were the first turning point in actually regulating Jewish lending.[22] All Jewish transactions were now to be recorded by a bipartite and later a tripartite chirograph or bond and copies were to be kept in *archae* or strong boxes which were administered by both Christian and Jewish officials. These local officials or chirographers were to enroll the debts and these in turn were to be checked by government officials who carried out regular scrutiny of the *archae*.[23] There were also strict rules which were laid down and issued to every *archa*. Henry III even tried to regulate the permissible interest rate on each transaction.[24] The activity of the officials of the Jewish Exchequer in the thirteenth century has preserved fairly complete details of payments of Jewish tallages, Jewish financial dealings and court cases (on the Jewish Plea Rolls) brought in front of the Justices of the Jews. It has preserved further lists of the bonds of deceased Jewish financiers. These inventories were particularly important to the crown as it often claimed a third of their estates before letting the relatives inherit. Lists of debts such as these, often highly abbreviated, pose problems of interpretation and, by their very nature, make it difficult to glean more than the type of detail outlined above.[25] By the early thirteenth century, however, more information on the nature of Jewish money-lending can be gained from local records such as the Norwich Day Book as well as details of actual extant bonds.

Norwich day book

The Day Book can be likened to a working ledger kept by the chirographers of the Norwich *archa* between 1225–27 and as such is extremely useful in revealing the mechanics of local lending . It records the making of new bonds, instalment payments and the aquittance of debts. It indicates that the chirographers who kept the day book had a steady trade of about four or five transactions a week. It shows that at this period most of the contracts contain the accepted penalty clause of *lucrum*, which appears at the rate of 2d or 3d in the £1 per week as well as in some cases a further rate of interest. Yet the Norwich Day Book does give some indications, even at this period, of trying to hide the interest within the agreement and often the sum lent is never clear.[26]

Furthermore, details of some of the transactions, made in Norwich, do help to give a better idea of profit margin and interest as well as the complications involved in arranging a loan. In 1226, Alan de Senior of Norwich owed Isaac son of Jurnet £9 6s 8d and was to give as interest thereof £1 every year. The interest was to be paid by instalments of 10s 0d at Easter and 10s 0d on 29 September. If the instalments were not paid, then there was to be a penalty of 2d in the £1 per week. At the end of five years Alan de Senior was to render £9 6s 8d, and if, in case of default, he had not, he again ran the risk of the penalty. Thus, for a loan of £9 6s 8d, he was to repay the principal, pay £5 and risk penalty interest of 2d in the £1 per week on it. The actual profit on the loan can therefore be seen, irrespective of penalty interest, to be of the order of 10 *per cent* per annum. In another transaction the profit rate is higher. On 24 December 1226, John son of Robert of Depham owed Samuel son of Isaac £4 13s 4d and agreed that by 2 February 1227 he would have paid pay him a first annual instalment of £1 6s 8d, the first of a series of repayments which were to last for fifteen years. After that date, John of Depham was to pay annually 8s 11d on 15 August, 8s 11d on 1 November and on 2 February 8s 10d, and finally, on 29 September two loads of wheat. The three annual cash payments during this period added up to £1 6s 8d, and the wheat was extra. Thus, the annual interest rate seems to have been approximately 25 *per cent*. Another bond shows yet a higher profit margin. On 26 May 1227, Andrew Wascelin acknowledged that he owed Aaron son of Jacob £2. He was to repay it according to the following terms: £1 on 25 March 1228 and £1 on 29 August 1228 and finally, to secure the withdrawal of the chirograph from the chest, a further £3. If de Wascelin was to clear his debt of £2 in one year the profit margin for Aaron son of Jacob would have been 150 *per cent* per annum.[27] Despite the differing range of profit margins revealed by the Norwich Day Book there are also once again some indications that the Jewish lenders in Norwich in the 1220s were also prepared to be diverse in medium of repayment. As Vivian Lipman noted there are some fifty examples of stipulated repayments in small amounts of commodities contained in the Norwich transactions.[28]

Bonds

By the mid-thirteenth century, a further impression of the complicated nature of credit transactions can be gained from one of the few inter-Jewish loans which have survived. Such agreements occasionally contain more information than those penalty clauses which Fuss has rightly described as not necessarily representative of the degree of interest attached to the original loan.[29] In a transaction made between Jacob son of Elias and his brother-in-law Moses, in 1251, Jacob promised to pay Moses £2 13s 4d. As security, Jacob's sister Hannah held a bond which was owed to her and Jacob by Robert Bataile from which Jacob promised to pay Moses the sum of £2 13s 4d. As further security for the loan Jacob deposited a bond for £4 owed to him by Robert de Elmswell with the Rabbi, Jacob Gabbay. In order that Moses might be able to obtain interest on his loan of £2 13s 4d, it was passed through the hands of a Gentile (to avoid the stigma of usury). The actual amount of interest that should accrue was agreed to be at 4d in the £1 a week, approximately 86 *per cent* per annum.[30]

Other transactions made in the Marches in the 1230s and 1240s reveal a similar degree of complexity. An inquest which followed the deaths of Hamo of Hereford in 1232 (who probably left an estate worth in the region of £12,000) and Ursell of Hereford, his son, who died in 1242 necessitated the writing down and recording of their debts by the Archbishop of York, the Bishop of Carlisle and a local William de Cantilupe.[31] This inventory of debts reveals much about the lending methods of what could be considered to be a family business as the debts involved twelve Jews. It also shows that the House of Hamo creditors came not only from the local area but also from Lancashire, Northamptonshire, Shropshire and Hampshire. These dealings included large transactions for £666 13 4d (1000m) to as little as 13s 4d (1m).[32] A bond, made in 1244, reveals the amounts that John de Balun, lord of the manor of Much Markle, had to repay for a debt of £70 over three years from Moses son of Hamo. In this case it indicates that he was to pay an interest rate of 17 *per cent* per annum.[33] The House of Hamo transactions also show that the Jews often lent as consortia and were also owed a few debts, which were to be repaid in cereal.[34] In 1244 Richard le Seiner of Bakinton owed Ursell son of Hamo six soams of corn annually, 'until the end of the world'. Nicholas de Dudewell of Weobley on the other hand owed £13 6s 8d (20 marks) and twenty soams of oats due at the rate of 6s 8d (1/2 mark) and half soam at every Michaelmas from 1238.[35] In his analysis of these dealings Joe Hillaby had little reason to doubt the validity of these commodity transactions. Indeed he commented that 'clearly these annual rent charges must have appeared to many small proprietors an attractive means of raising money in times of dire need'.[36]

The scribal extracts from a general *archae* scrutiny which took place in 1240, also provide some indication of lending patterns. A surviving roll from Lincoln shows that once again creditors often stipulated small repayments in commodities as well as the main loan such as the odd bushel of oats, white pease, rye, and beans and even ells of russet.[37] Other evidence from actual bonds made in the 1260s also show occasional agreements for commodities such as robes, herrings, cartloads of hay, firewood and even a cask of cider.[38] It is also clear that even when a debtor tried to liquidate his debt early the added stipulated commodity was still insisted upon. Such was the case with William le Moyne who paid £2 to Deulecres son of Solomon of Stamford in 1274 and was still expected to give him the agreed quarter of corn and of barley which had been originally stipulated in the contract note.[39]

This brief examination of credit agreements from the late eleventh to the mid thirteenth century indicates a number of important features of Jewish lending. In the first place, there were at least two methods of making a profit on a loan. The first was generally achieved by writing the usury or profit with the loan as the amount which was the stipulated repayment. The second was an interest or penalty charge *lucrum* which was made on the debtor's default and was generally charged at a rate of 43.3 *per cent* per annum. It can also be demonstrated that there were Jews and Christians who made agreements for commodities and it seems that in some cases insisted on their repayments as specified. It is also clear that it is difficult to establish an easily identifiable interest rate for Jewish lending from the type of detailed transactions that survive from this period. Even where detail is available there is still the need to remain open minded about the charges which were made between creditor and debtor. The basis of Jewish lending, as James Parkes observed, 'was usury – that is a charge for the loan beginning from the day on which the loan was made, calculated in the bond usually as a fixed sum due on the day appointed for repayment'.[40]

Jews and Christians: lending patterns, *c.*1270–*c.*1290

Jewish lending, according to Stacey, was limited in 1269 and 1271 and finally banned by the Statute of the Jewry in 1275.[41] In fact, Edward I's Statute of the Jewry did not actually close the *archae* system down. Neither did it bring an end to the creation of contracts nor, of course, were Jews expelled at this time. Rather, in the earliest years of his reign, Edward embarked on what the late Vivian Lipman termed the 'Edwardian Experiment'.[42] More recently Paul Brand has called the Statute of the Jewry of 1275 'the most radical of all the legislation concerned with the Jewish community'.[43] John of Oxnead's interpretation of the clauses in the statute which affected how the Jews were now expected to behave financially is explicit, 'It was forbidden for Jews throughout the whole of the Kingdom of England to give their own money to anyone else at usury, but they were to live from the profits of their own merchandise, having the same laws of the Christian merchant for buying and selling......'[44]

As Oxnead recognised, the Edwardian experiment tried to encourage Jewish moneylenders to make a living by commerce rather than by pure money-lending. Naturally they were expected to become members of a commercial world which by its very nature had to be driven by legal profit instead of overt usury. Such profit-bearing commercial transactions were considered to be free of usury because they involved risk.[45] However, for the Jew this economic re-adjustment, as has been observed elsewhere, was to take place alongside severe social restrictions, which disadvantaged him.[46] This did not go unnoticed by the Jewish community, which was, quick to point out that it could not compete with Christian merchants because Jews had to buy at dearer prices and could not manage to sell dearer. It also claimed that, despite continued royal protection, Christian merchants could take their goods far and wide but that if Jews took their merchandise out of the *archa* towns they might be robbed.[47]

Before considering the type of business engaged in by Christian merchants to make what was considered to be a non-usurious profit, it is important to understand some of the contemporary attitudes which allowed the taking of profit but circumvented the charge of usury. Despite the fact that officially both Church and Synagogue decried usury, in order to make profit both Christians and Jews practised it at all levels of society.[48] There were many legal and illegal ways in which this could be done. Usury evasion was probably as common in medieval society as tax avoidance is today. Many Christians clearly did not heed the Church's view of usury. The Crafty Old Codger, Covetousness, in Langland's *Piers the Plowman*, reflecting back from the mid fourteenth century, was quick to reply to Repentance who asked, 'Have you ever in your life practised Usury?'

> 'Nay, soothly', he seyde 'save in my youthe. I lerned amonge Lumbardes and Iewes a lessoun, to wey pens with a peys and peare the heuyest, and lene it for loue of the crose to legge a wedde and lese it; Such dedes I did wryte that if he his day breke. I have no maneres thorw rerages than thorw miseretur et comodat. I have lent lordes and ladyyes my chaffare, and ben her brocour after and boughte it my-self.[49]

Even Bishop Grossteste knew how to hide usury. He spoke of loans being made for 100 marks (£66 13s 4d) but of the sum of £100 being written down in the actual contract. He also suggested that the Jews were less greedy than the papal usurers.[50] Archbishop Langton with a very temporal view claimed that it was a greater sin to seek credit from a novice usurer rather than an established one just as it was more wicked to frequent a young rather than a seasoned prostitute.[51] In 1240 the Bishop of Worcester forbade members of his diocese from becoming wet nurses to the Jews and from giving them money to lend at interest.[52] The flouting of usury was so wide spread by the 1270s, that urged by the rulings of the Council of Lyons, Edward I when he returned as king of England in 1274 immediately issued orders against usurers in London.[53]

Yet kings and peasants needed finance and accordingly had to resort to methods which would give them access to credit but at the same time would not draw attention to the usury or profit margin. As Raymond de Roover observed,

> 'The Church's doctrine on usury was inadequate .....it overlooked the real economic and social conditions that allowed usury to exist. The fundamental truth is that people in need of financial help had to depend on the money-lender either because they had not been able to find a Christian soul willing to lend without interest or because they preferred to keep their troubles concealed from relatives and friends'.[54]

Medieval society was caught in a paradoxical situation which has been summed up as, 'He who practiseth usury goeth to hell, and he who practiseth it not tendeth to destitution.'[55] Those who provided credit naturally needed to do so and to take a profit.

But what laws did the Christians have for buying and selling, making advanced sale credits and possibly even lending money in order to avoid destitution? They could obviously make verbal agreements which contained unwritten usury. They could take their profit by using the *advantagium mercatoris*, or by making seemingly interest free loans as illustrated by Bishop Grosseteste.[56] However there had clearly been problems with repayments of loans and many Christians now wished for a record of the transaction on which they could depend. Michael Clanchy and others have pointed to the growing propensity for writing things down to make them legal.[57] By the 1270s there was an increase in the enrolment of Christian recognisances. These are as the late Michael Postan observed, 'the formal acknowledgement of the obligation of the debtor before a judicial tribunal'.[58] Richard Bowers has produced evidence from both the Close Rolls and the King's Remembrancer Memoranda Rolls which show this increase.[59] The Close Roll for the period 1272–1279 also has many examples of enrolled recognisances. Whilst there are difficulties in hazarding as to precisely what some of these debts were for it is quite clear that the creditor wished the debt to be recorded. Even a cursory examination of the Close Rolls show that members of the clergy were making officially enrolled recognisances.[60] There were also many recognisances owed to members of the royal household, members of the greater and minor nobility, London merchants (including the mayor of London, Gregory de Rokesle), provincial merchants and the various Italian *societias* (Nutus Fulbert, Hugh Pape and the Luccans) as well as some minor French merchants. There were even recognisances which were owed to two Jews, Benedict of Winchester and Aaron son of Vives, and which had presumably been included on the roll for their convenience.[61] It is quite plain that these social groups were not lending expecting nothing in return as the very reason that they recorded the transaction was so that they could enforce payment at a later date if they had to. It is equally clear that such recognisances must be seen as instruments of credit. In some cases we have details which show that they were trade agreements.[62]

Of particular interest are the credit operations of two London citizens, Bartholomew de Castello, a clerk, and Stephen de Cornhill, a draper. It is clear that Bartholomew de Castello, who was head of the royal mint, and Warden of the Exchange, was operating in the credit market on a very large scale.[63] His sixteen recognisances registered between 1272–9 were worth almost £1100.[64] His house in London was clearly a well-known landmark to men in search of credit or loans. Indeed in 1279, in a transaction made between Andrew de Sackville and Henry de Lenn, the clerk of Robert Burnell, the bishop of Bath and Wells, the sum was to be paid, 'in London in the house of Bartholomew de Castello on Mid-Lent day'.[65] (Table 2.2) The other prominent London citizen, Stephen de Cornhill, was owed debts worth £514 15s 6d and seems to have preferred more diverse methods of payment, which suggests that he was involved in the trading of commodities.[66] In October 1275, Geoffrey de Southorpe, a Northamptonshire knight, Hugh Ridel of Wittering, and William de Colewill, made an acknowledgement that they owed Stephen 'one hundred and twenty six quarters of wheat, well cleaned, and sixty quarters of barley which were to be rendered at Southorpe at Christmas.'[67] Similarly, in October 1276, Ela, the Countess of Warwick, acknowledged that she owed Stephen eight sacks of wool at the fixed price of eight marks or £5 6s 8d per sack.[68] No doubt such transactions bore profit of some sort which was as Postan observed disguised as a type of sale.[69]

It was in such circumstances that in 1275 the Jewish moneylender was ordered to compete by buying and selling as a legal merchant. The changes brought about by the Statute of the Jewry can be easily demonstrated by considering the business of the London Jew, Rabbi Elias Menahem.[70] In 1277, Master Elias received a special licence to carry on 'lawful trade in the realm according to the form of the late Statute lately provided by the council touching usury'.[71] Subsequently, until his death in 1284, Elias

Table 2.2 The recognisances of Stephen de Cornhill 1272–1279

Conusor	Year of enrolment	Details (debts other than money)	£	s	d
Robert de Derley	1275		18	5	0
John fil Philip	1275		8	6	4
Anselm Basset	1275		22	0	0
Geoffrey de Suthorp Miles, Hugh Ridel of Wittering co Lincoln and William de Coleville	1275	126 qtrs of 'well cleaned wheat' and 60 qtrs of barley to be rendered at Suthorp at Christmas [NB estimated price]	91	6	6
Andrew de Estley	1276		24	14	6
William de Bello Campo Earl of Warwick	1276		84	1	6
John son of Philip de Bobinton	1276		16	1	6
Nicholas fil Anketia de Pauling	1276		133	16	8
Eudo la Zuch	1276		37	12	0
Ela Countess of Warwick	1276	8 sacks of wool at 8 marks each	5	6	8
Robert de Pinkeny and Adam de Rugges	1277		4	0	0
Eudo la Zusch	1278		17	16	8
Roger Le Tayllur of Malling	1279		4	0	0
Alice the wife of John de Hulcote	1279		20	0	0
Walter de Huntercombe	1279		5	0	0
Walter de la Lynd	1279		9	12	0
Alan Plukenet	1279		13	6	8
Total value of debts			£514	14s	2d

Source: *Calendar of Close Rolls 1272 –1279*, pp. 234,247,250, 355, 356, 357, 361, 422, 492, 497, 568, 570, 578, 580,

began to make official recognisances for commodities. His recognisances were nearly always secured (as more ordinary merchant recognisances were) on his debtors' lands and chattels. The detail given in them regarding the condition of grain or wool is similar to that seen in Christian transactions. In case of the non payment of a commodity sometimes a price is specified.[72] This change can be mirrored by a provincial Jew's transactions such as those of Jacob of Brancegate of Lincoln who dominated the agreements which were registered in Lincoln between 1275 and 1290. Between 1278 and 1290 he was owed 32 bonds with a face value of £325 16s 8d. The promised medium of repayments included two for specie, seventeen for cereal and thirteen for wool.[73] There seem to be little difference between Elias' and Jacob's debts and those of other merchants who enrolled their recognisances to minimise the risk of non-payment. A further way in which the change, which had been initiated by the Edwardian legislation, can be seen is in the actual bonds themselves. It is significant that just before 1275 the penalty clause disappears from Jewish bonds. The early Edwardian bonds, which survive, do not bear an interest clause. Indeed there are very few post 1275 bonds which have survived and as has been noted elsewhere they tend to record debts in terms of money, wool and cereal.[74]

By the 1280s when as J. L. Bolton has observed 'credit sales were so ubiquitous' there was an increasing need for Christian trade to flow smoothly and for merchants to have the ability to recover their debts.[75] Such a system existed for Jewish debts in the form of the Jewish Exchequer. However it was the Chancellor, Robert Burnell, who now created a system for Christian Merchants. Burnell had himself been involved in financial transactions of his own, he had had dealings with the Jews and had been personally responsible for auditing the accounts of the Riccardi in 1279. Burnell now took action and made radical changes for the provision of credit and collection of debts.[76] In October 1283, at Acton Burnell, the chancellor, with others, produced radical changes in the provision of credit. The effect of this single medieval statute was comparable to that of 'Big Bang' of 27 October 1986 on the London Stock Exchange when access to trading was widened, negotiations made easier and divisions between brokers and jobbers abolished. Burnell's medieval solution to the provision of credit was to produce a recognisance with 'vicious teeth', as Bowers has put it, and to provide a system for recording the transaction as well as immediate recourse for retrieving bad debts backed by the government and debt collectors.[77] The Statute of Acton Burnell set up several centres for registration of debts in 1283 at London, York and Bristol and later, (after its re-enactment) in 1285, in Newcastle, Lincoln, Nottingham, Northampton, Shrewsbury, Exeter, Southampton, Norwich and Canterbury.[78] With the exception of Newcastle and Shrewsbury *all* of these centres also had Jewish *archae* with officials for recording Jewish debts. (Figure 2.1) Burnell now appointed officials to keep rolls of debts and to produce *lettres de obligaciun* or Certificates of Statute Staple on which both the seal of the debtor and the royal seal would be affixed.[79] This new system did not apply to Jews who were to continue to use the *archae* and the Exchequer of the Jews to reclaim their debts and did so until their expulsion in 1290.[80]

Burnell's statute made access to credit both wider and easier, encouraged lending and provided government approval for commerce. As is well known it also allowed the circumvention of usury and provided a mechanism for the collection of debts. Such

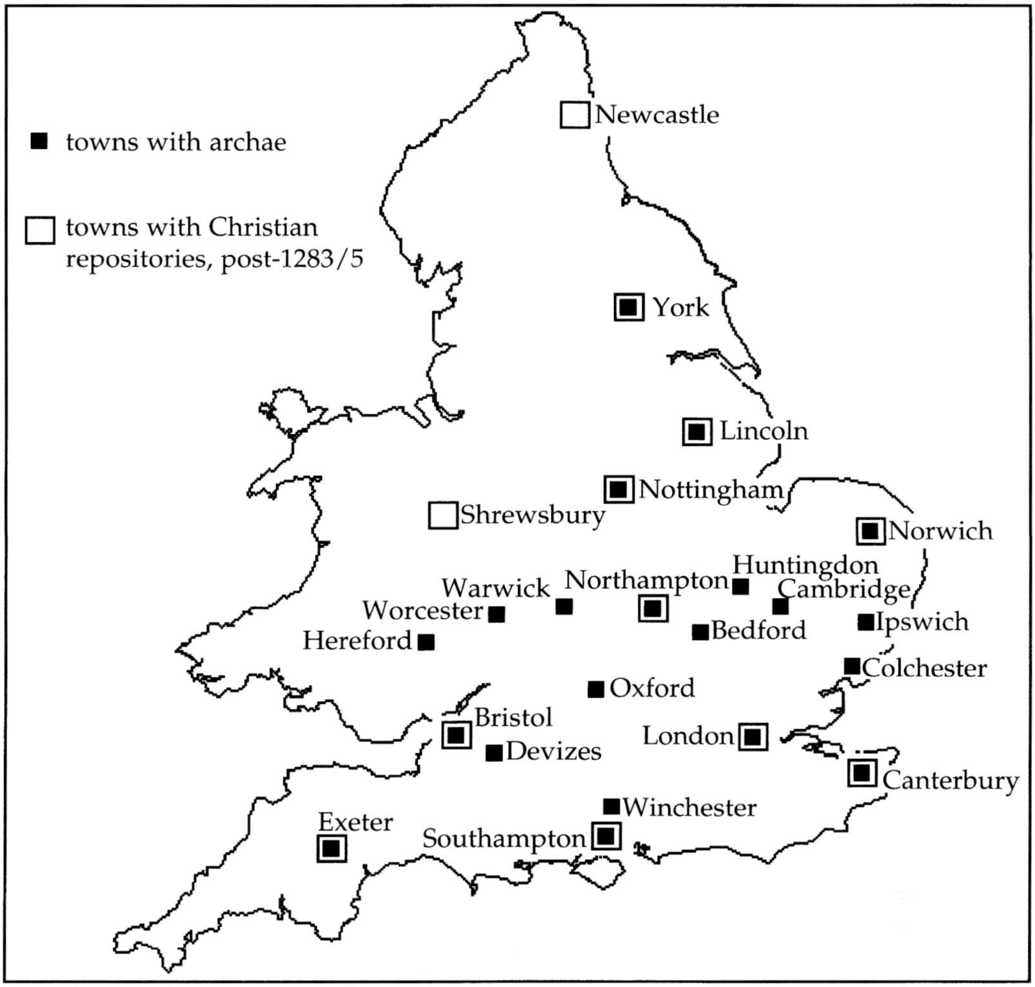

Figure 2.1 Towns with archae and/or Christian repositories in late thirteenth-century England

new opportunities were taken up by many Christians who could now become official lenders. The new certificates registered at Lincoln after the Statute of Acton Burnell show that the canons of the cathedral wasted no time and became active in the credit markets there. Philip of Willoughby, a dean of the chapter, and one of his chaplains, as well as others made frequent loans to both clerics and lay persons.[81] It is also clear that Philip of Willoughby made recognisances for the sale of wool.[82] Even the bishop of Lincoln's chaplain offered loans.[83] Similarly these new recognisances reveal the transactions of Lincoln merchants like William of Hepham who registered four loans in 1284 which were to be repaid in wool. These loans show that John and Stephen Ducket owed him one sack of wool priced at £9 6s 8d, Suspiro of Bayou owed him one sack at the same price, Richard of Thoresby owed him half a sack priced at £5 and

Richard Rudde of Barton (who is also known to have had dealings with Lincolnshire Jews) owed him two sacks of wool priced at £9 6s 8d.[84] The similarity between Hepham's recorded debts recorded in the new Lincoln Christian registry in 1284 and those of a local Jew, Ursellus Levi, recorded in the local Jewish *archa* between 1287 and 1290 are striking. By four bonds made during this period Ursellus was owed one sack of wool priced at £6 13s 4d by John, the parson of the church at Chedde. As late as May 1290 Ursellus was owed a further half sack of wool priced at £4 by Thomas of Poynton. In June 1290, Thomas son of Peter of Lincoln owed him one sack priced at £10 and, in July 1290, William de Brettevill of Houton owed Ursellus half a sack priced at £4.[85] Thus, in Lincoln in the 1280s Jewish and Christian merchants were operating amongst similar clients at the same level in the commodity markets using two different systems for recording their debts.

Jews and Christians: credit relationships, *c.*1170–*c.*1290

Having established that both Jews and Christians were involved in the evolution of credit facilities between the twelfth and thirteenth centuries it is now time to make some broader remarks on what can be gleaned from the records of their various credit operations and the extent to which their roles as lenders and borrowers altered over the period. As R. B. Pugh once observed, 'He who essays to reduce to intelligibility the credit instruments of the Middle Ages condemns himself to much drudgery without necessarily emerging from his labour with a clear mind'.[86] What exactly can be gained from such evidence? The detailed lists of the debts of dead usurer's like Aaron of Lincoln and Cade in the twelfth century and Master Elias in the thirteenth whose bonds had been taken over by the crown often have annotations and details of payments made to liquidate the debts as well as details of the debts themselves. However such records normally have one other detail in common; they nearly always carry details of the debtors and at times their geographical provenance.[87] Thus in some cases, as we have already seen, it is possible to trace not only their names, the amount owed but also the actual provenance of the debtor.

Systematic study of this information allows us to learn a little more about the debtors and their networks. A fairly cursory examination of Aaron of Lincoln's debtors in 1206 shows that, as would be expected, they come predominately from Lincolnshire and the eastern counties. (Table 2.4.) Yet it also becomes clear that he was able to provide finance for those from further afield.[88] Similarly the debtors of William Cade, who probably operated from London and the continent, seem to come predominately from Essex, London and Kent.[89] (Table 2.5.) It is interesting that in the late thirteenth century the London Jew, Master Elias, has a similar pattern to his clientele. This can be seen from a brief examination of his debtors which shows that he lent widely in Essex and Northamptonshire. The latter is perhaps due to his second marriage to a Floria a Jewess of Northampton.[90] (Table 2.6) Yet these were lenders on a large scale and in most cases with London connections.

What of the provincial Edwardian Jewry? The Statute of the Jewry of 1275 tended to restrict where the Jews could live. Although this was not entirely successful, most

Table 2.3 Mean averages of single loans from samples of various creditors' transactions in the twelfth and thirteenth centuries

Creditors	Date	Mean average of single loan
Aaron of Lincoln	1166–86	£39 19s 6d
William Cade	C12th	£46 14s 11d
House of Hamo of Hereford	1244	£56 5s 2d
Master Elias of London	1242–75	£26 7s 6d
Robert Burnell	1272–79	£39 4s 6d
Stephen de Cornhill	1272–79	£30 5s 6d
Lumbard of Cricklade	1270s	£4 9s 8d
Bonefey of Cricklade (his son)	1280s	£14 9s 10 1/2d
Jacob of Brancegate of Lincoln	1270–90	£10 3s 7 1/2d
The Riccardi	1270–95	£361 12s 2d

The figures above are clearly approximations taken from different surviving samples of debts but are used to give some indication of the lending capital and potential of each set of lenders

Source: Levy, 'Aaron's debts', pp.174–9; Jenkinson, 'William Cade', pp.220–7; Mundill, 'The Jews', pp. 212–3; PREJ1, pp. 65–8; Mundill 'Rabbi Elias', pp. 183–7; P.R.O. E/9/44; CCR 1272–9, pp. 38,113,121,132, 228, (bis) ,244, 337, 420, 416, 424, (bis), 430, (bis), 512, 568, 576, 578; CCR 1272–9, pp. 234, 247, 250, 355, 356, 357, 361, 422, 492, 497, 568, 570, 578, 580; Mundill, 'Lumbard and Son', pp. 165–9; P.R.O. E/101/249/32; Cohen, 'Plea Roll, pp.406–10, 418–9; P.R.O. E/101/250/9; P.R.O. E/101/250/12; Kaeuper, *Bankers to the Crown*, pp. 60–5.

Table 2.4 The geographical provenance of Aaron of Lincoln's debtors

Provenance	Number	(%)
Lincoln	64	37.2
Norfolk and Suffolk	28	16.3
Yorkshire	22	12.8
London and Middlesex	18	10.5
Hampshire	15	8.7
Warwick and Leicestershire	14	8.1
Wiltshire	3	1.7
Buckinghamshire and Bedfordshire	2	1.2
Cornwall	1	0.6
Northamptonshire	1	0.6
Northumberland	1	0.6
Oxfordshire	1	0.6
Staffordshire	1	0.6
Surrey	1	0.6

Source: Richardson, *The English Jewry under Angevin kings*, pp. 247–53; P.R.O. E/101/249/1.

Table 2.5 The geographical provenance of William Cade's debtors

Provenance	Number	(%)
Essex	33	19.1
London	28	16.2
Kent	17	9.8
Flanders	14	8.1
Unidentified	11	6.4
Lincolnshire	9	5.2
Yorkshire	7	4.0
Norfolk	7	4.0
Pont Audemer	6	3.5
Cambridgeshire	5	2.9
Northamptonshire	4	2.3
Oxfordshire	3	1.7
Northumberland	3	1.7
Wiltshire	2	1.2
Rouen	2	1.2
Middlesex	2	1.2
Hampshire	2	1.2
Berkshire	2	1.2
Bedfordshire	2	1.2
Worcestershire	1	0.6
Surrey	1	0.6
Suffolk	1	0.6
Staffordshire	1	0.6
Somerset	1	0.6
Shropshire	1	0.6
Nottinghamshire	1	0.6
Northumberland and Yorkshire	1	0.6
London and Bury St Edmunds	1	0.6
Leicestershire	1	0.6
Hertfordshire	1	0.6
Essex and Kent	1	0.6
Buckinghamshire	1	0.6

Source: Jenkinson, 'William Cade', 220–7.

Jews, after 1275, were confined to living in the *archa* towns. This geographical restriction in itself must have had a clear effect on their business. Bound by the necessity to live in an *archa* town a Jewish creditor must have dealt with a very local clientele which is helpful in identifying the geographical provenance of their debtors. It becomes quite clear that the Jews' clients were often rural and came from the hinterland surrounding the *archa*.[91] The actual logistics of seeking a loan also becomes a little clearer when we consider how, in 1274, Robert Fychet of Paxton in Somerset went into Exeter to

Table 2.6 The geographical provenance of the debtors of Master Elias of London, 1242–1284

Provenance	Number	(%)
Essex	6	15.4
Yorkshire	5	12.8
Unidentified	5	12.8
Northamptonshire	4	10.3
Herefordshire	4	10.3
Lincolnshire	3	7.7
Leicestershire	3	7.7
London	2	5.1
Warwickshire	1	2.6
Sussex	1	2.6
Surrey	1	2.6
Oxfordshire	1	2.6
Hertfordshire	1	2.6
Devonshire	1	2.6
Cambridgeshire	1	2.6
Buckinghamshire	1	2.6

Source: P.R.O. E/9/44.

negotiate a loan with Salamon the son of Salamon of Ilchester. This bond was witnessed by the two chirographers and the clerk of the Exeter *archa*. In a later legal case over the validity of the bond one of the witnesses testified that they had seen and drank with Robert Fychet of Exeter on that day.[92]

It has long been accepted that the type of Christian who borrowed from Jews in the period from 1150–1290 changed dramatically. Robert Stacey has recently viewed the Jewish communities of 1290 as, '...only an impoverished shadow of its former self, whose only significant role now lay in providing short term loans to peasants and craftsmen'.[93] By studying the debtors of the Jews of Cambridge Peter Elman proved principally that they were identifiable in a local context and that the Jews' clientele changed as attitudes and laws evolved. (Figure 2.2) He even went on to claim that 70 *per cent* of the Jew's clients were of the agricultural classes.[94] Such work can now be augmented by other studies of more local Jewish lending notably that of Joe Hillaby for Herefordshire and other studies for Lincolnshire and Kent. Hillaby's studies in particular illustrate the higher status of the Herefordshire debtors in the 1240s. (Figure 2.3) [95] Unlike the easily recognisable debtors of Aaron of Lincoln and William Cade in the late twelfth century it is more difficult to discover much about the debtors of the provincial Jewry in Edward I's reign. However because of their local nature it is possible to track down the provenance of a large proportion of them.

In the first place, the actual name used on the bond is obviously a method of identification in itself. The format of the names used on the bonds varied and might fall broadly into several categories: onomastic, locative, local locative, or descriptive.

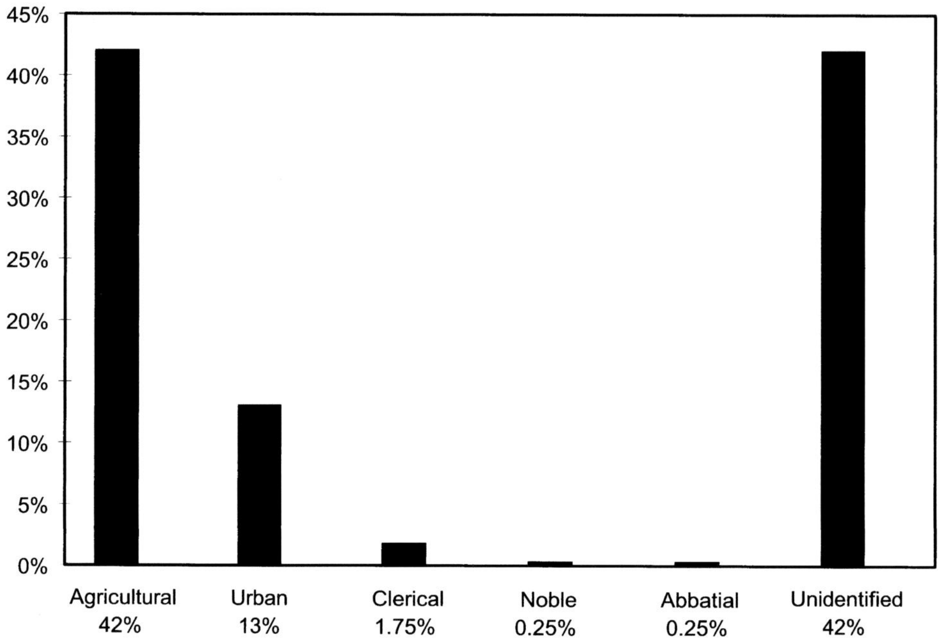

Source: Elman, 'Jewish finance', 1938, pp. 112–3; P.R.O. E/101/249/3, E/101/249/10, E/101/250/3; *C.C.R. 1254–6*, pp. 172–4.

Figure 2.2 Elman's categorisation of Cambridgeshire debtor, 1240–1290

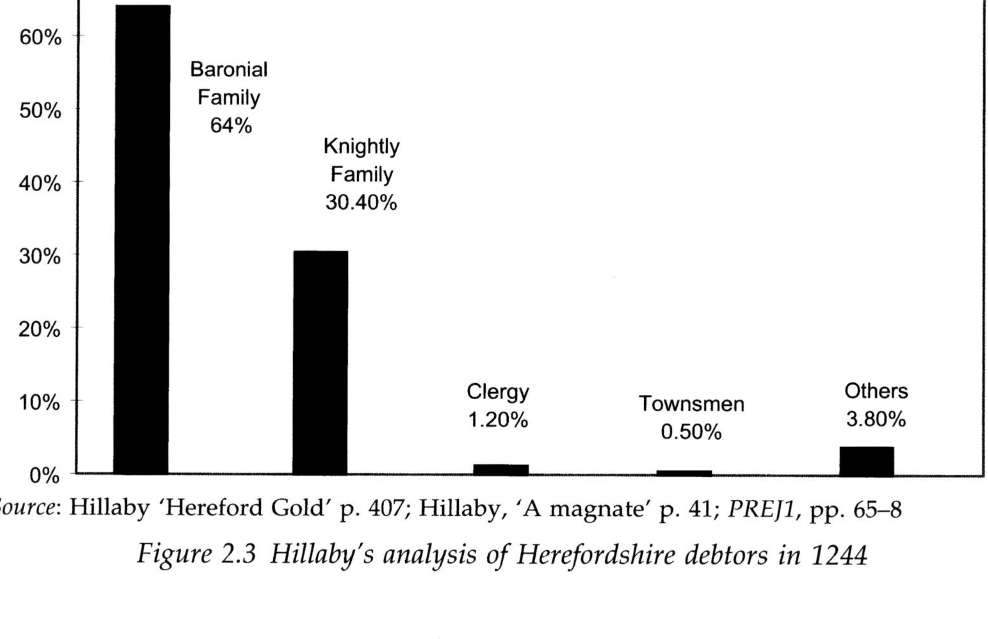

Source: Hillaby 'Hereford Gold' p. 407; Hillaby, 'A magnate' p. 41; *PREJ1*, pp. 65–8

Figure 2.3 Hillaby's analysis of Herefordshire debtors in 1244

Clearly simple onomastics with cognomen do not give much clue as to where the debtor came from but we can assume that in such instances they were probably known to the creditor and possibly the chirographer who wrote the bond. Local locatives like *de bosco, de la hethe, de la funtayne* are only of use in a very local context; for instance *de montibus* in Lincoln is a clear reference to Steep Hill. Descriptive names like *miles, carpentarius* and *capellanus* hint at the social position and occupation of the debtor. An analysis of the Jews' debtors from the bonds recorded in 1290 shows that there were 23 knights, 19 members of gentry families, 14 clerks, 13 women and over 50 artisans in debt. The vast majority were indeed agrarian.[96]

Fuller locative descriptors also allow us to trace the provenance of some local debtors. 'William, the son of Randulph of Stokes of Bube Clyne who lives next door to the house of William Quntyn of the same town' who had placed a bond in the Devizes *archa* can be positively identified as coming from the now lost village of Bupton in Wiltshire.[97] In Devonshire in the 1270s John Quynel, who is described as the rector of Shobrooke clearly came from that village but other records show that he had inherited a property in Exeter near to where his Jewish creditor lived.[98] Robert Kaynel de Yatton who had a bond deposited in the Devizes *nova cista* or new chest can be identified as a patron of the church at Yatton from 1265 onwards by a board in the back of the church.[99] Using such methods and the locative element of the description it is possible to make 'pathways to the medieval peasantry'. Thus provincial Jews both before and after 1275 operated on a very local level. Their debtors came from the surrounding hinterland. Research from the *archae* at Canterbury, Devizes, Hereford and Lincoln during the period from 1258–1290 shows that their debtors came from well within a 24 mile radius and in the main from a 16 mile radius and that by Edward's reign they tended to be from a lower level of society (Figure 2.4).[100]

Even one of the main changes brought about by the 1275 Statute of the Jewry, a preference for commodity bonds, does not on the face of it seem to affect dramatically the geographical pattern of the debtors.[101] The Statute made little difference to the debtors of the Jews who came from the village of Hackthorn some seven miles north of Lincoln. In the 1270s they made contracts for monetary repayment but by the mid-1280s they were making contracts for cereal and wool.[102] Likewise the debtors of the Canterbury Jews from the Romney marsh also change their contracts from monetary repayments to repayments in cereal.[103] A comparison of the clientele of Lumbard of Cricklade who died in 1277 and Bonefey who was exiled in 1290 show a change of repayment media but also a slight geographical shift.[104] Interestingly the debtors of the Jews of Nottingham and the Jewish creditors there do not seem to have even heeded the Statute as they continued to make monetary contracts of the type which were made before 1275 right down until the Expulsion at times alongside the commodity bonds. (Figure 2.5).[105]

Of course as far as some debtors were concerned the Statute of 1275 made little difference to their borrowing requirements. They were in debt and would seek credit where and when they needed it. The knightly debtor, Jordan Foliot had owed Benedict of Lincoln a debt of £10 in 1271 and a further £13 6s 8d in 1274.[106] In 1275 he was in debt to Roger of Evesham and used his lands in Norfolk as security.[107] By 1277 Jordan was actually in London when he made a recognisance with Manser son of Aaron and

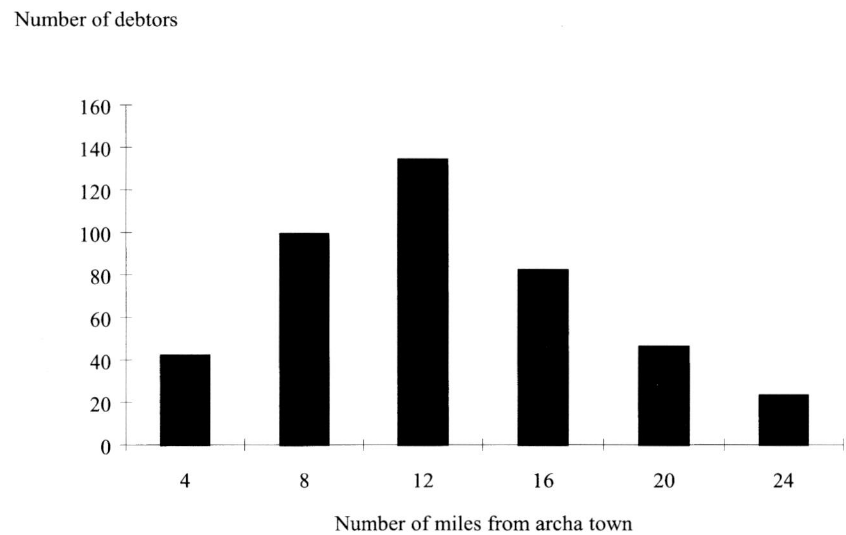

Source: Richardson, *The English Jewry under Angevin kings*, pp. 247–53; P.R.O. E/101/249/1.

Figure 2.4 Geographical distribution of Jewish debtors (Canterbury, Devizes, Hereford and Lincoln), 1258–1290

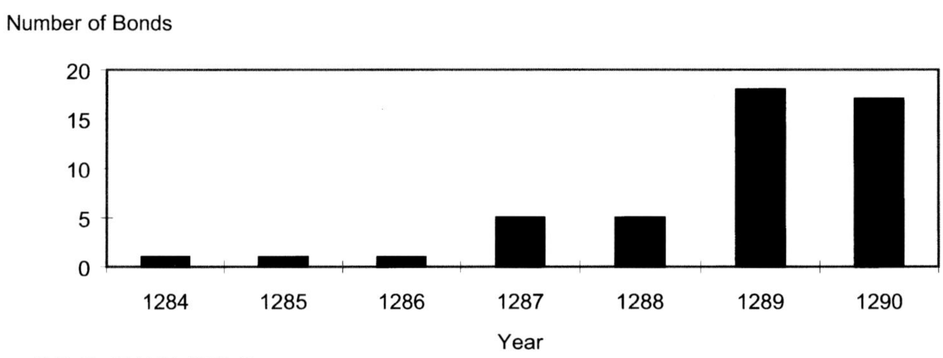

Source: P.R.O. E/101/250/8

Figure 2.5 Bonds stipulating monetary repayments in the Nottingham archa in 1290

promised to deliver four sacks of wool 'of worldly measure and of ancient weight' to the Jew's house in London.[108] In September 1279 he made a bond in Lincoln with Adam of New Market and promised delivery of 120 quarters of assorted cereal to Manser of Brodsworth.[109] In 1280 he made a recognisance in favour of Nicholas le Convers citizen of London for £18 10 0d. This was to be paid in three instalments in February, April and June 1280 and was secured on his lands.[110] In 1281 he acknowledged that he owed John de Kirkeby, clerk, £66 13s 4d half of which was to be paid in September 1282 and the remainder in October 1283. This transaction clearly was some form of liquidation of previous loans as an acknowledgement was made that with the exception of a rent of £2 from Jordan's chamber, which John received each year, all other debts between Jordan and John 'from the creation until May 1282' were annulled. This contract was witnessed by the testimony of Hamon Hauteyn, justice of the Jews.[111] It is likely that when Jordan died the family still experienced financial difficulties as in 1307 his widow Margery and his son and heir Richard were indebted for £410 by a recognizance in favour of Bishop Langton.[112] To an impoverished debtor, like Foliot, it mattered little what terms were negotiated or who granted them they still needed the credit.

Finally, in attempting to identify the debtors of the Edwardian Jewry, we should also consider some additional factors. Firstly, whoever made a bond with a Jewish creditor must have owned or had access to a personal seal. On the few surviving bonds from pre 1275 there are even fewer surviving seals. However those that do still have seals show that individuals like Susan the widow of Tonge, and William the carpenter of Selbire in Kent and Alan the son of Richard de Venella of Hackthorn and Geoffrey the son of Lawrence of Eresby of Lincolnshire all had seals which were personalised but with rather simplistic devices.[113] Some seals which might indicate either slightly higher social class or simply possession of a more ornate seal can be identified from the Lincolnshire debtors: Richard Rudde of Barton's seal had a rampant lion, Richard le Bret of Wrangle's an equestrian device and John Garnel of St Botulph's parish, Lincoln, had a dragon.[114] It also of course possible that seals might have been 'borrowed' from a guarantor. Ultimately sillography can only help a little in identifying such debtors.

Secondly, it also seems reasonable to believe that a debtor must have had some sort of security or promise of having the means to pay back the loan. The 1275 Statute of the Jewry limited the security for a debt to anything in the possession of the debtor, 'except the moiety of his land and chattels for his maintenance as aforesaid and the chief mansion'.[115] Thus it would be reasonable to believe that the Jews did not lend to anyone without security of some sort and may have been wary of lending to anyone of servile status.

Conclusion

Despite these caveats regarding likely wealth and status, it remains clear that over the two centuries of the Jewish presence in England there was a change from wide scale Jewish lending by large operators to small scale lending by small operators. Christians had also seen the way Jews had provided credit and had begun to apply it to Christian commerce. The stage was also set for the arrival of the Italians who quickly moved in on the higher levels of clients. Between 1270 and 1295 the Riccardi made a great impact in providing loans to the higher level of client. (Figure 2.6) R. W. Kaeuper has shown how the Riccardi of Lucca started to conduct making advances on wool. Prior John of Lewes used them for finance for over a decade. In 1283 he owed them £300. By 1286 not only had the debt risen to £600 (900 marks) but the priory had promised 23 sacks of wool at £8 13s 4d (13m) per sack. All was repaid by 1290.[116] In the period 1272–1295 the Riccardi made over seventy major loans worth a total of £25,312 14s 4d. These advances were made not only to the crown but to Archbishops, Bishops, Priors, Abbots, members

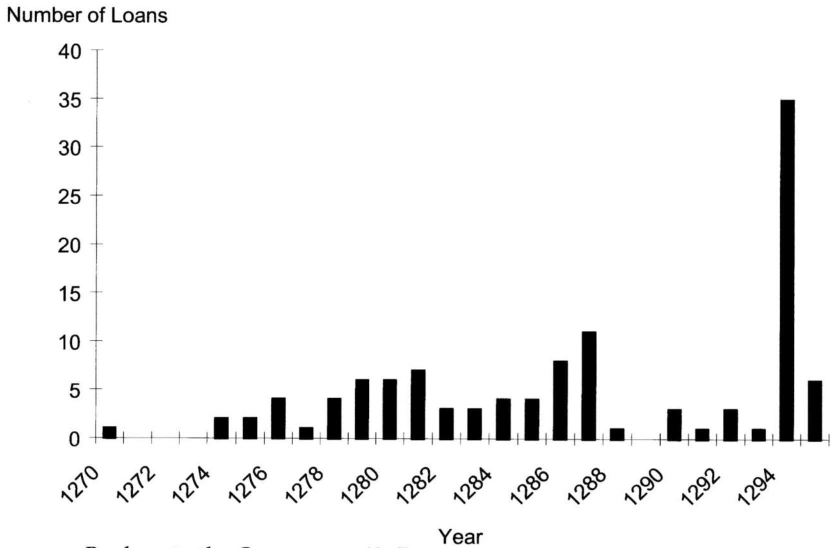

Source: Kaeuper, *Bankers to the Crown*, pp. 60–5

Figure 2.6 Major loans by the Riccardi, 1272–1295

of the government, members of the royal household as well as the aristocracy. They were lending to a clientele who consisted of the upper strata of Edwardian society, Kaeuper referring to the Luccans' clients as a *Who's Who* for the thirteenth century.[117]

But it was not just foreign merchants who could now enter the credit market. Many of the king's clerks who were, as Bowers describes, 'expert in law and familiar with Jewish and Italian innovations in lending', were able to take advantage of the new method of safer lending and to cash in.[118] Whilst the use of the Statute merchant has been fairly widely examined in the fourteenth century and the dealings of Walter Langton, bishop of Lichfield and Chester, Archbishop William Melton of York and the chancery clerks David Wooller, Henry Ingleby and Michael Ravendale have been closely scrutinised it is only fairly recently that their use in the late thirteenth-century century has been examined.[119] Examinations and case studies of Christian creditors tend to concentrate on the lending abilities of powerful men or *curiales*; however there are also many surviving examples of others using the system from relatively early on.[120] It was lenders such as these who were able to take over when the Jews were sent into exile in 1290.

Although, in the late thirteenth century, the Church might still have frowned on usury and men like Archbishop Pecham (even whilst borrowing over £3000 from the Riccardi) might have railed against royal usury and in particular the Jews before their expulsion: there was still a need for credit.[121] It does seem that the methods now used by the Jews' financial rivals and replacements came close to mirroring the Jewish system itself. Burnell's *lettres de obligaciun* (a distant cousin of the Jewish bond) and the system of registries in key towns for the recording of debt were as Rabinowitz observed, '.......convenient...since [they] afforded the easiest way of proving the debt and at the same time bound the debtor's property for its payment'.[122] Perhaps Mr Micawber bemoaning his own financial position and expressing antipathy towards the Jews of his day in Dickens' nineteenth-century London had in some way hit the nail on the head when he referred to bills as a 'convenience to the mercantile world for which we are originally indebted to the Jews'.[123] It was clearly the Jewish bond, the *archa* system, and the Edwardian Experiment which led to the development of the recognisance.

Notes

1 See, for instance, P. Geddes, *Inside the Bank of England* (Frome and London, 1987), p. 5; J. Giuseppi, *The Bank of England: a history from its foundation in 1694* (London, 1966), p. 5.

2 J. Clapham, *A Concise Economic History of Britain From the Earliest Times to 1750* (Cambridge, 1957), pp. 139–40; E. S. Hunt and J. M. Murray, *A History of Business in Medieval Europe 1200–1550* (Cambridge, 1999), p. 215.

3 M. Hook and A. Macgregor, *Medieval England Archaeological Collections in the Ashmolean Museum from Alfred the Great to Richard III*, (Oxford, 1997), p. 47.

4 Stacey, 'Jewish lending and the medieval English economy'; P. R. Hyams, 'The Jewish minority in medieval England 1066–1290', *Journal of Jewish Studies* 26 (1974), 270–93.

5 J. J. Rabinowitz, *Jewish Law* (New York, 1956), pp. 250–63.

6 *The Sunday Times Richest of the Rich* (Sunday Times Magazine supplement, March 2000), p. 8.

7 C. Roth, *A History of the Jews in England*, (Oxford, 1978), pp. 15–6. R. Bartlett, *England under the Norman and Angevin Kings* (Oxford, 2000), pp. 346–60.

8 Jacobs, 'Aaron of Lincoln', 162. J. Jacobs, *The Jews of Angevin England: Documents and records from Latin and Hebrew sources...... for the first time collected and translated* (London, 1893), pp. 108–9.

9 Jacobs, 'Aaron of Lincoln', 168–9.

10 P.R.O. E/101/249/1. Richardson, *The English Jewry*, p. 248 – '*Sciant presentes et futuri quod ego Robertus persona de Bitebroc debeo Aaron Judeo Lincollie sexcies viginti summas et v summas de avena ad mensuram de Stanford et Pleviavi eo quod ille due summe faciunt unam magnam scutellum ad mensuram Lincollie et totum hoc bladum reddam infra xv dies summonitionibus sue et hoc affidavi tenendum. Et ego Ricardus de Bitebroc sum plegius de toto blado predicto et deeo eidem Aaron ex parte mea xl summas de avena ad eandem mensuram redendas similiter infra xv dies summonitionis sue et hoc a ffiadvi tenedum*' . A summa was generally reckoned to be a horse load or a quarter of cereal.

11 Mundill, 'Anglo-Jewry under Edward I.

12 Jenkinson, 'William Cade'.

13 Jenkinson, 'William Cade', 211–2, as well as Walter fitz Robert, Guy Rufus, dean of Waltham and Richard of Ilchester, archdeacon of Poitiers.

14 Jenkinson, 'William Cade', 212.

15 *ibid.*, 221 *Pensa* = a wey = 256lbs or two sacks; *cum saccis*, with sacks; *vellera*, fleeces/pelts; one sack = 300 pelts.

16 *ibid.*, 221.

17 *ibid.*, 221, *Monaci de parco de Luda debent lxx. marcas quas receperunt de lana sua quam Willelmus debuit habere .vi. solidos.*

18 *ibid.*, 222–5. The Count of Alba Mira also owed 35 weys (70 sacks) and in Lincolnshire Guafridus de Navenbi owed 4 weys of wool (8 sacks).

19 Mundill, *England's Jewish Solution*, pp. 210–23 discusses toponyms and methodology of identification in relation to Edwardian Jewish bonds.

20 R. B. Dobson, *The Jews of Medieval York and the massacre of March 1190* (Borthwick Papers, 1974), pp. 17–37.

21 R. R. Mundill, 'Medieval Anglo-Jewry: Expulsion and Exodus' in F. Burgard, A. Haverkamp, G. Mentgen (Hrsg.) *Judenvertreibungen in Mittelalter und Früher Neuzeit* (Hannover, 1999), pp. 75–97; A. C. Cramer, 'The origins and functions of the Jewish Exchequer', *Speculum* 16 (1941), 226–9; M. T. Clanchy, *From memory to written record: England 1066–1307* (Oxford, 1993), pp. 68–73.

22 Jacobs, *Jews of Angevin England*, pp. 156–9; http://www.fordham.edu/halsall/source/1194ordjews.

html, *Online Reference Book for Medieval Studies*: English Jewry is Organised: The Ordinances of the Jews, 1194 © Paul Halsall, January 1999, Fordham University.

23 K. Scott, 'The Jewish arcae', *Cambridge Law Journal* 10 (1950), 451; H. Loewe, H.P. Stokes, I Abrahams, eds., *Starrs and Jewish Charters in the British Museum*, vol 1, (London, 1930), pp. xiv–xv; T. Stapleton, ed., *De Antiquis Legibus Liber Cronica maiorum et vicomitum Londoniarum* (Camden Society, 34, 1846), pp. 237–8.

24 Westminster Abbey Muniments (hereafter W.A.M.) 6719, W.A.M. 9002.

25 Mundill, *England's Jewish Solution*, pp. 6–8, reviews some of these sets of records.

26 W.A.M. 6686, 6687, 6693 and 9012; Levy, 'The Norwich Day-Book'; V. D. Lipman, *The Jews of Medieval Norwich* (London, 1967), pp. 84–86, 187–225.

27 Levy, 'The Norwich Day-Book', 248–9, 261, 263.

28 Lipman, *The Jews of Medieval Norwich*, p 164.

29 W.A.M. 6795, 6838, 6846, 6849, 6860, 6866, 6870. A. M. Fuss, 'Inter-Jewish loans in Pre-Expulsion England', *Jewish Quarterly Review* 65 (1975), pp. 235–40.

30 W.A.M. 6869.

31 *Calendar of Patent Rolls* (hereafter *CPR*) *1232–47*, p.5; *Calendar of Close Rolls* (hereafter *CCR*) *1237–1242*, pp. 354–5; *CCR 1242–47*, p.2; R. R. Mundill, 'The Jews in England 1272–1290' (unpublished Ph.D. thesis, University of St Andrews, 1987), 211–2.

32 *Calendar of the Plea Rolls of the Exchequer of the Jews* (hereafter *PREJ*), 1, pp. 65–8; Mundill, 'The Jews', 211–218; J. Hillaby, 'Hereford Gold: Irish Welsh and English land – the Jewish community at Hereford and its clients 1179–125. Part 1', *Transactions of the Woolhope Naturalists Field Club*, 44, 3 (1984), 358–419.

33 *PREJ* 1, p. 68 John de Balun owed (105 marks) £70 and had terms set for repayments over three years of (160 marks) £106 13 4d.

34 Hillaby, 'Hereford Gold', 381–92; *PREJ1*, pp. 65–8 Ursell was owed 77 soams of oats, 27 soams of mixed grain, thirty-nine and a half soams of corn and seven soams of pease.

35 *PREJ* 1, pp. 66, 68; Hillaby, 'Hereford Gold', table 9, 384–67 [please check this].

36 Hillaby, 'Hereford Gold', 411.

37 P.R.O. E/101/249/4; M.D. Davis, 'The Mediaeval Jews of Lincoln', *Archaeological Journal*, 38 (1881), 192.

38 Mundill, *England's Jewish Solution*, pp. 136, 156.

39 *PREJ* 2, p. 126.

40 J. Parkes, *The Jew in the Medieval Community* (London, 1938), p. 305.

41 Stacey, 'Jewish lending and the medieval English economy', p. 98.

42 Lipman, *The Jews of Medieval Norwich*, pp. 162–85; Mundill, *England's Jewish Solution* p. 14.

43 P. Brand, 'Jews and the Law in England, 1275–1290', *English Historical Review* 115 (2000), 1140.

44 *Chronica Johannis de Oxenedes*, ed. H. Ellis (London, Rolls Series, 39,1859), p. 247.

45 Parkes, *The Jew in the Medieval Community*, pp. 275–6, 293. Mundill, 'The Jews', 115–121.

46 C. Roth, *England in Jewish History* (The Lucien Wolf Memorial Lecture, London 1949) p.4; for the text of the Statute, see Mundill, *England's Jewish Solution* pp. 291–3. The Statute ruled that no Jew could live outside an *archa* town or travel outside it without wearing the Jewish badge of the Ten Commandments.

47 P.R.O. SC/6/54/2655; *Select Cases in the Court of King's Bench under Edward I*, ed. G.O. Sayles (Selden Society, 55, 1939), p. cxiv.

48 Mundill, *England's Jewish Solution*, pp. 108–115

49 Skeat, ed., *Langland The Vision of William*, i, p. 150, B. Text. Passus V., ll.241–6; 'No certainly not except in my younger days. I did pick up a thing or two then, I admit, chiefly from Jews and Lombards. They showed me how to weigh coins with a balance and clip the heavier ones, and then to lend them all out, all for the love of the Cross – the one on the back of the gold piece !!!! The borrower would give me a pledge he was almost certain to lose and that was worth more to me than the clipped coins. And you should have seen the agreements I used to draw up in case my debtors didn't pay on the nail. I've acquired far more properties through arrears of debt, than I ever could have got by showing kindness and lending', W. Langland, *Piers the Ploughman*, translated J.F. Goodridge (Penguin, 1959), p. 106.

50 S. Menache, 'Matthew Paris's attitude toward Anglo-Jewry', *Journal of Medieval History* 23 (1997), 154.

51 J. W. Baldwin, *Masters, Princes and Merchants – the social views of Peter the Chanter and his circle* (Princeton, New Jersey, 1970), p. 273.
52 Parkes, *The Jew in the Medieval Community*, p. 283.
53 *CCR 1272–79*, p.144.
54 R. de Roover, *Money, Banking and Credit in Medieval Bruges* (Cambridge, Mass., 1948), p. 149; N. Jones, *God and the Moneylenders: Usury and Law in Early Modern England* (Oxford, 1989), pp. 7–11.
55 P. Lacaita, *Comentum super Dantis Comoedium* (Florence, 1887), p. 579.
56 R. H. Britnell, '*Advantagium mercatoris*: a custom in medieval English trade', *Nottingham Medieval Studies* 24 (1980), 37–50.
57 Clanchy, *From memory to written record*, pp. 2–7; M. Bailey, 'The commercialisation of the English economy, 1086–1500', *Journal of Medieval History*, 24 (1998), 301.
58 Postan, 'Private financial instruments', p. 35.
59 Bowers, 'From rolls to riches' 65. The Close Rolls show that, in the period Michaelmas 1279 – Michaelmas 1280, 159 recognisances of debt were made; in the period Michaelmas 1289–Michaelmas 1290, 309 recognisances were enrolled. The King's Remembrancer Memoranda Rolls 1274–1275 show 78 recognisances, 1275–1279, 223 recognisances, 1289–1290, 359 recognisances.
60 These include Robert Burnell, then Archdeacon of York and later bishop of Bath and Wells who had made eighteen recognisances worth a face value of £695 6s 8d; others include Walter Merton, bishop of Rochester and Walter Gifford, the archbishop of York, representatives of Holy Trinity, London, Lesnes, Messenden, St James without Northampton, Stanley in Wiltshire, Vale Royal and even the Order of Friar Preachers. Mundill, 'The Jews', 134–5.
61 *ibid.*, 136–45. Jewish recognisances on the Close Roll itself show that Benedict of Winchester was owed 4 recognisances worth £72 6s 8d in cash terms and 202 qtrs of wheat, 20 qtrs of salt worth approximately £53 0s 0d: total £125 6s8d; Aaron son of Vives was owed two recognisances worth £49 13s 4d: *CCR 1272–1279*, pp. 326, 357, 358, 417, 495.
62 Parkes, *The Jew in the Medieval Community*, p. 276.
63 I am grateful to Martin Allen of the Fitzwilliam Museum, Cambridge for drawing my attention to M. Mate, 'Monetary policies in England, 1272–1307', *British Numismatic Journal* 41 (1979), 38–9. De Castello also had much to do with official of the Jewish Exchequer, Z.E. Rokéah, *Medieval English Jews and Royal Officials: Entries of Jewish Interest in the English Memoranda Rolls, 1266–93* (Jerusalem, 2000), pp. 114, 269.
64 *CCR 1272–1279*, pp. 109, 110, 113, 120, 235, 236, 256, 358, 422, 499, 578, 581, 582.
65 *CCR 1272–1279*, p. 554.
66 *CCR 1272–1279*, pp.234, 247, 248, 250, 355, 356, 357 (bis), 361, 422, 492, 499, 578, 581, 582. Cornhill was owed £418 2s 2d in cash repayments as well as 126 quarters of cereal, sixty quarters of barley, and eight sacks of wool worth £96 13s 4d.
67 *CCR 1272–1279*, p. 248. Wittering and Southorpe are a few miles south of Stamford. Geoffrey of Southorpe was a Northamptonshire Knight. Eleanor in 1280 secured the manors of Torpel and Upton through the debts of John de Camoys in the Jewry. In 1281 she farmed them to Geoffrey. Geoffrey already owed her £56 6 4 and by Easter 1285 owed a further £84 13 4 for three years as arrears in the farm of the manors. Later in 1285 he went to prison for debt. In 1285 he sold his manor at Southorpe to Stephen de Cornhill. He was freed in 1289. J.C. Parsons, *Eleanor of Castile: Queen and Society in Thirteenth Century England* (London, 1995), pp.131–2; E. King, *Peterborough Abbey 1086–1310 – a study in the land market*, (Cambridge, 1973), pp. 39–40.
68 *CCR 1272–1279*, p. 355.
69 As Postan has observed, 'Medieval loans were always disguised into or regarded as species of other transactions with which the Middle Ages were more familiar – especially those of purchase and sale'. Postan, 'Credit in medieval trade', p. 2.
70 Mundill, 'Rabbi Elias', 161–87.
71 *CPR 1272–81*, p. 212.
72 Mundill, 'Rabbi Elias', 168–70.
73 P.R.O. E/101/250/12.
74 Mundill, 'Anglo-Jewry under Edward I', 6. Lipman, *The Jews of Medieval Norwich*, 164. P. Elman, 'Jewish trade in thirteenth century England', *Historia Judaica* 1 (1939), 97.

75 J. L. Bolton, *The medieval English economy, 1150–1500* (London, 1980), p. 327.
76 Kaeuper, *Bankers to the Crown*, p. 84; Bowers, 'From rolls to riches', 67–8; Rabinowitz, *Jewish Law*, pp. 262–3; Mundill, 'The Jews', 150–4.
77 Bowers, 'From rolls to riches', 63; Kermode, *Medieval Merchants*, p. 238.
78 *Statutes of the Realm* (11 vols., Record Commission, London, 1810–1828), i, pp. 53–4, 100. Plucknett, *Legislation*, pp. 139–48.
79 Plucknett, *Legislation*, p. 140.
80 Mundill, *England's Jewish Solution*, pp. 121–2.
81 M. Prestwich, *Edward I* (London, 1988), p. 138. P.R.O. C241/13/101, C241/22/212, C241/23/93. I am grateful to Dr Pamela Nightingale for drawing my attention to some of Willougby's other transactions in York and Oxford, C241/44/50, C241/43/49, C241/43/32, C241/36/314.
82 *CPR 1292–1301*, pp. 310–1.
83 P.R.O. C241/17/64 C241/26/29. J. P. Bischoff, 'Economic change in thirteenth century Lincoln – the decline of a cloth industry' (unpublished Ph.D. thesis, Yale University, 1975), particularly chapter 3.
84 P.R.O. C 241/8/31, C241/8/34, C241/8/101, C241/8/195. Hepham actually rented some property to Jews – Lincoln Record Office (hereafter L.R.O.) Dean and Chapter Mss D (ii) 80/3/25. Richard Rudde of Barton W.A.M. 9170, L.R.O. Foster Library Transcripts A120, A144.
85 P.R.O. E/101/250/12.
86 R. B. Pugh, 'Some medieval moneylenders', *Speculum* 43 (1968), 288.
87 S. Levy, 'Aaron's debts sixteen years after his death', *Transactions of the Jewish Historical Society of England* 3 (1899), 174–9; Jenkinson, 'William Cade', 220–7; Mundill, 'Rabbi Elias', 183–7.
88 Levy, 'Aaron's debts', 174–9.
89 Jenkinson, 'William Cade', 220–7.
90 Mundill, 'Rabbi Elias', 183–7, 165, 171.
91 Mundill, 'Anglo-Jewry', 10; Nottingham Record Office Ms M24/182-8 – the Lassman papers
92 *PREJ2*, p. 194.
93 Stacey, 'Jewish lending and the medieval English economy', 100; S. T. Lieberman, 'English royal policy towards the Jews' debtors, 1227–1290' (unpublished Ph.D. thesis, University of London, 1983), 66–9, 116–7; M. Postan, *The Cambridge Economic History of Europe*, (Cambridge, 1966), p. 595.
94 P. Elman, 'Jewish finance in thirteenth century England with special reference to royal taxation', (unpublished M.A. thesis, University of London, 1936), 112–3, 140–7; P. Elman, 'Jewish finance in thirteenth century England with special reference to royal taxation', *Bulletin of Institute of Historical Research* 15 (1938), 148.
95 Hillaby, 'Hereford Gold', 400–15; J. Hillaby, 'Hereford Gold: Irish Welsh and English land – the Jewish community at Hereford and its clients 1179–1253: Four Case studies', *Transactions of the Woolhope Naturalists Field Club* 45, (1985), pp. 193–270; J. Hillaby, 'A magnate among the marchers: Hamo of Hereford, his family and clients, 1218–1253', *Jewish Historical Studies* 31 (1990), 23–82; J. Hillaby, 'The Hereford Jewry 1179–1290 – Aaron le Blund and the last decades of Hereford Jewry 1253–1290', *Transactions of the Woolhope Naturalists Field Club* 46 (1990), 432–87; Mundill, 'The Jews', 308–360 has detailed studies of the Edwardian clients of the Jews of Canterbury, Hereford and Lincoln; Mundill, *England's Jewish Solution*, pp. 209–48 has much of what follows.
96 Mundill, *England's Jewish Solution*, pp. 214–7; E.M. Carus Wilson 'The first half-century of Stratford upon Avon' *Economic History Review* 8 (1965), 52–57.; S. Reynolds, *An introduction to the history of English medieval towns* (Oxford, 1977), pp. 69–70; K. Wrightson, 'Medieval villagers in perspective', *Peasant Studies* 7 (1978), 213.
97 P.R.O. E/101/250/11; *Wiltshire Inquisitions Post Mortem*, ed. E. A. Fry (London,1908), pp. 152–3, 181; *Abstracts of Feet of Fines relating to Wiltshire for the reigns of Edward I and Edward II*, ed. R. B. Pugh (Devizes, 1939), p. 24.
98 P.R.O. E/101/250/2; Exeter Cathedral Archives, Medieval Deeds MS.52.
99 P.R.O. E/101/250/11; *Wiltshire Inquisitions*, ed. Fry, pp. 448–9.
100 P.R.O. E/101/250/6, E/101/250/11, E/101/250/5, E/101/250/12; Mundill, *England's Jewish Solution*, p. 235.
101 Mundill, 'Anglo-Jewry', 1–21.
102 W.A.M. 9162, 9130; P.R.O. E/101/250/12.

103 W.A.M. 9046, 9089, 9125, 9156, 9157; P.R.O. E/101/250/6.
104 Mundill, 'Lumbard and son', 137–70.
105 P.R.O. E/101/250/8; P.R.O. C/146/1360.
106 W.A.M. 9150; P.R.O. E/9/44.
107 *CCR 1272–1279*, p. 248; *CPR 1281–1292*, p. 324 seems to make it clear that Jordan also had Norfolk connections. In 1289 he rented a house in Norwich for one year. *PREJ* 3, pp. 65,294. S. Cohen, 'Plea Roll of the Exchequer of the Jews Michaelmas 1277 – Hilary 1279' (unpublished Ph.D. thesis, University of London, 1951), 397.
108 *PREJ* 4, p.120; Cohen, 'Plea Roll', 63, 308, 397 reveals that Jordan was also involved in other transactions between 1277 and 1278. In 1277, in partnership with Richard and William Foliot, he acknowledged that he owed the London Jew Aaron son of Vives 20 sacks of wool. In 1278, he owed Aaron Crespin 5 sacks of wool. In 1278, he also owed Benedict of London £20. In 1284, Benedict of London pardoned the Foliot family of all their debts P.R.O. E/9/44. Similarly, Aaron son of Vives also acquitted the family and issued a starrum in Norman French and signed in Hebrew, P.R.O. E/9/44.
109 His shared debt with Adam de Novo Mercato is on P.R.O. E/101/250/12 .
110 Rokéah, *Medieval English Jews and Royal Officials*, p. 240.
111 *ibid.*, p.273.
112 Beardwood, 'Bishop Langton's use of statute merchant recognisances', 68.
113 Clanchy, *From memory to written record*, pp. 257–9; H. Jenkinson, *A guide to seals in the Public Record Office* (London, 1968); H.S. Kingsford, *Seals* (London, 1920); P.D.A. Harvey and A. McGuinness, *A Guide to British Medieval Seals* (London 1996), pp. 79–88; W.A.M. 9028, 9036, 9092, 9162.
114 W.A.M. 9027, 9094, 9170.
115 Mundill, *England's Jewish Solution*, pp. 291–2.
116 Kaeuper, *Bankers to the Crown*, pp. 28–9.
117 *ibid.* pp. 34, 60–5, the latter for a detailed discussion of the debtors, who included earls, members of the royal family, and leading household officers.
118 Bowers, 'From rolls to riches', 65.
119 Bowers, 'From rolls to riches', 60–71; Beardwood, 'Bishop Langton', 55–70; L. H. Butler, 'Archbishop Melton, his Neighbours, and his Kinsmen, 1317–1340', *Journal of Ecclesiastical History* 2 (1951), 54–67; Pugh, 'Some medieval moneylenders', 275–91. See also below, pp. 69–89.
120 M. K. McIntosh, 'Money Lending on the Periphery of London, 1300–1600' *Albion* 20 (1988), 563–4; Mundill, 'The Jews', 139–40.
121 J. A. Watt, , 'The English Episcopate, the State and the Jews: The evidence of the thirteenth century conciliar decrees', in P. R. Coss and S. D. Lloyd, eds, *Thirteenth Century England: Proceedings of the Newcastle upon Tyne Conference* (Woodbridge, 1987), pp. 144–5; K. R. Stow, 'The good of the church, the good of the State: Popes and Jewish money', in D. Wood, ed, *Christianity and Judaism* (Studies in Church History, 29, Oxford, 1992), pp. 285–8, 294; Kaeuper, *Bankers to the Crown*, p. 61 shows that Pecham had made two agreements one in 1279 for 4000 marks, and a further loan in 1282 for 500 marks.
122 Rabinowitz, *Jewish Law*, p. 263.
123 C. Dickens, *David Copperfield* (Oxford, 1983), p. 630 –'Bills – a convenience to the mercantile world, for which, I believe , we are originally indebted to the Jews, who appear to me to have had a devilish deal too much to do with them ever since.......'.

Chapter 3

The business of statutory debt registries, 1283–1307

*Christopher McNall**

This paper examines the business of the debt registries established pursuant to the statutes of *Acton Burnell* (1283)[1] and *Merchants* (1285),[2] until the end of the reign of Edward the First, who died July 7th, 1307. These statutes, and the acknowledgments of debt entered into under them ('statutes merchant'), are very much the Cinderellas of the voluminous Edwardian legislative bundle. That is to say there has been little attempt in the realm of economic and commercial history, with the conspicuous exception of Pamela Nightingale's study of the history of the London grocers' company,[3] to scrutinise and collate the considerable mass of empirical material generated by the statutes as the means whereby a comprehensive and intimately-documented assessment of this particular facet of indebtedness during this period can be offered. However, no other extant set of documents possesses as much potential for this kind of endeavour as those which flow from the operation of these statutes. This seems to have escaped even M. M. Postan who, in his landmark article 'Private Financial Instruments in Medieval England',[4] discusses such acknowledgments as only one of the range of obligatory instruments available in the fourteenth and fifteenth centuries, without attempting to derive any hard conclusions from them. Accordingly, this paper aims to assess the character of the business of the registries, through description and analysis of the status of the parties making use of the registries, the sums recognised, and the purposes for which debt recognisances were entered into.

The statutory schemes

In outline, *Acton Burnell* provided that debtors could – the scheme was not mandatory – come before the Mayors of certain towns and cities to acknowledge ('recognise') debts. Such acknowledgments (or 'recognisances') were to be enrolled by a clerk appointed for that purpose, who also was to draw up a bond (a 'statute merchant') which, sealed with the seals of the debtor and a special Royal seal, was to be retained by the creditor. If the debt so recognised was not paid on the day agreed between the parties, the creditor could, on presentation of the statute merchant at the registry at which the recognisance had been entered into, seek an immediate sale of the debtor's movables and devisable burgage tenements.[5] If no buyer was found, or the debt remained unsatisfied, the goods and burgages were to be delivered to the creditor at an assessed price, to go in reduction of the debt. If any part of the recognised debt remained unrealised, the debtor was to be imprisoned unless or until some arrangement could be reached with the creditor. If execution could not be accomplished in the registry town, *Acton Burnell* allowed the Mayor of that town to certify the statute merchant to the Chancellor, who was authorised to issue a writ[6] to any sheriff in whose county the debtor had movables or burgages, ordering that the sheriff pursue statutory execution.[7]

Acton Burnell was soon succeeded by the statute of *Merchants* (often, *de Mercatoribus*) enacted in May 1285. *Merchants* retained the recognition and certification mechanisms of *Acton Burnell*, but the mode of enforcement of defaulted-upon statutes merchant was strengthened; on presentation of the statute merchant bond at the registry, the debtor immediately was to be arrested and imprisoned, remaining at his own expense in prison until agreement for the debt had been made. During the first three months' imprisonment, the debtor retained control of all his property, in order that he himself might levy and pay the debt. At the end of three months, the value of the debtor's movables was to be assessed, and sufficient of them to meet the debt and those costs allowed by statute were to be delivered to the creditor. If there remained a shortfall after this delivery, all the debtor's lands and tenements (and not just devisable burgages) were to be delivered to the creditor at an assessed annual value, and the creditor was to have an interest (a 'tenancy by statute merchant') in the debtor's real property until the debt was met from their annual issues. The debtor was to remain in prison until the debt and costs had been met.

The London Acton Burnell registry

London was one of three registries for which *Acton Burnell* expressly provided, the other two being Bristol and York, although other *Acton Burnell* registries (Winchester, Lincoln, Newcastle-upon-Tyne, York, and Shrewsbury) are known to have existed. [8] The idea of debt recognition was not new in 1283, and the London registry came into being against the backdrop of several existing modes for the recognition of debt. For instance, recognisances entered into in the Guildhall, before the chamberlain and aldermen of the City of London, are recorded in the Letter Books from 1276,[9] and, from as early as 1218,[10] recognisances entered into before the Treasurer and Barons of the Exchequer are recorded on the Memoranda rolls of the King's Remembrancer[11] and the Lord Treasurer's Remembrancer.[12] Recognisances are also known to have been entered into before the Steward and Marshal,[13] and their enforcement is noted on the rolls of the King's Bench.[14]

Despite the brief life of *Acton Burnell*, there is evidence sufficient to enable some conclusions on the activity of the London registry to be drawn. This evidence comes from the first Recognisance Roll ('Roll 1')[15] on which the statutory recognisances entered into before the Mayor[16] and the statute merchant clerk of the city of London were enrolled, and also the certificates[17] issuing from the London registry in respect of defaulted-upon recognisances entered into before it.

Roll 1 details all the business – 235 statutes merchant – of the London registry from January 8th to November 29th 1285. This period straddles the Parliament of Easter 1285, at which *Merchants* was enacted. However, since neither the entries on the roll change their form in any way indicative of a change in governing statute, nor the certificates issuing in respect of those recognisances certified from Roll 1[18] request that execution be according to *Merchants*,[19] the entirety of Roll 1 is considered as falling under *Acton Burnell*. Although Roll 1 begins a long step from the date of the statute,[20] the gap can, to some extent, be filled by certificates. Those from London record the name of the debtor(s) and creditor(s), the sum recognised, and the date(s) for repayment.[21] Sometimes, although not often, the date on which the statute merchant was entered into, as well as the date of the certificate, are given. These certificates enable the date of the earliest known operation of the London registry to be pushed back to December 20th 1283.[22] Accordingly, alongside Roll 1, are considered 167 certificates which (i) relate to statutes merchant stated to have been entered into before Henry le Galeys (Mayor until October 1284), Gregory de Rokesle (Mayor between October 1284 and July 1st 1285) and Ralph de Sandwich (appointed Warden, July 1st 1285), and which (ii) seek execution according to *Acton Burnell*, and (iii) for which no corresponding statute merchant can be located on Roll 1. It should be noted that, since a statute merchant only came to be certified when a defaulting debtor was outside the power of the Mayor, the certificates represent only a subset of all bad debts, which, in turn, is a subset of all statutes merchant, and, although it can be argued that the profile of a subset of 'bad' debts which the certificates offer cannot give an accurate idea of the profile either of 'bad' debts or of statutes merchant as a whole, this is the best which the available sources allow.

The profile of the debts before the London *Acton Burnell* registry is as follows:

Table 3.1 London Registry 1283–5: Acton Burnell statutes merchant

	Roll 1	Certificates	Roll and certificates
Number	224*	156**	380
Mean	13-5-0	24-11-0	17-18-0
Median	7-0-0	10-0-0	8-0-0
Lower Quartile	3-13-4	4-0-0	4-0-0
Upper Quartile	14-10-0	20-0-0	17-3-4
Lowest value	0-13-0	0-16-0	0-13-0
Highest value	200-0-0	648-16-6	648-16-6

All sums are in £-s-d
* Excluded are 11 statutes merchant for goods, or in which the sum recognised was illegible
** Excluded are 11 certificates which state no sum, or in which the sum recognised is illegible

Several phenomena fall to be noted. The first is that the 'entry' level (that is, the sum at which it was perceived worthwhile to enter a statute merchant) was below one pound, which suggests that the statutory procedure was perceived as convenient and readily accessible. The parties involved are also seen to span the gamut of society – from the humble (e.g. the sixteen shillings recognised[23] by one John de Maldon of Hertfordshire in favour of Ralph Sporon, a citizen of London) to the great (e.g. £80 recognised by Sir Richard de River in favour of Lord Edmund, earl of Lancaster, younger brother of Edward I)[24] and from relatively modest advances (e.g. the £4 recognised[25] by Ralph de Nevill, rector of Audham in Essex, in favour of Stephen de Cornhill, a draper and citizen of London) to much more substantial sums (e.g. £648-16s-6d recognised[26] by Sir Peter de Bermengham, a knight with interests in Ireland,[27] in favour of Baronchin Gualteri, a member of the Riccardi banking company of Lucca).

The above sums can be set against the background of pre-*Acton Burnell* non-statutory recognisances entered on the Close Rolls and in the London 'Letter' Books.

Table 3.2 Close Roll and Letter Book recognisances, 1276–83

	Close Roll*	Letter Book**
Number	401	422
Mean	45-6-0	14-7-0
Median	17-15-0	7-0-0
Lower Quartile	6-13-4	3-10-0
Upper Quartile	40-0-0	16-0-0
Lowest value	0-17-0	0-7-0
Highest value	1066-13-4	150-0-0

All sums are in £-s-d
* *Source*: Close Rolls, November 1279 – December 1283
** *Source*: *Calendar of letter-books, preserved among the archives of the corporation of the City of London at the Guildhall: Letter-book 'A' (c.1275 – 98)*, ed. R. R. Sharpe (London, 1899); January 1276 – December 1283

This *quantitative* discrepancy between the profiles of Close Roll and Acton Burnell recognisances suggests that Close Roll and statutory recognisances were also *qualitatively* different from each other. On the other hand, the similarity of the profiles of the pre-1283 Letter Book recognitions and those from the London *Acton Burnell* registry suggests that *Acton Burnell* recognisances were seen as an alternative to Letter Book recognisances. It then has to be asked what factors would have been taken into consideration by creditors; a schedule of the debts due to Gregory de Rokesle, a former Mayor of London and merchant[28] evinces some sophistication in the choice of the most appropriate means of recording and securing any particular recognisance.

Table 3.3 Gregory de Rokesle's debts, 1299

	per litteras	*per tallias*	*Exchequer recognisances*	*Certified Statutory recognisances*
Number	49	39	11*	9
Mean	13-01-0	3-15-0	28-12-0	23-15-0
Median	7-6-8	1-17-0	6-13-0	18-6-8
Lower Quartile	5-0-0	0-15-0	4-3-0	10-13-4
Upper Quartile	14-3-0	3-3-0	42-5-0	29-13-4
Lowest value	1-0-0	0-10-0	3-0-0	8-0-0
Highest value	66-13-4	50-0-0	70-0-0	66-13-4

All sums are in £-s-d
* Excluding a recognisance for five sacks of wool, with no price specified.
Sources: Public Record Office E 163/2/12; Statute Merchant certificates.

Here, although an obligatory writing (typically, a bond) seems to have been the most frequently resorted to option, recognisances – providing a measure of security – on the whole, seem to have been preferred for larger sums, with tallies employed for much smaller debts.[29] This gradient can also be seen as reflecting the ease in making – from tallies (on which nothing need even be written), through obligatory writings *simpliciter* (which could be composed anywhere), to recognisances (which could only be entered into before the appropriate forum, and which might have required the attendance of the parties, as well as the payment of a fee[30]).

The hypothesis that the London *Acton Burnell* registry was perceived as an alternative to the Letter Books is supported in one further way. Although *Acton Burnell* – and, subsequently, *Merchants* – expressly preserves other modes for the recognition of debts,[31] a marked decline in the number of Letter Book recognisances entered into after the advent of *Acton Burnell* is visible. During a twelve month period preceding the advent of *Acton Burnell*, 117 recognisances were entered in Letter Book 'A',[32] that is, about ten recognisances a month. Only about sixty recognisances are entered in the Letter Books during the 21 month period between the advent of *Acton Burnell* and *Merchants*,[33] that is, about three recognisances a month. However, a decline of Letter Book business coincidental with the advent of *Acton Burnell* in London does not suffice to prove, of itself, that decline to have been attributable to *Acton Burnell*. The incidence of Letter Book creditors 'migrating' to *Acton Burnell* can be investigated, and, it is contended, offers a sound measure of contemporary perception of the attractiveness of the statutory scheme. Between January 1276 and December 1283, the Letter Books identify 321 creditors; of these, 29 appear as *Acton Burnell* creditors; hence, about only about one in eleven of the pre-*Acton Burnell* Letter Book creditors resorted to the statutory recognisances: not a particularly pronounced movement. This would suggest *Acton Burnell*'s business to have been new, rather than a straightforward attrition of business from the other recognisance-taking forums in London.

The next question to be investigated is the size of the pool of persons resorting to the statutory mechanism. There are 412 individuals on Roll 1; 246 debtors and 173 creditors.[34] 259 individuals appear on the certificates, of whom 64 also appear on Roll 1. Hence, at least 607[35] persons used the London *Acton Burnell* registry. The size of this class can be compared with the pre-*Acton Burnell* letter books, in which, over the four years scrutinised, 685 individuals are named.[36] The categories of debtors or creditors are almost mutually exclusive; only 15 persons of the 607 (i.e, about one in forty) *Acton Burnell* parties appear both as debtors and creditors.

Although the London *Acton Burnell* registry drew in debtors identified as being from as far afield as Gloucestershire, Herefordshire, Staffordshire, Devon, Derbyshire, and Shropshire,[37] there is a pronounced London flavour to its business; about half of the entries on Roll 1 involve (whether as creditor, or debtor) persons identified as citizens of London,[38] and this is consistent with the certificates, of which a slightly smaller number – about four out of ten – involve persons so identified.[39] The discrepancy between the Roll and certificates (particularly the very small number of London debtors against whom certification came to be sought) is probably explained by the fact that the Mayor of London must often have been able to secure execution against defaulting London debtors, without need to resort to certification.

A key issue is the extent of mercantile involvement in the statutory process, especially given that the preamble to *Acton Burnell* made it clear that the statute was aimed at meeting a demand of merchant creditors:

> Whereas merchants until now have advanced their goods to various persons, and have fallen into poverty because they have had no suitable legal means by which they could speedily recover their debts at the day set for payment,[40] for this reason many merchants have forborne from entering the realm with their merchandise to the damage of merchants and all the Realm, the King by himself and his council has ordained and established ...

Indeed, there is a heavy mercantile component to the business of the London *Acton Burnell* registry. Merchants or tradesmen are involved in approximately two-thirds of the recognisances on Roll 1,[41] slightly more prominently as creditors (they appear in just under half of the recognisances: 116 of 235; 49%) than as debtors (about a third of all the recognisances: 79 of 235; 34%). The profile differs for the recognisances to which the London *Acton Burnell* certificates relate. Over a third – 60 of 167; 36% – of these are in favour of merchants or tradesmen, but there is only a small number by merchants – 7 of 167. It may be hypothesised that merchants or tradesmen – in London, at least – defaulted much less often that non-merchants, or, alternatively, that execution against them could be accomplished by the Mayor of London, without any need for certification.

Of these merchant creditors, there is a fair contingent of foreigners on Roll 1 and in the certificates; 66 individuals are named, amongst them 25 Frenchmen,[42] 18 Italians (particularly members of the great Lucchese trading companies),[43] nine Spaniards,[44] and a German.[45] By way of contrast, very few domestic merchants appear as creditors; only Leicester,[46] Great Yarmouth,[47] and Southampton[48] are noted.

Although the roll and certificates typically reveal little of the contexts of statutes merchant, some recognisances do make it clear on their face that they relate to the sale of goods. There are six statutes merchant like this on Roll 1 (four relating to wool,[49] and the remaining two to corn, and oats),[50] and six certificates.[51] The categorisation of such recognisances, when they appear, as 'mercantile' is, it is contended, supported by the fact that the enrolment often goes into the sort of detail usually encountered in a commercial sale of goods contract. For instance, a statute merchant on Roll 1 from January 1285[52] has the recognition of six sacks and six and a half stones of wool, to the value of £41-13s- 4d, to three members of the Riccardi company of Lucca,[53] by whom payment in full, it seems, had already been made. The weight of the wool was to be according to the 'Oxfordshire measure' and the wool, deliverable in three annual instalments between June 1285 and June 1287, was to be of the debtors' own stock or better. A further explanation of statutes merchant in favour of merchants would be as security for the repayment of loans. However, only one recognisance on Roll 1 states the statute merchant to have been entered into *'ex causa mutui'*,[54] and, likewise, only a single certificate.[55] Also included in the category of mercantile recognisances are those in which the identity of the parties is in itself strongly suggestive of such. For instance, Roll 1 identifies a variety of tradesmen as debtors, most prominently blanket-makers (twenty statutes merchant)[56] and leather-workmen[57] (sixteen statutes merchant). Almost all these latter are in favour of a small number of Spanish merchants,[58] and it can safely be postulated that these recognisances were associated with the purchase of leather by the debtors from the creditors.[59] A number of other tradesmen are also represented.[60]

A pattern reveals itself if the recognisances to different categories of creditor are ranked:

Table 3.4 London Registry: Acton Burnell statutes merchant, 1284–5

	foreign merchants	domestic merchants	all merchants	all others
Number	72	68	140	83
Mean	12-8-0	11-13-0	12-15-0	13-6-8
Median	8-9-0	6-5-0	8-0-0	6-0-0
Lower Quartile	4-6-8	2-16-0	3-12-0	4-0-0
Upper Quartile	16-0-0	12-0-0	13-17-0	20-0-0
Lowest value	0-16-0	0-17-0	0-16-0	0-13-0
Highest value	80-0-0	66-13-4	80-0-0	200-0-0

All sums are in £-s-d
**Source*: Recognisance Roll 1

The (perhaps surprising) result is that the profile of sums recognised in ostensibly mercantile or commercial contexts is less than in non-mercantile contexts. It is perhaps possible to attribute the relatively weak showing by merchants as symptomatic of any initial conservatism in resorting to an untried scheme. On the other hand, the figures could be seen as reflecting a widely disseminated confidence in the *Acton Burnell* scheme, and a willingness on the part of non-mercantile creditors to bring their debts within its provisions.

Roll 1 goes some way to identifying the non-merchants using the registry. There are 31 recognisances which identify at least one of the parties as a knight (*miles*), nine with clerks (*clericus*), eleven with rectors or vicars, and two with Priors.[61] However, as with recognisances to mercantile or commercial creditors, the roll (and certificates) often reveal nothing; for instance, it is probably never going to be known why two rectors recognised £16-13s- 4d to a Royal clerk,[62] or one chirographer was recognising to another.[63]

How long did creditors ordinarily advance money before expecting repayment? In respect of the 180 recognisances on Roll 1 for which the repayment period can be determined, the periods from the date on which the recognisances were entered into the day stipulated for repayment[64] were:

*Table 3.5 London Acton Burnell Registry: Roll 1 repayment periods, 1284–5**

	Number	Percentage	Cumulative Total	Cumulative Percentage
≤ 1 week	4	2	4	2
> 1 week ≤ 2 weeks	1		5	3
> 2 ≤ 3 weeks	4	2	9	5
> 3 ≤ 4 weeks	2	1	11	6
> 1 ≤ 2 months	41	23	52	29
> 2 ≤ 3 months	44	24	96	53
> 3 ≤ 6 months	61	34	157	87
> 6 ≤ 12 months	20	11	177	98
More than 1 year	3	2	180**	100

* *Source*: Recognisance Roll 1
** 55 statutes merchant for which the repayment date is not certain are excluded

Some points can be made. The first is that there does not seem to have been anything strange about entering into a recognisance for a debt payable almost immediately.[65] This strengthens the picture of the statutory recognisances as worth entering into.[66] The overall picture is one in which debts were repayable in the short to medium term; some repayment is due on about half of all recognisances within three months, and on almost nine out of ten within six months.

The London Merchants registry

From the fact that a certificate relating to the final entry on Roll 1 seeks execution according to *Acton Burnell*, it would appear that *Merchants* did not come into effect in London until at least November 25th 1285, the end date of Roll 1. The evidence presented here as to the business of the London *Merchants* registry, accordingly, is derived from Rolls 2–5 and certificates of *Merchants* recognisances issuing from the London registry. Rolls 2–5 are the only Edward I *Merchants* rolls to have survived.[67] They are:

Roll 2[68] (February 20th, 1291 – February 15th, 1292)	287 entries
Roll 3 (*Circa* February 16th, 1293 – February 16th, 1294)	219 entries
Roll 4 (late November, 1295 – November 16th, 1296)	141 entries
Roll 5 (November 30th, 1298 – November 19th, 1299)	171 entries[69]

The profiles of the debts recognised on these rolls and those certificates which relate to statutes merchant which are not to be found on the surviving rolls are as follows:

Table 3.6 London Registry 1285–1307: Merchants statutes merchant

	Roll 2 (1291-2)	Roll 3 (1293-4)	Roll 4 (1295-6)	Roll 5 (1298-9)	Rolls 2-5	London Merchants Certificates (1285-1307)	London Certificates and Rolls
Number	265	195	137	166	763	1220	1983
Mean	23-5-0	32-10-0	24-10-0	42-0-0	30-0-0	26-10-0	28-12-0
Median	10-0-0	13-16-8	12-0-0	20-0-0	13-6-8	12-0-0	12-0-0
Lower Quartile	6-0-0	5-0-0	4-2-6	7-10-0	5-8-4	5-6-8	5-6-8
Upper Quartile	21-6-8	32-0-0	24-13-4	40-0-0	30-0-0	25-0-0	26-13-4
Lowest value	0-10-0	0-10-0	0-10-0	1-10-0	1-10-0	0-13-4	0-10-00
Highest value	368-13-4	400-0-0	500-0-0	1000-0-0	1000-0-0	1000-0-0	1000-0-0

All sums are in £-s-d

The picture is a fairly static one: there is little expansion or contraction in the volume of business over the period studied, nor any decided shifts in the debt profiles.

Looking to the identity of those using the *Merchants* registry, the percentage of recognisances in favour of known merchants or tradesmen[70] are reasonably consistent, but well below the level of mercantile involvement on Roll 1; that is,

Roll 2: 14%;[71] **Roll 3:** 28%;[72] **Roll 4:** 17%;[73] **Roll 5:** 20%[74]

This contraction is reflected in the fact that only nine of the creditors named as London *Acton Burnell* creditors appear as such on the *Merchants* rolls. The tribulations and eventual expulsion of the Italian bankers in the 1290s by Edward I probably stands to explain some of this, but, otherwise, several prominent *Acton Burnell* merchant creditors simply disappear. The nomenclature of *Merchants* also points towards a perception that the 1285 statute was not just for merchants. The late thirteenth century treatise *Fleta* has the statute as *De Debitoribus et Creditoribus*, which mirrors the naming of the statute in certificates[75] and bonds[76] from the Bristol registry. Since most certificates refer to it as 'the statute issued lately at Westminster', the attribution '*De Mercatoribus*' is perhaps accidental.

The diminished, although subsisting, level of mercantile and commercial business is reflected in the thousands of certificates revealing the variety of things which could be the subject matter of a statute merchant; sacks[77] of wool,[78] various types of grain (most commonly, wheat,[79] barley,[80] oats,[81] and rye[82]), beans,[83] 'cars' of lead,[84] horse-loads ('seams') of iron,[85] tin,[86] loads ('lasts') of herring,[87] lime,[88] wine,[89] cloth,[90] peat,[91] horses,[92] and sheep.[93] This stands to be qualified in so far as it is almost always the case that, where the statute merchant stipulates for the delivery of goods, a monetary sum is also named,[94] and the debtor's performance cast as delivery (*solutio*) of the goods or payment of the money, e.g. *sex saccis lane de proprio instauro suo de L. et de K. precii sexaginta libris quam lana vel precium soluisse debuit* (my emphasis).[95] Such statutes merchant seem to have been entered into in connection with genuine transactions; for instance, the prices per sack of wool are both consistent across registries,[96] and tally with known market prices.[97] The same is true of statutes merchant for grain.[98] However, it is not possible to exclude, with any degree of certainty, the possibility of chevisance; namely, money-lending against fictitious sales, used as a device to circumvent restrictions on usury.[99] The correspondence between the value of the goods recognised and the sum named suggests that the latter was the purchase price, and did not incorporate any penalty in case of the debtor's failure to deliver the goods.[100] This is perhaps slightly surprising given that there was a way in which this could easily have been accomplished. There is no evidence that buyer/creditors in commodity transactions themselves entered into statutes merchant for the payment of the price. This is consistent with a model of advance payment by the buyer/creditor;[101] in theory, the purchase price would have been recoverable using the statutory procedure in the event of non-delivery.[102]

Hence, a significant proportion of the recognisances have no apparent mercantile or commercial connection. The pattern observed in relation to Roll 1[103] asserts itself in relation to the *Merchants* rolls.

The certificates sometimes reveal the range of non-commercial, ecclesiastical, and even familial, purposes for which statutes merchant were entered into. As to the latter, there are certificates relating to statute merchants entered into by debtors in favour of their fathers,[104] mothers,[105] brothers,[106] sisters,[107] and sons.[108] These were probably associated with familial, or dynastic, settlements, although this is made explicit only very occasionally; for instance, statutes merchant where the debtor is said to have entered into the recognisance in order to buy the marriage of the creditor's son,[109] or upon marriage to the creditor's daughter.[110] A lengthy enrolment on the plea roll of the court of Common Pleas for Michaelmas 1294 shows how complicated such arrange-

Table 3.7 London Merchants registry: statutes merchant to different classes of creditors: means

Recognition:	Roll 2	Roll 3	Roll 4	Roll 5
To foreign merchants	21-0-0	40-10-0	14-0-0	54-10-0
To domestic merchants	8-10-0	12-0-0	21-0-0	30-0-0
To all merchants	18-5-0	33-15-0	19-10-0	46-15-0
To all others	25-0-0	32-5-0	25-10-0	41-0-0

All sums are in £-s-d

ments could be.[111] Transacted between a prospective father-in-law (F), his daughter (D), and prospective son-in-law (S), it can be broken up into three parts. The first was an agreement whereby F and S covenanted that F would enfeoff S and D of all F's lands to hold to S and D and the heirs of their bodies, rendering F an annual rent for his life. This was coupled with an agreement that when F had made a fine before a Royal court that all F's lands were to be the right of S and D and their heirs, S and D were to refeoff F of all the lands for his life, except certain lands which were to remain to S and D in perpetuity, and others which were earmarked to go to F's wife as her dower if F were to predecease her. On refeoffment, the annual rent was to cease. The third element recited in the enrolment was the statute merchant; two days after the covenant between F and S, S entered into a statute merchant for 400 marks in favour of F; 180 marks was payable on the wedding day. The statute merchant was to be lodged a third party until a fortnight after the marriage of S to D. Only then, and no sooner, was the statute merchant to be delivered to F. S and D were to promise by charter to perform all the due services, and this was also to be lodged with the third party, to be delivered to S and D when everything had been fully accomplished.

In non-commercial contexts, statutes merchant for the following purposes were certified; bailiffs in a county administration acknowledging debts to their sheriff;[112] and for the relief of fees.[113] Statutes merchant stated to have been entered into for the fruits of a church,[114] for tithes,[115] and for tithes of sheaves,[116] reveal a decided non-secular component in statutes merchant. A Register of the early 1320s[117] which appears to have belonged to a religious house (the writs are overwhelmingly religious and there is not much interest in family property) nevertheless contains a number of writs in connection with statutory recognisances, although it should be noted that execution on statutory recognisances – especially the delivery of lands under *Merchants* – would probably have generated mortmain difficulties,[118] and a Year Book report of 1341 describes a Prior getting *Merchants* execution into the debtor's lands as being 'in fraud of the statute'.[119] Despite this, there are statutes merchant in favour of the entire panoply of ecclesiastics: Archbishops,[120] Bishops,[121] Deans and Chapters,[122] Abbots and Convents,[123] Abbesses,[124] Archdeans,[125] Canons,[126] Rectors,[127] Vicars,[128] parsons,[129] chaplains,[130] and clerks.[131] Ecclesiastics also feature, although to a much lesser extent, as debtors: for instance, Adam, the Abbot of Quarr on the Isle of Wight, recognised one sack of wool, price 18 marks, to a merchant of the Frescobaldi society of Florence.[132] Statutes merchant by ecclesiastics might have been unattractive to creditors, since statutory execution against clerics was much restricted: *Merchants* provided that they could not be imprisoned pursuant to a statutory recognisance, and enrolled cases suggest that there could be no tenancy by statute merchant in ecclesiastical lands.[133]

However, the very absence of detail on the face of the statute merchant bond or in the enrolled recognisance does, in almost all cases, hamper assessment of the underlying nature of the transaction, and this can only be laid bare with the assistance of extrinsic evidence, such as plea rolls. For instance, in *Stirkeland v Goldington*, a case heard at the Westmorland Eyre in 1291,[134] a statute merchant seems to be used as an instrument to disguise an illegal (since usurious) loan. The jury found that S, obliged in the York Jewry, needed money to acquit himself there. He agreed to sell G ten sacks of wool for £30; the suspiciously low price puts us on notice that the transaction was in fact a loan with interest.[135] A day was set for S to receive the money. However, when S came, G insisted, ostensibly from considerations of S's 'mortality', that the date of delivery of the wool be brought forward a year – from Whitsun 1288 to Whitsun 1287 – and refused to hand over any money to S unless S entered into a statute merchant guaranteeing delivery at that time.[136] S, 'fearing disinheritance' by the Jewry, agreed. A case in the London Mayor's Court in 1307 also scratches the surface of an otherwise unremarkable statute merchant. The claimant, Sir John de Fresyngfeld, contended that he had instructed Deveneys, his servant, to obtain credit on his behalf. Deveneys did so, obliging himself to creditors for just under £20.[137] Fresyngfeld entered into a statute merchant for £40 in Deveneys' favour, on condition that Deveneys would not be entitled to more money than he in fact managed to raise for Fresyngfeld and any damages which Deveneys might incur for failure to repay the money borrowed on time. The defendant sought, and obtained, execution on the statute merchant.[138]

There is no means of ascertaining, for any registry other than London,[139] the proportion of statutes merchant defaulted upon, and for which certificates came to be issued. It will be recalled that certified statutes merchant represent the intersection of two subsets of all recognisances taken; that is, defaulted upon statutes merchant for which execution in full could not be secured by the certifying Mayor in the registry town. For the London registry, the proportion of statutes merchant certified can be assessed via a comparison of the five Recognisance Rolls and statute merchant certificates issued during the reign of Edward I.[140] This exercise indicates that a certificate was issued in respect of approximately one in six of all recognisances on the Rolls:[141] a large proportion. There is nothing notable about the average sums of the recognisances certified: that is, they are neither especially big nor small; for instance, of the twenty-two *Acton Burnell* recognisances on Roll 1 which came to be certified, the average sum was £16-15-0.

Business of other registries

Without any extant surviving Recognisance Rolls for any registry other than London during this period, the certificates are the only means for assessing the business of other registries. These, with the earliest known dates of their operation, were;

Appleby-in-Westmorland:	December 28th 1285[142]
Hereford:	February 1290[143]
Nottingham:	December 1290[144]
Chester:	October 1291[145]
Exeter:	August 1292[146]
Norwich:	October 6th 1298[147]
Oxford:	April 4th 1307[148]

Merchants also instituted 'flying' registries at major fairs,[149] staffed by the London statute merchant clerk, and two merchants elected for that purpose. The following are known to have operated:

Boston (St.Botulph's) Fair (Lincs)	before late July 1286[150]
St. Giles' Fair (Winchester, Hants)	before late September 1286[151]
St. Ives' Fair (Hunts)	before early May 1287[152]
Stamford Fair (Lincs)	before late March 1288[153]

The profiles of the debts recognised in all registries, from the certificates, are:

Table 3.8 All certificated statutes merchant, 1283–1307

Registry	Number	Mean	Median	Lower Quartile	Upper Quartile	Lowest value	Highest value
Appelby	34	10-18-0	3-9-8	1-5-10	12-0-0	0-11-00	83-6-8
Bristol	205	21-13-0	11-0-0	6-0-0	24-0-0	0-18-00	431-1-6
Exeter	303	14-6-0	7-5-1	3-18-0	13-6-8	1-0-0	133-6-8
Hereford	232	19-16-0	8-13-0	3-6-8	20-0-0	1-0-0	1000-0-0
London	1529	26-16-0	12-0-0	5-6-8	26-13-4	0-13-4	1000-0-0
Lincoln	833	15-16-0	7-13-7	4-0-0	16-0-0	1-0-0	1000-0-0
Newcastle	47	18-10-0	9-11-7	4-0-0	16-0-0	0-15-00	200-0-0
Nottingham	313	15-11-0	8-4-9	3-6-8	17-13-4	0-13-4	300-0-0
Norwich	274	11-15-0	5-6-8	2-10-0	12-0-0	1-0-0	200-0-0
St.Botulph's Fair	125	14-6-0	8-0-0	4-0-0	16-0-0	1-0-0	232-0-0
Shrewsbury	635	14-1-0	6-13-4	3-6-8	16-0-0	0-9-1	200-0-0
Winchester	457	16-3-0	8-9-0	4-0-0	18-2-9	0-13-4	300-0-0
York	1383	14-16-0	6-13-4	3-0-0	15-15-0	0-6-8	1000-0-0

All sums are in £-s-d

In contrast to the 'standing' registries, the business of the Boston registry – for which the greatest number of certificates has survived – was predominantly (although by no means exclusively) mercantile: of the eighty creditors named in the certificates, only about one in three are *not* identified (or otherwise identifiable) as merchants, or trading for commodities. Several merchants are particularly prominent, and involved in a number of statutes merchant – Gaylard Buschon, a merchant of Cahors is involved in fifteen statutes merchant, and Jacob Hugelyn, a merchant of Lucca, in ten, and merchants of Besançon, Bordeaux, Douai, La Rochelle, Perigord, Toulouse, Florence, Piacenza, and Lubeck all appear. The nature of mercantile business is distinguishable from other business, in that the mean sum certified in favour of foreign merchants is £15-10-0, in comparison with business in favour of all others, where the mean was £11-19-0.

Despite the efforts made after 1285 to extend the territorial coverage of the statutory scheme, examination of the direction of writs requested by statute merchant certificates during the entire period of this study reveals that this was coverage was, in fact, patchy. Bearing in mind that the certificates represent only a portion of all statutes merchant entered into, the first phenomenon to be noted is that the influence of the statutory registries seems to have been strongly localised; that is, for any given registry, a considerable majority of those debtors in respect of whose recognisances certificates issued, seem to have come from nearby. Distributed equally over forty counties, the proportion of writs requested to each county would be 2½ *per cent*. Of the ten counties above this average[154] there was a statute merchant registry in nine,[155] and these ten counties accounted for about seven out of ten (71%) of all writs requested. Over a fifth of all writs requested were to the sheriff of Yorkshire (1947 from 8926: 21.8%), and further tenths to the sheriffs of Lincolnshire (1042: 11.7%), and Shropshire (807: 9%). Approaching the matter from a different angle, four in every five writs sought are to the sheriffs of the counties in which registries were located.[156] For instance, of the 2029 requests for writs made by the Mayor of York, almost nine of every ten (1805: 89%) were that writs be sent to the sheriff of Yorkshire. When writs requested to be sent to the sheriff of the next most mentioned county, Lincolnshire, are factored in, this is pushed up to over 90 *per cent*, and this is consistent across registries.[157] At the opposite end of the scale, there are counties to which a disproportionately low number of writs were requested; there are 18 counties where the number of writs requested was less than half the average. Nine of these counties – Worcestershire, Warwickshire, Oxfordshire, Northamptonshire, Buckinghamshire, Bedfordshire, Huntingdonshire, Rutland and Cambridgeshire – form a large block across the south Midlands, falling roughly within a polygon described by the London, Winchester, Hereford, Shrewsbury, Nottingham and Norwich registries at its apexes.[158] Together, they account for only about one thirteenth of all writs requested. Counties at the 'extremities' of England – Cornwall, Cumberland, Northumberland,[159] Lancashire, Dorset and Sussex are also underprovided in this sense. Even for the fair registries, the picture of the sphere of influence mirrors the general picture. For instance, in respect of Boston Fair, over four in every ten writs are requested to the sheriff of the 'home county', Lincolnshire, and almost three quarters of certificates (74%; 111 of 150) request writs to sheriffs of eight counties thirty miles or less from Boston: Lincolnshire, Norfolk, Leicestershire, Huntingdonshire, Nottinghamshire, Northamptonshire, Cambridgeshire and Rutland.

Conclusions

The evidence presented above enables the construction of certain hypotheses regarding the fiscal climate at the very end of the thirteenth century to be tested. The general picture presented by Pamela Nightingale from the evidence of pepperers' credit activities is that an increase in mercantile capital[160] was followed by a credit slump in the 1290s.[161] However, the picture which can be derived from the data adduced in this paper is at some variance with that summary. Between 1283[162] and 1298–9[163] a distinct upward trend in the size of the sums recognised before the London registry is visible: over that period, the mean sum recognised more than doubles (from £17-18s to £42),[164] and, furthermore, the overall debt profile over this period shifts consistently with the mean: both the median and the upper quartile values evince similar growth. However, this trend is not uniform, since there is a dip in the mid 1290s, indicated by a slimming down of the figures in Roll 4 (1295–6), which is also reflected in the mean values of statutes merchant in favour of different classes of creditor.[165] Alongside this, and over the whole period studied, there is a marked contraction in the volume of business, that is, the number of recognisances entered into, although this always appears to be at fairly buoyant levels.

Several wider conclusions can also be drawn: the first is that the business of the statutory registries – the fair registries aside – can never be said to have been predominantly mercantile. Secondly, the appearance of parties from all walks of life – both religious and secular – reveals a society aware of the possibility of being able to secure a debt under the statutory procedures – often as a means of guaranteeing, or underpinning, another transaction – and quick to avail itself of that possibility where available (although it is seen, from the provenance of defaulting debtors, that large parts of the country were far from the nearest registry). The statutes were certainly no paper tigers – judging from the sheer volume of certificates, there was a distinct alacrity to make use of the statutory provisions for enforcement, where necessary.

Notes

* Cardiff Law School. Some of this material derives from my 'The recognition and enforcement of debts under the statutes of Acton Burnell (1283) and Merchants (1285), 1283–1307' (unpublished D.Phil. thesis, University of Oxford, 2000). I am extremely grateful to my colleague Dr. Peter Clifford for his generous assistance with calculation of the statistics in this paper.

1 *Statutes of the Realm*, i, pp. 53–4. The statute is dated October 12th 1283.

2 *Statutes of the Realm*, i, pp. 98–100.

3 Pamela Nightingale, *A Medieval Mercantile Community: the Grocers' Company and the politics and trade of London 1000 – 1485* (Yale UP, 1995).

4 Postan, ' Private financial instruments', 37–9.

5 Lands and tenements of burgage tenure were subject to the custom of the borough in which they lay, and, in general, were characterised by the payment of an annual rent which operated in discharge of all other services. The degree of freedom of devise varied: in some boroughs it was deemed that land which the tenant held by inheritance (rather than by purchase) constituted part of his patrimony, and, accordingly, alienation *inter vivos* and devise were prohibited; Morley de Wolf Hemmeon, *Burgage Tenure in Medieval England*, (Cambridge, Mass., 1914).

6 There is an *Acton Burnell* writ on the Close Roll: Public Record Office (hereafter, P.R.O.) C 54/102 m 6d (captioned, *forma brevis de pecuniam levandam super statutum*), and *Merchants* writs in Bodleian

Register 'R' (dating from c. 1318–20), transcribed *Early registers of writs*, ed. Elsa de Haas and G. D. G. Hall (Selden Society, 87, 1970), pp. 223–6.

7 For another, general, account of the statutes, see Plucknett, *Legislation*, pp. 138–46.

8 From certificates of statutes merchant issued by them, and preserved at the Public Record Office in Class C 241.

9 See *Calendar of letter-books, preserved among the archives of the corporation of the City of London at the Guildhall: Letter-books 'A' (c.1275 – 98), and 'B' (c.1275 – 1312)*, ed. R. R. Sharpe (London, 1899, 1900). At the 1321 London Eyre, this practice was asserted as having existed 'time out of mind', *Select cases concerning the law merchant. Volume iii. Statute recognizances and special assizes*, ed. H. Hall (Selden Society, 49, 1932), pp. 50 nr 31.

10 Bowers, 'From Rolls to Riches', 60, 63 n. 10.

11 PRO E 159: Exchequer: King's Remembrancer: Memoranda Rolls and Enrolment Books.

12 PRO E 368: Exchequer: Lord Treasurer's Remembrancer: Memoranda Rolls. In 1262, these rolls begin to include a separate series of *recogniciones.*

13 The Marshalsea court is known to have kept rolls from 1276 onwards, although none earlier than 1316 has survived. For a plea before the Steward and Marshal in 1272 enrolled in the 'Westminster Abbey Domesday', see *Fleta. Volume iv. Books 5 and 6*, ed. G.O. Sayles (Selden Society, 99, 1983), p. xxvi (Appendix I).

14 e.g. PRO KB 27/149 m 19 (Salop) (M 1296).

15 Held at the Corporation of London Record Office, Guildhall, London.

16 Or, from July 1st 1285, the Warden; see Gwyn A. Williams, *Medieval London: From Commune to Capital* (University of London Historical Studies, vol 11, 1963), pp. 252–61.

17 PRO Class C 241 – Chancery: Certificates of Statute Merchant and Statute Staple.

18 The latest of which (RR 1 nr 235) was enrolled on November 25th 1285, and is the final entry on the roll. The corresponding certificate is C 241/6 nr 144.

19 e.g. RR 1 nrs 143 (C 241/6 nr 207; /7 nr 373); 207 (/10 nr 15); 235 (/6 nr 144). These were all entered into after Easter 1285. It is assumed that the statute under which the certificate seeks execution is reliable, since certificates issuing from the London registry seem to have been careful in specifying which of the two statutory execution procedures was applicable during this 'transitional' period, e.g. C 241/6 nr 121 describes the statute as issued ...*apud* <W> *Acton Burnell*. The deleted W is perhaps 'W(estm)' ('Westminster', i.e. *Merchants.*) The certificates often refer to *Merchants* as *novo statuto edito apud Westm.*

20 October 12th 1283. There is some indication that Roll 1, as originally composed, might have begun in November 1284; unlike the other London rolls, it lacks a heading, there are perforations for stitching at the head of the first membrane, and entries number 38 and 140 (about a hundred apart) are captioned 'C' (*centum*). It is postulated that at least 60 entries from the beginning have disappeared.

21 Repayment was often stipulated to be by instalments; e.g. RR 1 nr 39: £20 repayable in four 10-shilling instalments per year for ten years; and C 241/1 nr 25: £192 repayable in four instalments – £83-13s-4d, £50, £25, and £33-6s-8d.

22 C 241/2 nr 59.

23 C 241/6 nr 161.

24 C 241/10 nr 21.

25 C 241/7 nr 322.

26 C 241/1 nr 88; /8 nr 388.

27 The Mayor of London requests that the Chancellor issue a writ to the Justice of Ireland instructing him to levy statutory execution against Bermengham there.

28 See R. H. Britnell, 'Sedentary long-distance trade and the English merchant class in thirteenth century England', in P. R. Coss and S. D. Lloyd, ed., *Thirteenth Century England. Volume 5. Proceedings of the Newcastle-upon-Tyne Conference, 1993* (Woodbridge, 1995), pp. 129, 135 n. 49.

29 No recognisances in Rokesle's favour have been located on the surviving Recognisance Rolls, and only a single Letter Book recognisance; for 13 marks: Letter Book 'A' 39.

30 Resort to the statutory registries was not free: *Acton Burnell* (and, subsequently, *Merchants*) provided that a fee of one penny for every pound recognised was payable 'to sustain the costs of the (statute merchant) clerk'.

31 *E ne soyent pas le Chauncelier Baruns del Escheqere Justices del un Baunc e del autre e iustices erraunz forclos de prendre reconoissaunces de dettes de ceus qi devaunt eus le voderunt fere.*
32 Letter Book A 51–70 (June 11th 1282 – May 27th 1283).
33 Letter Book A 79–90 (October 1283 – July 1285).
34 Seven individuals appear both as debtor and creditor: 412 = (246 *minus* 7) + 173.
35 (259 *minus* 64) + 412.
36 26 individuals appear both as debtor and creditor: 685 = (390 *minus* 26) + 321.
37 RR 1 nrs 9, 105, 106 (Gloucs); 61 (Hereford); 115 (Staffs); 21, 114, 154 (Devon); 174 (Derbyshire); 64 (Salop).
38 121 of 235: 61 with citizens of London as debtors, 45 as creditors, and 15 with both parties.
39 65 of 156: 3 with citizens of London as debtors, 59 as creditors, and 3 as both parties.
40 The Close Roll text of the statute identifies it as *Statutum editum pro mercatoribus ad debita sua celeriter recuperanda;* PRO C 54/100 m 2d.
41 137 of 235; 58 recognisances have persons identified as merchants or tradesmen making recognition in favour of other merchants or tradesmen (i.e, recognisances which look exclusively mercantile or commercial), a further 58 identify at least one of the creditors as a merchant or tradesman, and 21 recognisances identify at least one of the debtors as a merchant or tradesman but with no indication whether any of the creditors was mercantile.
42 e.g. RR 1 nrs 18–9 (Toulouse); 26, 46 (Bergerac); 10–1 (Burgundy); C 241/12 nr 15 (Paris); /8 nr 132 (Cahors); /2 nr 56 (Reims).
43 e.g. RR 1 nrs 21, 31, 87 (The Riccardi of Lucca); 94 (The Eubaldi Cardelini of Lucca); 71 (The Rusticati of Piacenza).
44 e.g. RR 1 nrs 181, 209–11 (Peter Fort, 'merchant of Spain'); 144, 146–7 (Simon Peres, 'merchant of Bures').
45 e.g. RR 1 nrs 9, 139–40 (John Graunt, 'mercator Alemann').
46 RR 1 nr 118.
47 RR 1 nr 84.
48 RR 1 nrs 220, 225.
49 RR 1 nrs 3, 31, 79, 102.
50 RR 1 nrs 185–6
51 C 241/1 nr 111 (one sack of wool, price 10 marks 4 shillings); /6 nrs 15 (11 carts of lead), 42 (3 sacks of wool), 164 (52 quarters of wheat).
52 RR 1 nr 31.
53 On whom, see, generally, Kaeuper, *Bankers to the Crown.*
54 RR 1 nr 97.
55 C 241/6 nr 69; such attribution is also rare in the London Letter Books. There are only two instances before *Acton Burnell*; Letter Book A 32, 45.
56 19 'Chaloners' (e.g. RR 1 nr 13) and one 'burreller' (a maker of burel, a kind of cloth); RR 1 nr 178.
57 'Tawers' (*allutarius*), e.g. RR 1 nrs 15, 17, 33.
58 e.g. to Peter Fort, *mercator Castri Novi de Vallibus* (e.g. RR 1 nrs 209–13), Simon Peres (e.g. RR 1 nr 144). Interestingly, these merchants do *not* appear as creditors in the pre-*Acton Burnell* Letter Books, in which there are many recognisances (e.g. Letter Book A 10; 13; 16; 17 *et passim*) associated with the sale of leather; this perhaps supports the idea of *Acton Burnell* generating its own business.
59 Similarly, taverners or vintners recognising in favour of French merchants; e.g. RR 1 nrs 18; 52.
60 e.g. taverners (e.g. RR 1 nrs 18, 30, 52); goldsmiths (nrs 150, 194, 228); drapers (nrs 71, 109); furriers (nrs 174, 229–30); pepperers (nrs 20, 78); smiths (nrs 35, 134); tailors (nrs 187, 204); a tanner (nr 2); a butcher (nr 49); a tiler (nr 75); a vintner (nr 108); two chirographers (nr 126); a barber (nr 129); a spicer (nr 140); a baker (nr 148).
61 Knights: e.g. RR 1 nrs 7; 9; 14; Clerks: e.g. nrs 12; 73; 76; Priors: nrs 37; 95; Rectors or vicars; e.g. nrs 45; 64; 73.
62 RR 1 nr 96.
63 RR 1 nr 126.
64 Or, where repayment was to be by instalments, for the first instalment to fall due.
65 e.g. RR 1 nrs 189 (£2, recognisance Sept 25th 1285); 190 (Sept 25th); 191 (Sept 26th); all payable Michaelmas (September 29th 1285).

66 Although such recognisances were also encountered in the Letter Books (e.g. Calendar Early Mayor's Court Rolls 66 (1300); 'payable tomorrow') and Great Yarmouth (e.g. Norfolk Record Office, Y/C4/2 m 3; 1280).

67 The fate of the other Edward I London rolls (probably about forty, based on the assumption that, after *Merchants*, which prescribed that the roll was to be in duplicate, there would have been two rolls per year: one in the possession of the Mayor and one the clerk) is unknown.

68 Of which a small portion is transcribed, *Select cases concerning the law merchant. Volume iii*, ed. Hall, pp. lxxviii – lxxix. See note 9, above.

69 Accordingly, the total number of *Merchants* entries is 818.

70 Or – where no party is identified as a merchant or tradesman – in respect of goods sold.

71 38 recognisances. A further 10 recognisances have persons identified as merchants (all domestic) as debtors, with no merchant as creditor. Hence, as few as 15% of the recognisances on Roll 2 could be mercantile.

72 55 recognisances. A further 16 recognisances have persons identified as merchants (all but one domestic) as debtors, with no merchant as creditor. Hence, as few as just over a third – 36% – of the recognisances on Roll 3 could be mercantile.

73 24 recognisances. A further 13 recognisances have persons identified as merchants (all but one domestic) as debtors, with no merchant as creditor. Hence, as few as about a quarter – 26% – of the recognisances on Roll 4 could be mercantile.

74 32 recognisances. A further 13 recognisances have persons identified as merchants (all domestic) as debtors, with no merchant as creditor. Hence, as few as about a quarter – 26% – of the recognisances on Roll 5 could be mercantile.

75 e.g. C 241/31 nr 132.

76 e.g. The bond transcribed in Michaelmas 1294, at PRO CP 40/106 m 120 (Gloucs).

77 Or fells; C 241/16 nr 64 (200 sheepskins (*vellera*), price five pence each).

78 About 450 statutes merchant in total. There is a clear regional bias to these; almost half (209) were entered into before the York registry, and 110 at Nottingham. The quantities of wool recognised ranged from three stones (e.g. C 241/27 nr 91) to 24 sacks (C 241/45 nr 267). By way of comparison, a list prepared by the Riccardi of Lucca of all the wool which they had bought in 1294 (E 101/126/7/12) describes 44 purchases; the average purchase was about three sacks, which is about the same as the amounts recognised in statutes merchant.

79 About 140 recognisances, for quantities between 2 and 290 quarters.

80 About 100 recognisances, for quantities between 2 quarters, 1 and a half bushels, to 92 and a half quarters.

81 About 80 recognisances, for quantities between 2 and 120 quarters.

82 About eight recognisances, for quantities between 3, and 14 quarters.

83 About 10 statutes merchant in total; e.g. C 241/3 nr 14; 16 and a half quarters of *fabar et pis.*

84 About 30 recognisances in total; e.g. C 241/9 nr 199; 27 'cars' at 2 shillings a car. A 'car' (*charre*) was about 2100 pounds in weight.

85 About 5 recognisances in total; e.g. C 241/34 nrs 192; 6 and a half 'seams' (*summa*) at 15 shillings a seam.

86 e.g. C 241/22 nr 65: 49 marks recognised at the Exeter registry by a Cornwall man to Edmund of Cornwall, first cousin of Edward I, *pro stagno ab eodem domino empto*. The same parties appear in C 241/22 nr 134 and /26 nr 5.

87 C 241/15 nr 35; /49 nr 60; /51 nr 7.

88 About 6 recognisances in total e.g. C 241/5 nr 16; /7 nr 148.

89 About 12 statutes merchant in total e.g. C 241/14 nr 20.

90 e.g. C 241/7 nrs 75, 76, 77.

91 C 241/32 nr 75.

92 C 241/8 nr 430.

93 e.g. C 241/15 nr 28; /54 nr 69: recognitions *pro ovibus*.

94 By way of exception, there are scattered instances where the debtor recognises to 'pay' a particular thing with no expressed monetary alternative (e.g. C 241/35 nrs 112; 145; 324; 457; /36 nrs 28; 31). However, most of these certificates are curious in some respect; e.g. the word *precii* is present, but

followed by a blank (C 241/35 nr 324); certificate specifies that the debtor has rendered up (*soluisse*) neither the goods *nor the money* (C 241/35 nr 112); 'repeat' certificates *do* specify monetary values (e.g. C 241/36 nr 262; /45 nr 102). There is a hint on the Plea Rolls that, where a quantity of goods was recognised without any price, the sheriff was to be ordered to 'make up' the goods recognised pursuant to a writ of *fieri facias* e.g. an order to *fi.fa.* three sacks of wool on *Acton Burnell* recognisance (CP 40/64 m 125 (Essex) (M 1286)). However, in this instance, a corresponding certificate (C 241/6 nr 42) makes no mention of *fi.fa.*, but orders straightforward *Merchants* execution.

95 RR 1 nr 102.

96 With a very small number of exceptions, between eight and twelve marks a sack.

97 T. H. Lloyd, *The movement of wool prices in medieval England*, (Economic History Review Supplement, 6, Cambridge, 1973). However, there is no way of knowing, unless the creditor happens to name a suspiciously low price that the transaction was a genuine sale. For instance, a usurious loan *could* be disguised by the naming of a current price for the commodity recognised by the debtor, but the creditor advancing less money.

98 D. C. Farmer, 'Some grain price movements in thirteenth century England, *Economic History Review* 2nd ser., x, (1957–58), 207, 212.

99 Elizabeth Zwanzig Bennett pays some attention to this phenomenon in her thesis, 'Debt and Credit in the Urban Economy: London 1380–1460' (unpublished Ph.D. thesis, Yale University, 1989), 56–9, but has no evidence of its existence before the early fifteenth century.

100 It should not pass, however, without remark, that the question of usurious loans is a difficult one, especially since considerable lengths would, it may be hypothesised, have been gone to in order to disguise such transactions.

101 e.g. RR 1 nr 31.

102 However, the availability of the statutory procedures does not eliminate the risk of the buyer/creditor being unable to recover the payment from an insolvent, or recalcitrant, debtor; for instance, a statute merchant for four sacks of wool, price £7 per sack and payable at June 1291 was certificated at least three times before August 1293; C 241/17 nr 80 (October 26th 1292); /23 nr 75–2 (March 12th 1293); /22 nr 158 (August 6th 1293); perhaps also /22 nr 151 (3 sacks, £21).

103 See above, Table 4.

104 e.g. C 241/42 nr 5: Robert son of Hugh Gatehill, in favour of Hugh.

105 e.g. C 241/35 nr 172: Nicholas, son of Hugh of Hastings, in favour of Beatrice, wife of Hugh.

106 e.g. C 241/74 nr 34; Hugh son of Nicholas Selby, in favour of William, son of Nicholas.

107 e.g. C 241/34 nr 58: Hugh son of Nicholas Selby, in favour of Agnes, sister of Hugh.

108 e.g. C 241/27 nr 79: Thomas Anlakeby senior to Thomas Anlakeby junior.

109 C 241/35 nr 216.

110 C 241/36 nr 108.

111 CP 40/106 m 120.

112 e.g. four Lincolnshire bailiffs recognising to John Gobaud, sheriff of Lincolnshire; C 241/42 nrs 47, 51–3.

113 C 241/21 nr 30.

114 e.g. C 241/34 nr 187; /45 nr 133; /54 nrs 9, 10.

115 C 241/20 nr 43.

116 e.g. C 241/35 nr 353; /47 nr 41.

117 MS Cambridge University Library Hh vi 5. I am grateful to Jeffrey Hackney for drawing my attention to this Register.

118 Although this acted as no deterrence to some; for instance, the nefarious uses to which Bishop Walter Langton put statutes merchant have been well documented by Alice Beardwood; see, for example, 'Bishop Langton's use of Statute Merchant recognisances', *Medievalia et Humanistica* 9 (1955), 54; 'The Trial of Walter Langton, Bishop of Lichfield, 1307 – 1312', *Transactions of the American Philosophical Society* New series, 54 (1964); 'Records of the trial of Walter Langeton Bishop of Coventry and Lichfield 1307–1312', *Camden Society* 4th ser., 6 (1969).

119 YB Michaelmas 15 Edward III (Rolls Series) 424 nr 61. However, there must have remained some incentive for religious to take statutes merchant from secular debtors, given the small, though consistent, contingent of ecclesiastical creditors on the London rolls.

120 e.g. John de Romeyn (York) C 241/27 nr 81; Thomas de Corbridge (York) C 241/53 nr 109.

121 e.g. Robert Burnell (Bath and Wells) e.g. C 241/2 nr 242; William Louth (Ely) e.g. C 241/32 nrs 32–3 (Lincoln registry); Oliver (Lincoln) e.g. C 241/28 nr 29, Thomas (Exeter), e.g. C 241/53 nr 44.
122 e.g. The Dean and Chapter of St Ethelbert's, Hereford, C 241/21 nr 28, /32 nr 216.
123 e.g. The Abbot and Convent of Wellbeck, Nottinghamshire, C 241/45 nrs 110–1, 130.
124 e.g. The Abbess and Convent of Godstow, Oxford, C 241/37 nr 73.
125 e.g. William of Hamelton, Archdean of York, C 241/34 nrs 97–8 *et passim.*
126 e.g. William of Puntington, Canon of Exeter, C 241/35 nr 25.
127 e.g. Thomas, Rector of St Nicholas Coldway, London, C 241/2 nr 17.
128 e.g. Benedict of Utterby, Vicar of Cadenay, Yorkshire, C 241/35 nr 180.
129 e.g. Robert of Seffield, Parson of Brampton, Norfolk, C 241/44 nr 14.
130 e.g. Robert, *domus* chaplain of Melford Hospital, Leicester, C 241/23 nr 91.
131 C 241 *passim*
132 C 241/32 nr 191.
133 e.g. YB Trinity 10 Edw II (T 1317): 55 SS 174 nr 9, *per* Bereford C.J.
134 PRO JUST 1/987 m 34.
135 The jury at the Eyre presented the defendant creditor as a usurer, specifically in respect of his dealings with Stirkeland; Goldington had made seven pounds from the loan of two pounds, and 22 marks for lending 10 marks (JUST 1/988 m 8d). I am grateful to Dr. Paul Brand for drawing my attention to this enrolment.
136 This is consistent with the model of advance payment for goods postulated above.
137 No such recognisance has been located on the Recognisance Rolls.
138 *Calendar of Early Mayor's Court Rolls preserved among the archives of the Corporation of the City of London 1298–1307*, ed. A. H. Thomas (Cambridge, 1924), p. 259 (1307). The recognisance (RR 4 m 1 nr 15) does not suggest any of this context, nor does a certificate issued on it (C 241/18 nr 57).
139 And, for London, only for the sample of five years represented by the surviving Recognisance Rolls.
140 Restricting the analysis to the Edward I certificates may mean that statutes merchant first certified after 1307 will be missed, but it is suggested that, Roll 5 ending in 1299, that there cannot have been many of these.
141 164 certificated of 1053:

Roll 1	235 statutes merchant	22 certificated	(9 %)
Roll 2	287 statutes merchant	37 certificated	(13 %)
Roll 3	219 statutes merchant	45 certificated	(21 %)
Roll 4	141 statutes merchant	23 certificated	(16 %)
Roll 5	171 statutes merchant	37 certificated	(22 %)

142 C 241/7 nrs 77; 279; 379; /8 nr 152; Appleby may have had an *Acton Burnell* registry. Neither the absence of any recorded appointment of an Appleby *Acton Burnell* clerk, nor any *Acton Burnell* certificates issuing from Appleby, is conclusive: not all appointments were recorded and, given the remote and rural nature of Westmorland, no certificates may have issued.
143 Appointment of clerk, CPR 1281–1292, p. 346; earliest known activity, February 2nd 1292 (C 241/21 nr 27).
144 Appointment of clerk, CPR 1281–1292, p. 448; earliest known activity, March 12th 1291 (C 241/15 nr 127).
145 Appointment of clerk, CPR 1281–1292, p. 449; earliest known activity, February 2nd 1293 (C 241/25 nr 188). The King, by a writ dated June 28th 1291 (PRO E 159/65 m 5d), ordered the Barons of the Exchequer to have a *Merchants* seal made for the Chester registry.
146 Appointment of clerk, CPR 1281–1292, p. 505; earliest known activity, January 8th 1293 (C 241/22 nr 183).
147 C 241/32 nr 46.
148 C 241/53 nr 231; the only other certificate (C 241/53 nr 225) relates to a recognisance payable on May 1st 1307. The first statute merchant clerk for Oxford was appointed in August 1306; CPR 1301–7, 461.
149 'Flying' registry is my term.
150 C 241/2 nr 188; /6 nr 11; payable September 29th 1286. Boston Fair operated for one month from the Nativity of John the Baptist (i.e., June 24th); Ellen Wedemeyer Moore, *The Fairs of Medieval England – An Introductory Study* (Toronto, 1985), pp. 298 – 9 (1258 document).

151 C 241/18 nr 114; payable November 11th 1286. St. Giles' fair operated for 15 days from September 8th. There are only seven extant certificates, relating to 4 statutes merchant; C 241/2 nr 233; /9 nr 240; /18 nrs 114, 159; /35 nr 207; /7 nrs 127, 362.

152 C 241/7 nr 26 (recognisance payable May 25th 1287). There are nine certificates, relating to 6 statutes merchant C 241/7 nrs 25, 26; /8 nrs 10, 16 245, 246; /9 nr 16; /12 nr 130; /36 nr 18. St. Ives' fair operated for one month from Easter day.

153 C 241/2 nr 255 (recognisance payable June 24th 1288). There are only two more certificates, C 241/ 9 nrs 255; 308. Stamford Fair ended the night before Palm Sunday.

154 Derbyshire; Devon (Exeter); Essex (London); Hampshire (Winchester); Herefordshire (Hereford); Lincolnshire (Lincoln); Norfolk (Norwich); Nottinghamshire (Nottingham); Shropshire (Shrewsbury); Yorkshire (York).

155 The exception was Derbyshire, which is the county nearest to the average.

156 Counting the home counties of Bristol as Somerset *and* Gloucestershire, and London as the area under the jurisdiction of the sheriffs of London, Essex, Middlesex, Kent and Surrey.

157 64% from Appleby to Westmorland (47 from 74); 78% from Bristol to Somerset and Gloucestershire; 83% from Exeter to Devon; 85% from Hereford to Herefordshire; 80% from Lincoln to Lincolnshire; 60% from Newcastle to Northumberland; 42% from Nottingham to Nottinghamshire; 89% from Norwich to Norfolk; 87% from Shrewsbury to Shropshire; 70% from Winchester to Hampshire.

158 The Oxford registry is not included in this analysis. It appears to have come into existence only at the very end of the period studied.

159 The scarcity of certificates suggests either that the business of the Newcastle-upon-Tyne registry was very light, or most debtors were within the power of the Mayor (and, accordingly, certification was not needed).

160 Nightingale, *A Medieval Mercantile Community*, pp. 85–6, 86 n 2.

161 *ibid.*, p. 115 n 4 and accompanying text.

162 see Table 1.

163 see Table 6.

164 It should be noted that Table 8 suggests that debts recognised before the London registry were higher than those recognised before any other registry.

165 see Table 7.

Chapter 4

The English parochial clergy as investors and creditors in the first half of the fourteenth century*

Pamela Nightingale

The subject of credit in the middle ages, linked as it is with the religious prohibition of usury, inevitably revives the old, but still-unburied, arguments about religion and the rise of capitalism. Weber's thesis that the economic doctrines of the Catholic Church delayed the advent of modern capitalism whereas the Calvinist creed promoted it, has most recently found some support from Professor N. P. Jones in his *God and the Money-lenders*, where he argues that it was essentially the new climate of Protestant thought which allowed England at the end of the sixteenth century to develop unhindered along capitalist lines. Protestantism, he claims, sanctioned self-aggrandisement, and relegated economic behaviour to the realm of the private conscience, whereas, in his view, medieval theologians made economic behaviour subject to the control of the Church and the moral strictures of the community in ways which inevitably hindered credit and investment.[1] Brian Holderness also considered, in his innovatory study of Anglican clerical creditors after the Reformation, that as late as the sixteenth and seventeenth centuries the tensions engendered in these clergy by contemporary ecclesiastical strictures against usury, 'almost certainly induced or reinforced hesitation and ambiguity' in their lending. He considered that the medieval Church's tolerance of lending money at interest illustrated its failure to enforce obedience on its members, rather than any developments in its doctrine.[2]

Medievalists have long taken issue with such views, arguing that the Catholic Church had refined and adapted its teaching on usury to meet the needs of an expanding commercial economy in which credit became ubiquitous at all levels of society. By the middle of the thirteenth century canonists had proposed as many as thirteen exceptions to the ban on taking interest. These included the lender's sharing in the risk, and his loss of profit on the capital. They also laid a new emphasis on the lender's intention, which necessarily meant that in his conscience he had to make a private judgement.[3] Although the laws against usury were by no means a dead letter, they produced relatively few cases in the medieval English church courts.[4] Those which did occur were only for the taking of excessive interest. For example, a chaplain, John de Fransham, was denounced in Norwich in 1289–90 because he was 'an excessive usurer'.[5] Londoners did not object to the taking of interest at ten *per cent* on the funds of the City's orphans,[6] and it is probable that interest at about this level was not deemed to be usurious.[7] Loans of cash given by religious houses at low interest were seen as acts of charity,[8] while lenders of large sums over £25 seem to have escaped the attention of the church courts entirely.[9] Before, as after, the Reformation, it is argued, 'much depended on the conscience and understanding of the parties involved'.[10]

It is well known that monastic houses, the episcopate, and the higher clergy (that is, dignitaries) in the middle ages both lent and borrowed money; but little is known about the contribution of the 40,000 or so parochial clergy as investors and creditors.[11] Yet they, rather more than the theologians, are likely to illuminate the local community's views about credit and investment in later medieval England. For, if the clergy, who were under a strict obligation to seek out usurers among their flock, could be seen acting openly as professional money-lenders, it is unlikely that the laity felt any inhibitions about doing the same.[12] The record of the clergy as creditors is also important because it indicates how much the commercial world could expect to draw on capital and credit from those whose occupations, or social standing, officially separated them from trade.[13]

Materially the parochial clergy were well equipped to become money-lenders in their communities. There was a long medieval tradition of churches serving as places of safe deposit,[14] while the clergy were frequently called upon to act as the executors of wills, and therefore might have money to invest on others' behalf.[15] Although there was considerable variation in their incomes, most of the beneficed clergy enjoyed a standard of living at least the equal of the richer peasants, and many received ample revenues which gave them surpluses to invest.[16] Parochial fees and offerings put into their hands a steady supply of coin, which was a significant advantage in a society which rarely had enough. Also, it has been calculated that the tithes of the 9,000 or so parishes accounted for between six and eight *per cent* of the kingdom's total harvest of corn.[17] Similarly, incumbents profited from all other harvests of the land and sea, and took a share, through personal tithes, of the profits of trade and industry.[18] Celibacy, too, had financial advantages. Officially, at least, the clergy had no wives or children to provide for, and so they were under no economic or social pressure to invest in land to build up a family holding. Their greatest material need was to provide for their own old age; they therefore had every incentive to invest in the most profitable way for their future.

Some statistical evidence about the extent to which the clergy acted as investors and creditors in England can be gained from the certificates of unpaid debt which have their origin in the Statute of Acton Burnell of 1283 (11 Edw. I).[19] They provide a sample of all the credit originally registered under this system in London and the chief provincial towns, and they cover the whole of England. Although the certificates reveal only the credit which was unpaid, it is likely that they reflect one-fifth of the loans, and therefore provide a large sample of those originally registered. Although the certificates do not represent the small sums recorded in manorial courts, the Statute Merchant did not restrict the size of recorded loans and 83 certificates exist for fourteenth-century debts which were under the maximum of 40s. imposed on borough and baron courts.[20] Although the great majority of the certificates are for sums well above 40s., the fact that one is for 6s. 8d. shows that the system did not exclude the ordinary level of debt to be found in villages and small towns, where even in the late fourteenth century, it was likely to be under ten shillings.[21]

The certificates make it plain that parochial clergy from all over the kingdom felt no

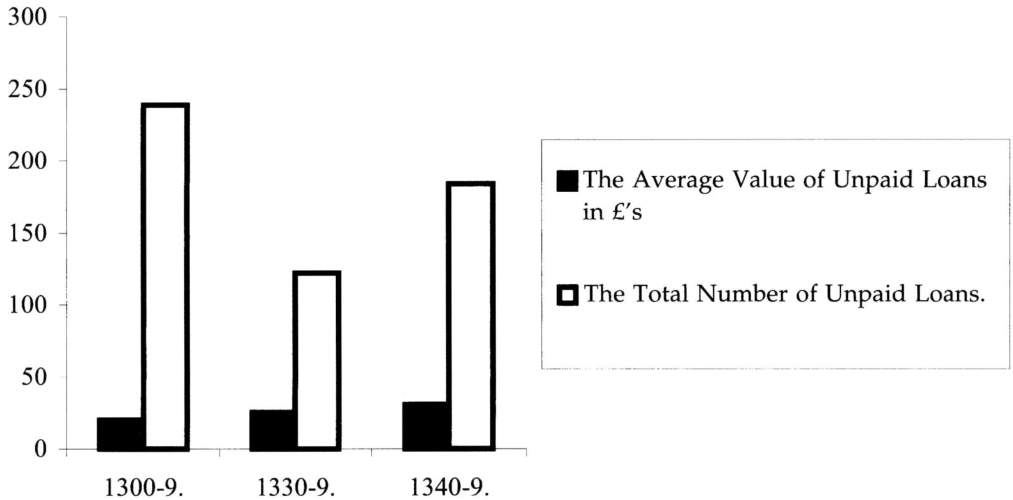

Figure 4.1 The total number and average value of unpaid loans advanced nationally by parochial clergy

misgivings about appearing before the mayor and clerk of their nearest large town and registering a loan or similar transaction. No interest was ever declared either in the rolls which recorded the loans, or in the certificates of debt which were sent to the Chancery. However, it is unlikely that medieval people were any more reluctant than their sixteenth-century counterparts to conclude that no-one lent money, certainly not sums of any magnitude, unless he benefited from the loan.[22] If the clergy aroused any indignation by registering their loans publicly, it was scarcely strong enough to deter them or make them fear a public denunciation, or any discipline from their bishops.

For the first decade of the fourteenth century, certificates survive for 239 loans made by parochial clergy which have an average value of £20. [Figure 4.1] In the 1330s, when the economy was in recession, the number of certificates falls to 122 with an average individual value of £25. For the 1340s there are 184 certificates for clerical loans, whose average value had now increased to £30 12s.[23] Exact comparisons with the two intervening decades from 1310 to 1329 are not possible, because between 1311 and 1322, as a result of the work of the Ordainers, the system was restricted solely to merchants. The sample indicates that, although the parochial clergy accounted for only a small proportion of national creditors the sums they lent were large (£20 was equivalent to 1,600 days' wages for a skilled craftsman). Moreover, just as the average value of their debts was rising, so, too, was their share of the total number of creditors. It rose from 3.7 *per cent* in the first decade to 4.5 *per cent* in the 1330s, and then to 5.3 *per cent* in the 1340s. As a class it seems that in the first half of the fourteenth century the parochial clergy were becoming more important to the economy as creditors.

The clergy who made these large loans described themselves as rectors, parsons, vicars, or chaplains. In fact the terms 'rector' and 'parson' were synonomous, so that the two must be counted as one category.[24] Not surprisingly, the parsons and rectors in

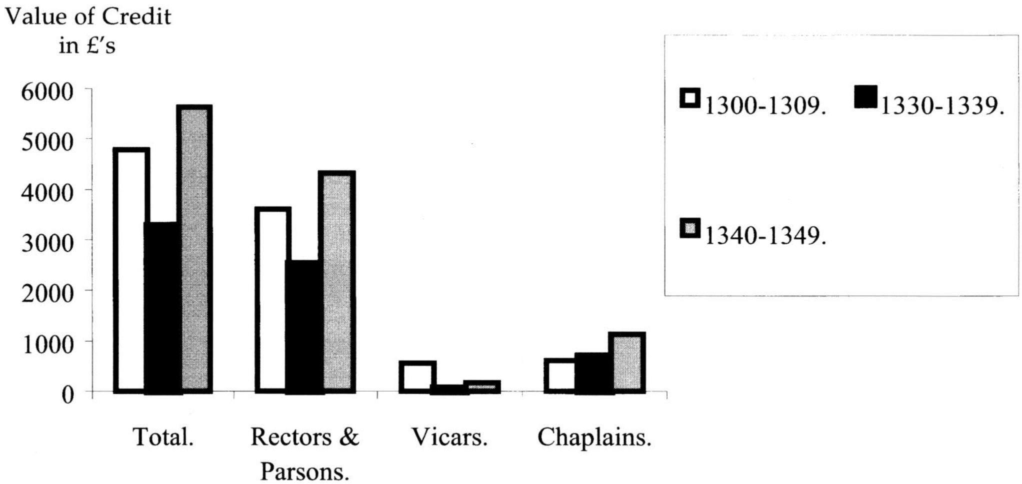

Figure 4.2 The value in £s of unpaid credit given nationally by beneficed and unbeneficed clergy

the certificates reveal themselves as economically superior to the less fortunate vicars and chaplains. Figure 4.2 shows that the former provided a consistently high proportion of the clerical creditors with 62 *per cent* of the certificates in 1300–9, 66 *per cent* in the 1330s, and 66 *per cent* in the 1340s.[25] Moreover, the gap of more than one-third between the average amount of credit they gave, and that given by vicars and chaplains combined, widened by the 1340s. In a few cases very large sums might be lent by incumbents who were not only pluralists but were also men who acquired much of their wealth from outside the parochial sphere, including the profits of government office. Such were important Chancery clerks like John Markingfield, who described himself as the parson of the church of Escrick in the East Riding of Yorkshire when in 1306 he lent £1,000 to the son of a Yorkshire knight.[26] But the number of instances of this kind were few, and unlikely to have any marked effect on the averages, if only because the same John Markingfield, this time as rector of Axminster in Devonshire, was two years later lending such relatively small sums as 60s. and £4 6s. 8d.[27] In contrast with the incumbents, vicars did not increase their average level of credit during this time. It remained, in the 1340s, at just over £15 – the same as in the first decade of the century. Moreover, their share of the total number of parochial clerical creditors fell in this period from 14 *per cent* to 6 *per cent*, and even dipped as low as 1.5 *per cent* in the 1330s. The income of perpetual vicars was allocated when the rectory was appropiated, and although it might include the lesser tithes, it was usually worth less than half that of a rectory, and was less capable of expansion.[28] Chaplaincies, too, suffered from fixed stipends, set at 5m. in 1362.[29] But chaplains seem to have had more opportunities, and more leisure to make money. This could explain why their average credit increased from £11 in the 1300s to £22 in the 1340s. Probably this was because more chaplains were in towns at a time when the rural economy in the 1320s and 1330s was suffering from recession.[30] Also, the growing number of perpetual chantries may explain why the chaplains' share of clerical credit increased slightly from 23 *per cent* to 28 *per cent* between the first and fifth decades of the century.

The divisions among the parochial clerical creditors were not only those of status and wealth. They were also geographical. Some counties had no certificates issued for them at all throughout the first half of the fourteenth century. These were Cheshire, Cumberland, Lancashire, and Rutland, the first three, no doubt because of their relative poverty and remoteness, and Rutland because of its small size. In the first decade of the century clerical creditors were to be found in 29 counties, but in only 17 in the 1330s as the economy contracted. The 1340s saw a recovery with 24 counties having at least one clerical creditor. But they were only significant as a group in a handful of counties. These are, in descending order of importance Norfolk, Derbyshire, Yorkshire, Devonshire, and Lincolnshire. Even so, those in Lincolnshire, Devonshire and Derbyshire quickly faded away after the first decade of economic expansion. Yorkshire's showed more staying power, but it is only in Norfolk that one can see the parochial clergy emerging as a really significant group of creditors throughout the first half of the fourteenth century.

One might surmise that the counties where the parochial clergy were most able to amass the capital they needed to become creditors were those which yielded the highest parochial tithes. The tithes of corn alone in many benefices were equal to the average amount of credit given by incumbents. For example, in 1296 the rector of Combeinteignhead in Devonshire was owed 30m. for the church's tithe of corn and cider, and also in some parishes in Yorkshire and Norfolk tithe-sheaves alone could be worth up to £60.[31] The tithe system, too, brought the clergy into close contact with the commercial economy and made them frequently creditors of merchants who bought their tithe-produce. The parson of Brington in Huntingdonshire was owed £46 13s. 4d. for corn by two men, one from nearby Catworth, and the other, presumably a merchant, from Godmanchester, which was ten miles or more away.[32] The rector of Sigglesthorne, in the East Riding of Yorkshire was owed £24 in 1344 by two merchants from Hull,[33] and the same sum was owed by a York merchant to the parson of the church of Spofforth, more than ten miles away in the West Riding.[34] It could be significant that the parochial clergy's share of between 3.7 and 5.3 *per cent* of all creditors is not far removed from their estimated share, through tithes, of the corn produced in the kingdom.[35]

It is certainly true that the expansion of clerical credit in the first decade of the century broadly reflected that of the laity, as did its general decline in the 1330s. The prominence of clerical creditors in Norfolk also accords with that county's leading position in the 1334 Lay Subsidy Rolls. The more surprising prominence of clerical creditors in Derbyshire in the first decade of the century could be linked with a recovery in the county's production of lead.[36] However, one cannot assume that there was necessarily a straightforward connection between the value of tithes in a particular county and the parochial clergy's record as creditors. In many counties a good proportion of tithes were diverted far afield into the coffers of impropriators.[37] In Derbyshire, for example, of 56 rectories which had been appropriated by about 1300 the tithes of only 22 remained in the county. The rest, along with other payments like mortuaries, went to enrich dignitaries like the Deans of Lincoln and Lichfield.[38]

Furthermore, it is noticeable that where there were large towns and a wealthy merchant class incumbents were not prominent as creditors. London is the most obvious example, since only six parochial clergy from the City appear as creditors in the certificates throughout the first half of the century. The easy availability of mercantile credit in London seems also to have stifled any competition from the clergy of the whole of Middlesex. The latter produced no incumbent and only one solitary vicar as a creditor in the certificates for those 50 years. In York, too, only three incumbents appear as creditors in the same period. It is true that many town parishes were poor, had no glebe, and could collect little in the way of agricultural produce as tithes, but this cannot explain the failure of Middlesex to produce clerical creditors. By contrast the parishes of St Aldate, St Ebbe, and St Michael at the Northgate in Oxford all had clerical creditors, encouraged, no doubt, by limited competition from a small merchant class and by a large population of students in need of loans. Incumbents in the larger towns had also to face competition as money-lenders from the higher clergy at cathedral churches such as Lincoln, Hereford, St Paul's in London, and York Minster.

It is, therefore, not surprising that the beneficed parochial clergy appear more often as creditors in the countryside. Although the sums lent were normally beyond the means of individual peasants to repay the certificates include cases, particularly common in Shropshire, where incumbents gave credit to groups of villagers. For example, seven men of Staunton, in Shropshire, including their reeve, with the reeve of a neighbouring village, owed 11m. in 1311 to their rector.[39] Two stockherds, a shepherd, and another local man from Acaster in the West Riding of Yorkshire owed 15m. to the neighbouring rector of Stillingfleet across the River Ouse.[40] Possibly there is a connection in both examples with the local wool-trade, in which the parochial clergy could have been acting as middle-men, much as monasteries did.[41]

Certainly the Derbyshire certificates show that some clerical creditors were taking an active part in lay enterprises. The parson of Ilkeston, in partnership with a layman, was advancing money for iron worth almost £10, and was obviously involved in the trade.[42] Close to Derby itself, at Morley, where a coal-mine was worked, the parson, John Goffyn, was the creditor in no fewer than twelve certificates between 1301 and 1307 which represented an investment of over £143. Some of his loans look very much like the financing of miners, since they were given to groups of local men, like the eleven to whom he lent £21 in 1302, and a similar group of ten the following year.[43] In Nottinghamshire the parson of Hickling was owed four loads of lead by a Derbyshire man, either because he needed it for the roof of his church, or because, he, too, was involved in the trade.[44] Mercantile and financial interests could also explain the local clergy's membership of the Guild of Holy Trinity, Coventry.[45]

Chaplains, in particular, who lacked parochial responsibilities and most needed to supplement their incomes, had the leisure, and often the urban connections, to be closely involved in trade and finance. For example, a chaplain of Leominster in Herefordshire was owed £20 for wool by a merchant of Evesham in Worcestershire,[46] and two chaplains of Hereford were owed £10 and £20 by two other merchants of Evesham for wool.[47] Geoffrey de Lanum, a chaplain of York, issued eight certificates between 1300 and 1309, which show him extending credit to a variety of trading partners, including a goldsmith from Beverley, a knight, and others who owed him

Figure 4.3 Norfolk's clerical creditors as a proportion of national clerical creditors

wool.[48] A chaplain from Leake in Nottinghamshire lent money to a dyer of Nottingham, and a chaplain of Newnham in Hertfordshire, lent £120 to William le Taverner of Hitchen in 1335, £22 in 1337 to Ralph le Butler of Baldock, and in 1342 200m. to John Barat of Baldock. The names of his first two debtors, and the size of the loans, suggests that he was deeply involved in the wine trade.[49] Other chaplains were giving credit to a corn-blader, a linen-draper, butchers, and a smith, as well as to merchants.[50]

It is in Norfolk, though, that one can study in greatest detail the developing pattern of the clergy's activity as creditors and investors. Figure 4.3 shows how Norfolk alone was responsible for 25 *per cent* of the kingdom's clerical creditors in the first decade of the century, for an astonishing 56 *per cent* in the 1330s, and for 29 *per cent* in the 1340s. Is this prominence of the Norfolk clergy as creditors to be explained chiefly by the county's exceptional agricultural productivity from which the clergy benefited through tithes? The total number of debts registered at Norwich, lay and clerical, suggest not. For although those registered at Norwich [Figure 4.4] show the county's prominence in the national economy, with 12.5 *per cent* of the kingdom's total in the first decade of the century, 23 *per cent* in the 1330s, and 13.5 *per cent* in the 1340s, Norfolk's share of national clerical creditors was always at least twice as large as its share of combined lay and clerical creditors. This indicates that there was more to the exceptional record of its clergy as creditors than can be explained by their profiting from tithes.

The unusual character of the Norfolk clergy's record as creditors is emphasised by the clergy's normal preference for safe investments in property. Investment in urban housing was always attractive to clergy who needed somewhere to live when they retired from the parochial ministry. Buying a house which they could let until they needed it, particularly in a cathedral town where they might pick up part-time chaplaincies in old age, made economic sense. It offered security, and the possibility of

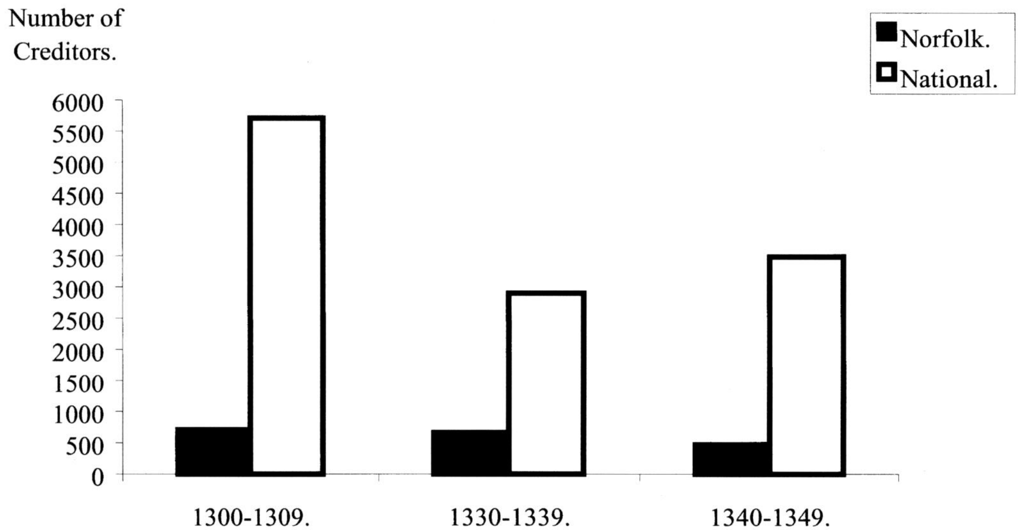

Figure 4.4 Norfolk's share of combined national lay and clerical creditors

rising rentals and capital values. Deeds registered in Norwich show that the Norfolk clergy, too, found long-term investment of this kind most attractive, particularly in times of economic difficulty. The combined acquisitions of property in Norwich by rectors, parsons, vicars, and chaplains of the county rose from 21 in 1300–9 to 80 in 1330–9, whereas the same decades saw the number of statutemerchant certificates in which Norfolk clergy were creditors rise from 62 to 69, that is by a mere 10 *per cent* compared with a rise of 74 *per cent* for their investments in property. Chaplains accounted for more than half of the clergy who invested in property. Undoubtedly some of them served in Norwich parishes and needed a house to live in, but where their places of residence are given, it is clear that many buying houses there lived elsewhere in the county, while beneficed clergy came from almost every hundred in Norfolk to purchase property in the city.[51] In one or two cases investing in real property seems to have been akin to balancing their portfolio. One of the most prominent clerical lenders, John de London, parson of South Creake, acquired various properties in Norwich in the five years before his death in 1327, while in 1326 he was also pursuing three defaulting debtors.[52] Similarly, Simon le Doo, rector of Rackheath, was lending money in 1326, while he was also investing in property at Norwich.[53] But they were the exceptions; it seems that in general the more cautious clergy invested in the property market, while the more daring and speculative lent the sums of money recorded in the statute merchant certificates.

What one has to explain is why there were so many more clergy in Norfolk than elsewhere who were willing to take the risks involved in lending money, and why their share of the total number of certificates of debt isssued in Norwich rose [Figure 4.5] from 10.6 *per cent* in the first decade, to 12.8 *per cent* in the 1330s, and then to 14.6 *per cent* in the 1340s. If one compares the terms under which the clergy of Norfolk lent their

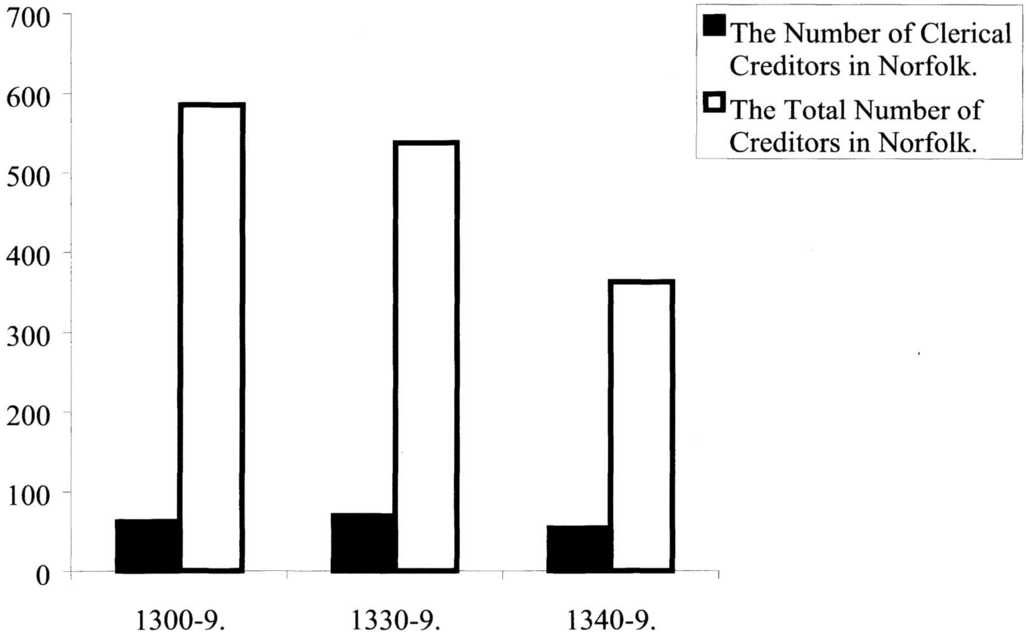

Figure 4.5 The total number of unpaid creditors (Norfolk) compared with unpaid clerical creditors (Norfolk)

money with those set by parochial clergy elsewhere, there is not much difference between them. For both groups credit was short-term, although it was given on average for four-and-a-half months in Norfolk compared with five months elsewhere.[54] Furthermore, there was virtually no difference between the length of time taken by clerical creditors in Norfolk, and those elsewhere, to pursue their defaulting debtors. The consistency is striking. For both groups in the first decade of the century about 40 *per cent* took less than three months, 26 *per cent* between three months and a year, and about 20 *per cent* over three years. In later decades, as economic conditions became less favourable, and creditors saw less likelihood of recovering their money quickly, so the proportion enforcing payment in less than three months fell to under 30 *per cent*, while those taking more than three years grew to 26 *per cent*. The risk of tardy repayment, or of losing capital, seems to have been as high in Norfolk as elsewhere.

There was, though, one substantial difference between clerical creditors in Norfolk and those elsewhere, and that was in the average value of the credit they gave. [Figure 4.6] The Norfolk men gave an average of £8.6 in the first decade compared with an average of £20 given by parish clergy elsewhere. The gap narrowed in the following decades but still Norfolk's average remained lower at £17.5 in the 1330s compared with £25.2 nationally, and at £26 in the 1340s compared with *c.* £30.6 nationally. The explanation cannot lie in the greater poverty of the Norfolk clergy, even though many livings in the county were appropiated and the stipends of vicars averaged only 5m.[55] Certainly few Norfolk vicars appear as creditors, and almost none after the

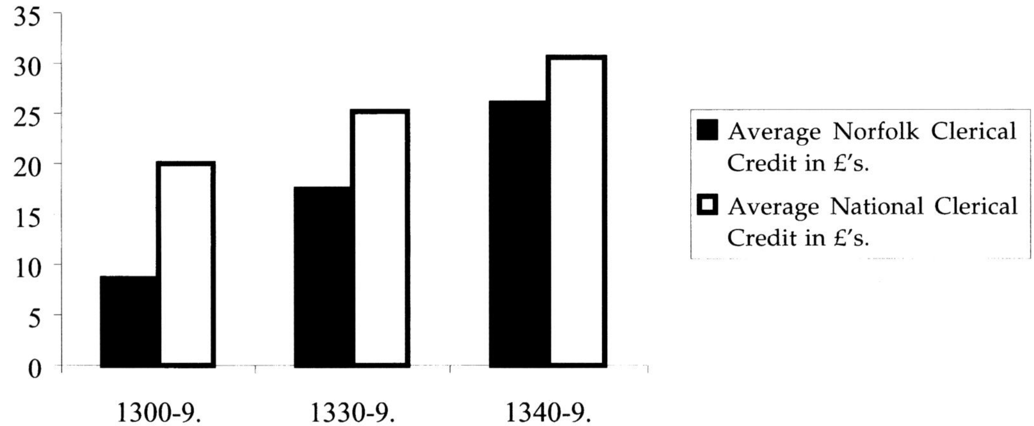

Figure 4.6 The average amount of credit advanced by Norfolk clergy and by national clergy

expansionary first decade of the century. But this is also true of vicars elsewhere. Moreover, in Norfolk the vicar of Bacton and the vicar of Loddon, who between them were responsible for ten certificates in those early years, lent at *c.* £7 18s. almost the same average sum as the rest of the Norfolk clergy, and in one case the loan was for £25 6s. 8d.[56]

There is, in fact, no discernible link between the value of individual benefices and vicarages in Norfolk and the personal wealth and money-lending activities of their incumbents. For example, the income of the benefice of Shelfanger was, according to the taxation of Pope Nicholas, divided into two portions worth £10 each, yet its parson, John Ward, was robbed in 1312 of goods and chattels worth £100. There is no indication that he lent any money.[57] Similarly, Tilney, one of the richest livings in Norfolk, was worth £80 in the Taxation, but produced no certificates for clerical creditors. The Rector of Brampton lent prolifically, but his church was too poor to appear in the Taxation.[58] The attitude of the incumbent to risk counted far more than the value of his living in determining both the extent to which he would lend money, and the nature of his investment, but perhaps most important of all was the number of local opportunities he had for profitable investment.

Since the clergy of Norfolk produced so many more certificates than any other county, the most satisfactory explanation for the lower value of their loans, and the shorter terms of repayment, is that they were advancing credit to more people lower down the social scale than did clergy elsewhere. This deduction gains credence from the fact that whereas only 2.7 *per cent* of the Norfolk clergy's debtors were described as knights, the sons of knights, or lords of manors, in all the other counties of England this social class accounted for 6.7 *per cent* of the clergy's debtors. Unfortunately, too few of the Norfolk certificates record the occupations of the debtors to permit wider comparisons, but in those cases where their trades are given they include, besides merchants, a Norwich goldsmith, two butchers, a rural linen-draper, a brewer, a shepherd, a carpenter, a cordwainer, and a smith. All the tradesmen were recipients of small loans.[59]

Enough has already been uncovered about the economy of Norfolk in the first half of the fourteenth century – in particular about its progressive commercialised agriculture, and linen and worsted industries – for it to be no surprise that there was a high demand for credit in most parts of the county. The structure of its society, with a high proportion of free peasants who lived in small families with relatively loose bonds of wider kinship, meant that loans were more likely to be raised in the market place than from the extended family. There is also no doubt that cash was available in its villages and small market towns to make possible a network of rural money-lenders. A record of the criminal accusations laid against the inmates of Norwich gaol between 1307 and 1316 reveals their victims' wealth in sheep and cattle, and household possessions, as well as the large amounts of cash and silver plate which could be kept in people's houses, such as the 44 marks of silver stolen from a house in the relatively poor village of Gasthorpe, silver worth £100 stolen in Walsham, and the 40 marks of silver stolen from Alan le Barker of Tuttington.[60]

This cash fuelled the expansion of credit in Norfolk in the first decade of the century, and, significantly, more than two-thirds of the certificates of debt were issued by creditors who lived outside Norwich.[61] Furthermore, credit in the countryside was expanding at a faster rate than it was in the town, encouraged by thriving exports of wheat, barley, wool, and ale, and by the expansion of the linen and worsted industries in the hundreds of South Erpingham, Tunstead, and Eynesford.[62] It seems that the rural economy of Norfolk was far more commercialised, generated a greater demand for credit, and offered more opportunities for profitable investment than elsewhere, particularly in financing new industries. It is significant that it was loans to men in the cloth hundreds, principally South Erpingham, which account for nearly half the 76 certificates produced by clerical creditors in Norfolk in the first decade of the century.

A few clerics were outstanding as creditors. Robert de Bayfield, the rector of Brampton, near Cawston in the Hundred of South Erpingham, was responsible for 23 certificates, as many as were issued by one of Norwich's wealthiest drapers, Robert de Holverston.[63] Between 1300 and 1311 Bayfield lent sums ranging from 35s. to 39m. (520s.), mainly to debtors in the hundreds of South Erpingham and Tunstead, but also to men from Suffolk, where he may have spent his earlier career.[64] Another significant clerical creditor was William, the vicar of Bacton, in Tunstead Hundred, who issued eight certificates between 1304 and 1311. His speciality seems to have been supplying the neighbourhood, and therefore the cloth-workers, with herrings bought from Yarmouth merchants, to whom he may well have been supplying cloth in return.[65] In the 1330s, following a period when Norfolk's cloth industry, particularly its linen manufactures, was unable to compete with overseas products, only William de Saltby, the parson of Blickling, again in South Erpingham Hundred, stands out with five certificates.[66] However, in two of these transactions he was joint-creditor with the Chancellor of Salisbury, which would explain how he could lend £173 6s. 8d. to two Suffolk men in 1337.[67] Capital could be imported from wealthy patrons, or from the higher clergy, through the clerical network to fund enterprises which seemed to offer good profits.

Capital could also come from the clergy's connections with merchants, and this distinguishes John Leech's exceptional record as a creditor in the 1340s. He was the parson of Barney, a modest village in North Greenhoe Hundred, where he was a neighbour of the wool-brogger and exporter, William Athelwald of Egmere.[68] The main branch of the Athelwald family at nearby South Creake had been wool-exporters at least from the beginning of the century, and it can be no coincidence that John de London, the parson of South Creake, was also an outstanding creditor in the 1320s.[69] Connections with the Athelwalds also encouraged other parochial clergy to invest: in 1333 William Athelwald advanced £32, in partnership with the parson of Letheringsett, for four sacks of wool and £4 in cash.[70] From 1339 Athelwald began a new partnership with John Leech, which produced eight certificates and lasted until Athelwald's death in 1343. John Leech was then responsible for another eight certificates as a creditor either on his own, or in partnership with other clergy. His loans extended over a large area covering six hundreds and ranged from 60s. to £73. It can be assumed that they were generally advances for wool. Another parson who was probably engaged in the same trade was Edmund Gonville, the founder of St John's College, Rushworth. He was lending money, at least from 1339, particularly to Norwich merchants: firstly, as the incumbent of Rushworth, and lastly of the rich living of Terrington.[71]

These few clergy who show every indication of being venture-capitalists on a considerable scale were, though, the exception to the general run of clerical creditors who produced usually no more than one certificate a piece. What made the Norfolk clergy so distinctive is that they were more numerous in the countryside than clerical creditors elsewhere. The fact that Norfolk's cloth industry developed in rural areas away from the control of Norwich's merchants, and outside the normal financial sphere of the city's higher clergy, made it initially dependent on local creditors in the countryside. The profits offered by such investment made it attractive to the parochial clergy who most likely knew their debtors personally and could carefully assess the risks. Also, Norfolk's success in weathering the economic depression of the 1330s so much better than other counties, meant that although far more of the clergy in that decade took the safe course of investing in urban property, their more adventurous colleagues did not abandon commercial or personal loans.

How, though, does one account for the clergy's growing share of credit in Norfolk, and for the increasing average value of their loans? The answers are important not only for Norfolk but to understand the same trends elsewhere. Do these developments imply that the clergy's attitude to risk was generally less subject to economic constraints than mercantile credit, and that it was more responsive to the needs of the community? Part of the answer appears from analysing in more detail the average value of their loans. [Figure 4.7] As the economy contracted, the proportion of clerical loans in Norfolk under £5 fell from 35 *per cent* in the first decade to 4 *per cent* in the 1340s. During the same period the proportion over £30 grew from 9 to 40 *per cent*. Since this shift cannot be explained by inflation it is likely that it is connected with another important change in the pattern of their lending: a move away from loans made to men in their own hundred to debtors much further afield. [Figure 4.8] In the first decade of the century 42 *per cent* of their debtors had been in their own hundred, 23 *per cent* in contiguous hundreds, and 35 *per cent* further away. In the 1340s 22 *per cent* were in the same hundred, 15 *per cent* in contiguous hundreds, and 62 *per cent* elsewhere. The

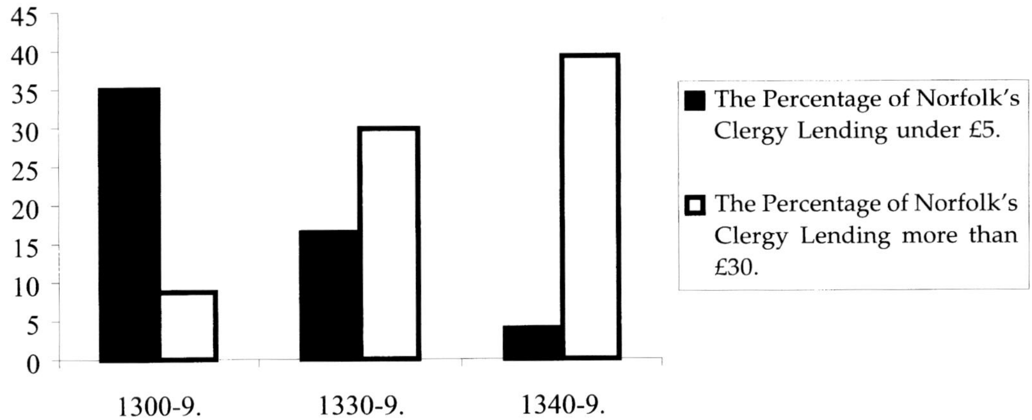

Figure 4.7 The percentage of Norfolk clergy's lending (i) under £5 and (ii) more than £30

clergy of Norfolk became far less parochial as creditors. The explanation for both developments seems to be that, just as the clergy increased their investment in property over this period, so they protected themselves against the greater possibility of default by choosing men of more substance to lend to. This meant lending larger sums to debtors with good security – preferably in land – but who inevitably lived further afield.

Thus economic interests, rather than the moral influence or local needs of the community seem to have motivated the parochial clergy as creditors and investors in the first half of the fourteenth century. Caution and safety seems to have been the guiding principle of the majority, and once the expansionary first decade of the century was over, fewer clergy in all parts of the kingdom were prepared to take the risk of lending large sums of money. Only in Norfolk, where the economy was particularly robust, did the parochial clergy have the confidence to continue lending money on any scale. Even so, their investment in urban property grew more quickly than their investment in trade or industry, and they increasingly chose to lend to people of means, or with good security, rather than support more risky enterprises in their own neighbourhoods. There is no indication, though, that high clerical taxation in the 1330s and 1340s,[72] any more than the prohibition of usury, inhibited their actions as investors and creditors. Indeed, the partial recovery of clerical lending generally in the 1340s indicates that once the economy had improved, more parochial clergy were willing to lend money, but like the clergy of Norfolk, they lent larger sums to people who offered better security. It is inconceivable that they chose to do so, instead of investing in property, if their loans had not offered a greater financial return.

It is, therefore, most unlikely that religious scruples explain declining investment in trade and industry in the later middle ages, particularly as men of the same religion had helped create the expansion of credit in the thirteenth century. It seems that creditors, clerical as well as lay, were influenced most in their decisions to lend or invest by their observation of their local economy. The clergy were rarely entrepreneurs

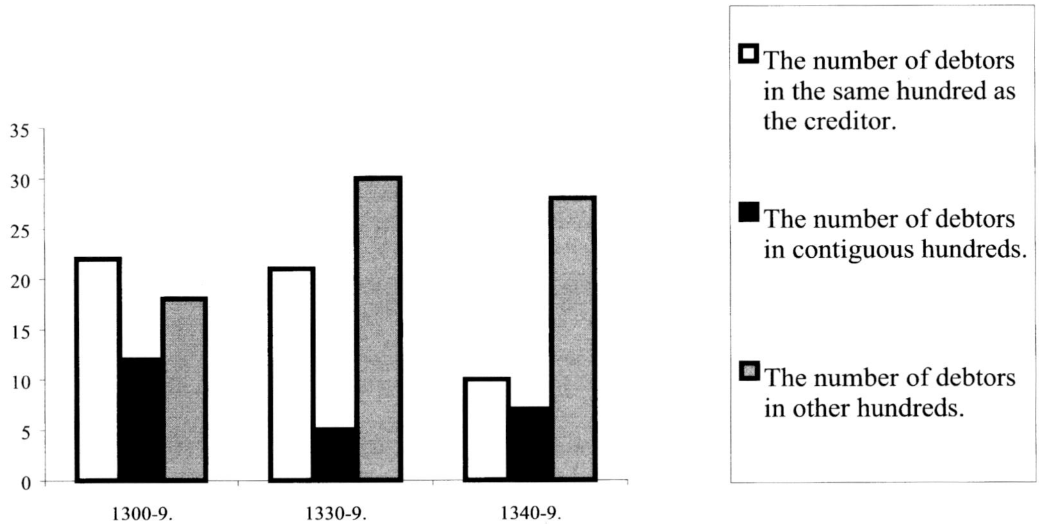

Figure 4.8 The hundreds of Norfolk clergy and their debtors (where both are known)

and initiators of economic development, but their need to provide for their own old age, and the commercial awareness which the tithe system gave them, made the bolder among them keen to exploit local opportunities for investment and profit wherever these offered high enough returns. Accordingly, the parochial clergy could be a significant source of capital for new rural ventures, such as the Norfolk cloth industry. Even so, the clergy of Norfolk protected themselves by giving credit for even shorter periods than elsewhere, so that, once there were signs of economic contraction, they could, like the merchant class, quickly move into safer and more utilitarian investment in urban property.[73]

In these ways the parochial clergy of Norfolk during the decades studied were not very different in their behaviour from the richer peasants who withdrew credit from the needy in times of bad harvest and took advantage of the market to invest cheaply in land.[74] This meant that the rural population could not find much local help when bad harvests or depression struck. Hence the migration of the poor to towns, and the advance of the wealthier urban capitalists, both features of the Norfolk economy by the middle of the fourteenth century.[75] Neither the moral tenets of the community, nor the private conscience of the individual made much difference to creditors' strategies, which inevitably put their own economic survival before the needs of their debtors. The short-term nature of most credit, which reflected the high degree of risk creditors felt they were running, and their natural preference for investing long-term in property or land, were a serious handicap to commercial and industrial development. But in their attitudes as creditors these parochial clergy were only reflecting the general shortage of liquid capital and the economic insecurity of their time.

Notes

* I am grateful to the Leverhulme Trustees, the University of Oxford, the Grocers' Company of London, and the Economic and Social Research Council (Award No. R000271010) for supporting my work on certificates of debt.

1 Jones, *God and the Moneylenders*, pp. 145–60, 173–4, 200–3.

2 B. A. Holderness, 'The clergy as money-lenders in England, 1550–1700', in Rosemary O'Day and Felicity Heal, eds., *Princes and Paupers* (Leicester, 1981), pp. 205, 197.

3 Gilchrist, *Church and Economic Activity*, pp. 65–9, 112–15.

4 Helmholz, 'Usury and the medieval English church courts', 368–70.

5 Woodcock, *Medieval ecclesiastical courts*, p. 87; Helmholz, 'Usury and the medieval English church courts', 370, 375; *Leet Jurisdiction in the City of Norwich during the 13th and 14th Centuries*, ed. W. Hudson (Selden Society, vol. 5, 1891), p. 35.

6 S. L. Thrupp, *The Merchant Class of Medieval London* (Chicago, 1948), p. 107.

7 Helmholz, 'Usury and the medieval English church courts', 374–5; Gilchrist, *Church and Economic Activity*, pp. 69, 113–14.

8 Rubin, *Charity and Community*, pp. 224–5.

9 Helmholz, 'Usury and the medieval English church courts', 375.

10 *ibid.*, 378–9.

11 J. R. H. Moorman, *Church life in England in the thirteenth century* (Cambridge, 1946), p. 53. He estimated that at the end of the 13th century there were 9,500 parishes and at least 40,000 priests to man them.

12 W. A. Pantin, *The English church in the fourteenth century* (Cambridge, 1955), pp. 198–200; R. E. Rodes, Jr, *Ecclesiastical administration in medieval England* (Notre Dame, Indiana, 1977), pp. 169–70; G. R. Owst, *Literature and the pulpit in medieval England* (Oxford, 1961), p. 259.

13 The clergy were officially forbidden to take part in trade: P. Heath, *The English Parish Clergy on the Eve of the Reformation* (London and Toronto, 1969), p. 3.

14 Gilchrist, *Church and Economic Activity*, p. 3; R. K. Morris, 'The Church in the Countryside: Two Lines of Inquiry', in, Della Hooke, ed., *Medieval Villages: A Review of Current Work* (Oxford University Committee for Archæology, Monograph No. 5, Oxford, 1985), p. 50.

15 N. P. Tanner, *The church in late medieval Norwich, 1370–1532* (Pontifical Institute of Medieval Studies, Toronto, 1984), p. 8. Some dioceses required them to be one of the executors. For example, in the Diocese of Norwich, where there was no such obligation, between a quarter and a third of lay testators from 1370 to 1517 chose at least one member of the secular clergy as an executor: *ibid.*, p. 14.

16 Rose Graham, 'The taxation of Pope Nicholas IV', *English Historical Review, 23 (1908)*, pp. 444–53.

17 R. Britnell, 'Urban demand in the English economy, 1300–1600', in, Galloway, ed., *Trade, Urban Hinterlands, and Market Integration*, p. 5.

18 R. N. Swanson, 'Standards of Livings: parochial revenues in Pre-Reformation England', in C. Harper-Bill, ed., *Religious Belief and Ecclesiastical Careers in Late Medieval England* (Studies in the History of Medieval Religion, vol. 3, (Woodbridge, Suffolk, 1991), pp. 151–95.

19 As amended by the Statute Merchant of 1285 (13 Edw. I). These certificates constitute class C. 241 in the Public Record Office. The figures given in this article refer to the date when a transaction was first registered as a debt, *not* when the certificate was received by the royal Chancery.

20 The Statute of Gloucester in 1278 limited borough courts and courts baron to hearing actions for claims under 40s. (*Select Pleas in Manorial and Other Seignorial Courts*, ed. Maitland, p. lvi). There are two Statute-Merchant certificates for 6s. 8d: C.241/9/53; 9/273. At least three parochial clergy recorded loans of 20s., *e.g.* C.241/40/110; 46/295; 55/203.

21 Clark, 'Debt litigation', p. 252; Britnell, *Colchester*, p. 108.

22 Jones, *God and the Money-lenders*, p. 59.

23 All the calculations refer to transactions for which there is clear evidence in the certificates; any readily-identifiable duplicates have been excluded.

24 The certificates show that, whereas in the 1300s the rectors slightly outnumber the parsons as creditors (78 certificates to 70) by the 1330s the parsons outnumber the rectors by 7 to 1. Possibly by the latter date the term rector was too closely associated with the unpopular impropiators who siphoned off the bulk of the parochial revenues.

25 W. M. Ormrod, 'The Crown and the English economy, 1290–1348', in, B. M. S. Campbell, ed., *Before the Black Death: Essays in the Crisis of the Early Fourteenth Century* (Manchester, 1991): tables 5.1, 5.2, 5.3 (pp. 153, 161, 163). Royal and papal taxation of the religious and secular clergy was about one-third higher in the 1330s than in the first decade of the century.

26 C.241/47/64.

27 C.241/68/90; 68/107.

28 P. A. Bill, *The Warwickshire Parish Clergy in the later Middle Ages* (Dugdale Society, Occasional Papers, no. 17, Oxford, 1967), pp. 4–5, 8, 11.

29 G. H. Cook, *Medieval Chantries and Chantry Chapels* (London, 1947), pp. 48–9. The mark was the equivalent of 13s. 4d.

30 E. Miller and J. Hatcher, *Medieval England: towns, commerce and crafts, 1086–1348* (Harlow, 1995), pp. 421–5.

31 Combeinteignhead (Devon.): C.241/32/283. Harthill, £41 6s. 8d.; Sandal Magna, £56; Fishlake, £40 (all in Yorks.); Gimingham, and East Ruston, both in Norfolk and both worth £53 6s. 8d.; this latter information is derived from, Swanson, 'Standards of Livings', pp. 192–4.

32 C.241/99/39.

33 C.241/121/414.

34 C.241/126/300.

35 R. N. Swanson, 'Standards of Livings', pp. 191–4.

36 There are 17 certificates for incumbents in Derbys. (the next highest total after the 40 for Norfolk). At least two Derbys. incumbents, those of Middleton and Wingfield, were not far from the lead mines: C.241/65/122; 81/101.

37 Heath, *English Parish Clergy*, p. 29. Of some 9000 parish churches in medieval England probably more than a third had been appropiated before the Reformation. In some counties the proportion was far higher, *e.g.*, 63% has been calculated for Yorks. and 50% for Lincs: A. Hamilton Thompson, *The English Clergy and their Organisation in the Later Middle Ages* (Oxford, 1947), p. 115.

38 *Victoria County History (Derbys.)*, ii, pp. 10–11.

39 C.241/74/356; 46/315; 69/257; 128/33 & 36. See also for Devon., C.241/53/29 & 35. For Derbys: C.241/36/284; 43/73.

40 C.241/95/28.

41 E. Power, *The wool trade in English medieval history* (Oxford, 1941), p. 45.

42 C.241/44/7.

43 C.241/36/284; 43/73. See also, C.241/36/180; 43/71; 40/61; 43/69; 50/153.

44 C.241/65/185 (1308).

45 Harper-Bill, *Warwickshire Parish Clergy*, pp. 22–3.

46 C.241/106/123.

47 C.241/106/122 & 126.

48 C.241/36/146; 55/36; 56/22; 61/189 & 135; 63/14; 70/172; 84/104.

49 C.241/69/202; C.241/110/38; C.241/109/212.

50 C.241/128/94; 36/265; 63/195; 106/41; 109/15.

51 *E.g.*, in the hundreds of Eynesford, Depwade, South Erpingham, Humbleyard, Holt, Clavering, and Taverham.

52 C.241/97/8,11; 102/175; *A Short Calendar of Deeds relating to Norwich enrolled in the Court Rolls of that City*, ed. W. Rye (Norwich, 2 vols.: 1285–1306 (1903); 1307–41 (1915)), ii, pp. 107, 114, 136, 139, 142.

53 C.241/105/333; *Short Calendar of the Deeds relating to Norwich*, ed. Rye, ii, pp. 153, 155, 158.

54 The average is based on the evidence for 1330–49, since many certificates before 1330 do not give all the necessary information.

55 *Victoria County History (Norfolk)*, ii, p. 236.

56 C.241/90/11.

57 *Taxatio Ecclesiastica Angliæ et Walliæ, Auctoritate Papæ Nicholai IV, circa A.D. 1291*, eds, T. Astle, S. Ayscough, and J. Caley (Record Commission, London, 1802), p. 84; *Crime in East Anglia in the Fourteenth Century: Norfolk Gaol Delivery Rolls, 1307–1316*, ed. B. Hanawalt (Norfolk Record Society, vol. 2, 1976), no. 330.

58 *Taxatio Ecclesiastica*, p. 80.

59 C.241/36/265; 42/41; 57/125; 77/58; 102/175; 103/199; 109/15; 15/188.

60 *Crime in East Anglia*, ed. Hanawalt, *passim*, esp. nos. 91, 146, 175, 216, 363, 417, 448. R. E. Glasscock, *The Lay Subsidy of 1334* (British Academy, Records of Social and Economic History, New Series, vol. 2, 1975), p. 205.

61 Pamela Nightingale, 'Norwich, London, and the Regional Integration of Norfolk's Economy in the First Half of the Fourteenth Century', in Galloway, ed., *Trade, Urban Hinterlands and Market Integration*, pp. 86–7.

62 *Ibid.*, pp. 92–3.

63 *Ibid.*, p. 87.

64 C.241/34/132; 35/102; 33/38; 35/100; 88/4; 36/32; 33/39; 33/36; 33/51; 33/44; 50/88; 50/90; 45/78; 44/14; 53/106; 50/89, 221; 57/125; 85/13; 62/147; 63/166; 67/48; 80/2.

65 C.241/80/169; 53/81; 55/90; 80/130; 61/39; 65/140 & 141; 71/157.

66 Nightingale, 'Norwich, London, and the Regional Integration of Norfolk's Economy', pp. 94–6.

67 C.241/109/114, 122 & 275; 110/84; 118/510.

68 Glasscock, *Lay Subsidy of 1334*, p. 197.

69 See p. 97 above; Nightingale, 'Norwich, London, and the Regional Integration of Norfolk's Economy', p. 92.

70 C.241/105/25.

71 C.241/111/305; 130/152 & 157; 117/300; 119/114; 130/151. For Gonville's foundation of the College of St John the Evangelist of Rushworth, see, E. K. Bennet, 'The College of St John Evangelist of Rushworth', *Norfolk Archæology*, vol. 10 (1888), 277–380.

72 W. M. Ormrod, *The Reign of Edward III* (New Haven and London, 1990), pp. 136–7, 205.

73 Nightingale, 'Monetary contraction and mercantile credit', 569–70.

74 Schofield, 'Dearth, debt, and the local land market', 9–17.

75 Nightingale, 'Norwich, London, and the regional integration of Norfolk's economy', pp. 97–99.

Chapter 5

Access to credit in the early fourteenth-century English countryside

Phillipp R. Schofield

We are, as yet, insufficiently aware of the particulars of the market integration of the medieval English peasantry and the implications of that integration. In certain cases, the particulars look to speak for themselves. It was once a standard of the literature – but is no more – that peasants produced a cash crop – typically, wheat – for rent and the remainder for consumption. Market involvement was accounted for in essentially internalised way – peasants ventured into the market when they needed to for reasons of their own consumption or were obliged to in order to meet the demands of lordship.[1] Undoubtedly, this defensive or responsive marketing was true for a great deal of market involvement throughout the middle ages but historians have grown interested in ways in which peasants entered the market aggressively, with a plan of campaign.

That such 'positive' integration existed is increasingly a standard of the historiography of the medieval peasantry. There already exists an extensive historiography which acknowledges the capacity of the peasantry to engage in a range of transactions beyond the local community. In particular, investigations of peasant involvement in small-town trade, production for semi-urban and urban markets, have shown the potential for villagers to trade and to sell produce for profit and not simply to raise cash for rent. Work by, amongst others, Hilton, Dyer, and Smith on small-towns and the market involvement of the peasantry has illustrated the inter-relationship between market and village.[2] Christopher Dyer, in particular, has shown that the peasantry were actively engaged in markets beyond the village and their immediate neighbourhood.[3] Studies of towns and their marketing strategies have also revealed the relationship of urban markets with their hinterlands, as, for example, in the work of Kowaleski on medieval Exeter.[4]

In fact, discussion of integration has developed to the point where the wealthier sections of the peasantry are perceived as significant and direct contributors to the national economy. Masschaele's recent study of 'peasants, merchants and markets' aims to show that the villein tenants of the larger customary holdings were significant producers for the market economy.[5] Historians have also identified clear indication in the records of medieval taxation that wealthier peasants were producing substantial taxable surpluses and, thereby, funding the functions of the state.[6] These observations, based on close analyses of lay subsidy assessments and returns – those pre-dating 1334, in particular – have also revealed the developed degree of stratification in the medieval village.[7] Biddick, Masschaele and Raftis have all, to varying degrees, commented on the measurable distinctions of wealth amongst the medieval peasantry and have explained this not solely in terms in shifts of family size and wealth according to life-cycle but as a consequence of trade and market involvement.[8]

As part of this investigation into the market involvement of the peasantry, there have also been significant attempts by historians to investigate efforts on the part of the peasantry to raise credit beyond the village. Kowaleski's investigation of borough court litigation in fourteenth-century Exeter reveals that villeins from the town's hinterland bought and sold produce within the town. For the most part, villagers came to Exeter to buy more than they came to sell; they appeared in the Exeter borough courts mostly as defendants and as debtors. But they also saw Exeter as a source of cash loans.[9] Kowaleski does not attempt – it was certainly not part of her remit to do so – to investigate the purpose of these cash loans, or indeed the stature of those outsiders who bought, sold and raised credit in the town's market. From a rather different perspective, Robin Mundill has considered the debtors of Jews in thirteenth century England. Mundill has elaborated on his earlier work in this volume and has gone as far as anyone in identifying peasant debtors beyond their villages and manors.[10] His focus, in this context, has however been upon the geography of debt, something to which brief return will be made a little later. McIntosh has also, from the particular perspective of the ancient demesne manor of Havering-atte-Bower, described the indebtedness of villagers to lenders from beyond the manor.[11]

There has as yet, however, been no clear attempt to examine the implications of such credit-raising at the local level nor to distinguish between those peasants who attempted such endeavours.[12] Can we identify the peasants who entered credit markets beyond the vill and can we begin to discuss their apparent intentions or the effect of employing such credit within their own communities? This chapter offers some observations directed at this question. We will begin with a brief discussion of 'extrinsic' credit and the potential to identify peasants as debtors and creditors beyond the manor, their range of activity and their economic profiles. Thereafter, discussion will return to village credit, its role and nature before, finally, some of the implications within the manor or vill for credit relationships external to the manor and village will be discussed. In order to maintain some consistency of social, political, economic and demographic conditions, the early fourteenth century will offer a focus for discussions.

Extrinsic credit

To investigate the extrinsic credit of the peasantry is, in part, to proceed beyond the local records of seigneurial courts. The potential areas of investigation are considerable, since there is a broad and varied survival of medieval sources in which debts are recorded, either as formal records of debt as recognisances or as pleas of debt, detinue or covenant. The earliest and still most important statement on this, remains that made by M. M. Postan in the first volume of the *Economic History Review*.[13] Postan identified various records of debt, including listings of recognisances, inventories of debts and accounts. Since he wrote, investigators have begun to analyse a range of sources, most especially those which shed light on mercantile credit.[14] Though he did not venture upon the 'uncharted sea of ...the various local court rolls', Postan was prescient in recognising their value, as well as pleas of debt in other fora.[15] We have already discussed the work of certain historians who have attempted to examine courts other than manor courts in search of peasant commercial activity: Kolaweski has used the Exeter borough courts, and Dyer has also used borough courts to comment on peasant debtors and creditors. Farmer has also drawn our attention to the records of piepawder and fair courts as potential sources for the investigation.[16]

In the following section of this chapter, in order to offer a further exploration of the extension of credit to villagers from beyond their own communities and to attempt a limited prosopographical analysis of litigants, credit relationships recorded in the rolls of a county court will be investigated. An examination of one of the earliest surviving records for a county court, the Bedfordshire county roll for 1332–3, will seek to relate information contained there to other national and local records. There are published lay subsidy taxation lists from 1332 for Bedfordshire and Buckinghamshire.[17] A search has also been made for some of the Bedfordshire litigants in local records.[18]

Both the Bedfordshire county roll and a near contemporary sheriff's return of writs were transcribed by G.H. Fowler in the first half of the last century, as was the shorter record of proceedings of a Bedfordshire County Court in 1327/8.[19] Fowler, in his edition of the county roll for 1332/3, carefully distinguishes between pleas recorded in the county roll, identifying seventy-six separate pleas across the nine sessions of the county court between 1332 and 1333. Of these seventy-six pleas, seventeen were pleas of trespass, one of which was later changed to a plea of debt, thirteen were pleas for illegal distraint, three were pleas of account, two were for breach of covenant. There were four (additional) pleas, each of different form: observance, restoration of charters, repair, and detinue. Thirty-seven, almost fifty *per cent* [48.6%] of the pleas were for debt.[20]

The Bedfordshire county roll for 1332/2 records the names of twenty-nine plaintiffs and thirty-nine defendants in pleas of debt. There were, amongst both plaintiffs (five) and defendants (three), a few individuals who appeared in more than a single plea. By cross-referencing the names of debt litigants recorded in the county rolls with those named in contemporary lists of payers of the lay subsidy, it is possible to glean some information on the range of litigants pursuing or being pursued in the county court. The lay subsidy provides a useful source for identifying and locating the litigants but also offers a partial opportunity to consider the relative wealth of the litigants and their position within their particular communities.

The potential for linking individuals named in the county roll with listed payers of the subsidy varies from individual to individual, with some litigants more easily identified in the subsidy list than others. To begin with creditors, fifteen of the plaintiffs were described in the county roll by their place of origin/residence. The combined information of name and place of origin/residence have been treated here as a reasonable basis on which to attempt an accurate identification of the same individual in both sources, the county roll and the lay subsidy. As we will also see, however, there are additional features in the documentation which encourage a degree of confidence in attempting linkages even where the additional check of place of origin/residence is not available. Of the fifteen plaintiffs described by name and place of origin/residence, only two are also closely identifiable in the 1332 lay subsidy for Bedfordshire.[21] In addition, four plaintiffs can also be 'found' in the lay subsidy lists, although not living in the vill by which they are identified in the county roll, such as Thomas Rous, described as 'of Wootton Bourne' in the county court, and who, listed amongst the subsidy payers for the vill of Shelton, paid over 9s. to the 1332 subsidy, or Ralf Marchal of Ampthill, who, in 1332, paid 5s. to the subsidy at Bedford.[22] Some of the plaintiffs clearly came from beyond the county. Two plaintiffs look to have come from Hertfordshire (Baldock (three instances), Hitchin).[23] In two cases, plaintiffs who were described according to place of origin in the county court, but are unidentified in the subsidy lists themselves, share surnames with individuals who were both listed in the subsidy and were resident in the plaintiff's supposed place of origin.[24] In three other instances, plaintiffs unidentified in the subsidy lists share surnames with individuals found in vills other than that of the plaintiff's supposed place of origin.[25] The names of fourteen individuals, including, unsurprisingly, two of the three Hertfordshire creditors discussed above, cannot be found in the subsidy lists while the names of four individuals who are not identified by place of origin in the county roll can be found in the subsidy lists.[26] In these last cases, cross-identification of the individual in the county roll with the individual named in the subsidy list cannot be made with any real confidence. Finally, one plaintiff, who cannot be identified in the subsidy list, shares a surname with an individual listed in 1332.[27]

As to the thirty-nine defendants, twenty-five were identified in the county roll by place of origin and, of these, nine can be closely identified in the 1332 lay subsidy list by their stated place of location.[28] A further five can be identified by simple name search of the subsidy list allied to a probable locational identification, in that they are recorded in the subsidy as living in a village adjacent to the one with which they are identified in the county roll.[29] Of the other eleven defendants identified by location in the county roll, seven cannot be found in the lay subsidy list for 1332, whilst two shares surnames with individuals listed in 1332.[30] One, Thomas Hayroun of Riseley, shares a surname with an individual listed in the same vill in the 1332 subsidy list, although he does not appear himself in the subsidy list for that year whilst one other, John Daye, appears as resident in a vill other than that with which he is identified in the county roll.[31] Of the remaining fourteen defendants not supplied with locational identification in the county roll, three names cannot be found in the subsidy list whilst the names of eleven individuals can be found and are, generally, of a sufficiently distinctive quality to suggest that they may, in most cases, belong to the same individual named in the county roll.[32]

The process of cross-referring litigants in the county roll with payers of the 1332 lay subsidy has, therefore, revealed a number of individuals who we can, with some reasonable degree of certainty, identify in both sources as one and the same. If we reject those who cannot be closely or reasonably closely identified in both the county roll and the subsidy lists, we can retain information on nine plaintiffs and twenty-six defendants. The lay subsidy, allied to the locational information in the county rolls, allows us to identify some of the county roll litigants according to place, and to hazard the suggestion that some of the creditors and debtors were rural dwellers. Linkage of litigants with lay subsidy lists also affords an opportunity to construct a crude measure of the relative wealth of the litigants, the economic 'range' of creditors and debtors, and the economic relationships underlying individual credit relationships. A combination of the locational information from the county roll and subsidy list and the measures of 'wealth' extracted from the subsidy list presents us with limited opportunities, in the absence of extensive court roll series for the same Bedfordshire vills during the early fourteenth century, to identify some of the litigants as villagers.

To begin with the location of the litigants and the extent to which we can identify them as villagers, it seems to be the case that whilst most of the identifiable plaintiffs came from within the immediate hinterland of the larger towns of Bedford, Ampthill or Hitchin/Baldock in Hertfordshire, their debtors were slightly more dispersed [maps 5.1 and 5.2]. Debtors were to be found in smaller population centres, as well as local market centres, such as Cranfield, Blunham, Potton, Marston, Shefford and Arlesey.[33] Where locational information survives for both creditors and debtors, as it does in fifteen cases, agreements can be grouped according to three 'types': agreements made between creditors and debtors resident within the same vill (4);[34] agreements made over short distances, typically of no more than five miles (3); agreements made over longer distances, that is, of between five miles and twenty-five miles (8). Given the small size of the sample, the slight preponderance of credit agreements over a longer distance cannot be treated as anything more that mildly suggestive of a tendency for debtors from smaller communities to seek credit from lenders in larger communities allied to the probability that credit agreements conducted over distance were, when they collapsed, more likely to be contested in county or other more central courts rather than more local tribunals. Richard Bazeley of Baldock, for example, a plaintiff in three separate instances, appears to have extended credit to those living in eastern Bedfordshire, contracting, as he did, loans with men from Millo, Ickwell and Potton.[35]

Just as there may have been a distinctive geography as regards creditors and debtors, so also may there have been distinctions of economic status. In terms of average measures of 'wealth', mean lay subsidy payments by creditors and debtors were very similar, at 59.5d. and 61.77d. respectively. However, although the average for creditors looks to be representative, the average payment for debtors is clearly skewed by two or three substantial individuals and a median value of 37.2d. comes closer to reflecting the typicality of subsidy payments by debtors. According to the lay subsidy lists, the wealthiest creditor was Thomas de Stodleye who paid 9s. 6½d. in 1332 whilst the wealthiest debtor was Walter de Huntyngfeld who paid 18s. 1½d.[36] John Osemond, a shepherd at Marston, was the poorest creditor identifiable in the subsidy list, paying 16d.[37] Amongst debtors, there were individuals such as Geoffrey Joye at Ickwell (16d.) and William Bonseriaunt at Shefford (13½d.) who paid very small sums in 1332 but most debtors, as we have seen, paid a little more.[38] The majority of debtors were at the mid-lower end of the lay subsidy payments but this is still likely to have placed them, for instance, well inside the upper third of wealthiest villagers.[39]

There are, of course, a number of potential pitfalls in this method, in addition to the uncertainties associated with attempting a simple correspondence of names in two separate series of documents, even where they are closely contemporary. Even if we are content that we are dealing with the same individuals, can we be sure that we have

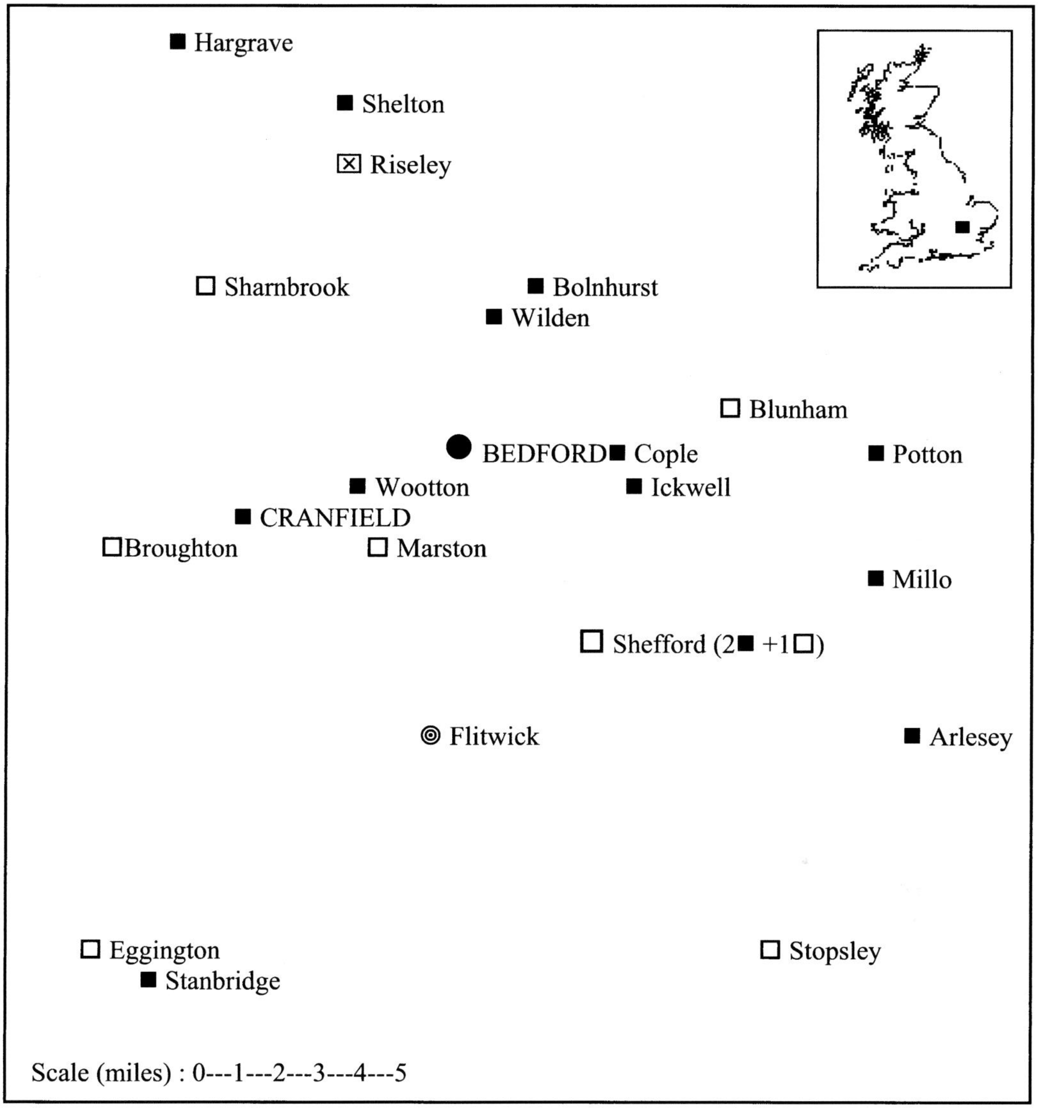

■ – defendants identifiable in 1332 lay subsidy by name and location.
◎ – defendants identifiable by name and proximate location.
☒ – defendants identified by local family name only.
□ – unidentified defendant.

Figure 5.1 Location of defendants in Bedfordshire County Court, 1332/3. Pleas of debt.

identified their economic status appropriately? It is, for example, clearly the case that certain individuals were assessed for the lay subsidy in more than one vill, assuming that, for instance, the Simon Cranfield who paid 2s. 1½d. at Goldington was the same man who paid 3s. 9d. at Southill.[40] While, therefore, we can use the simple information

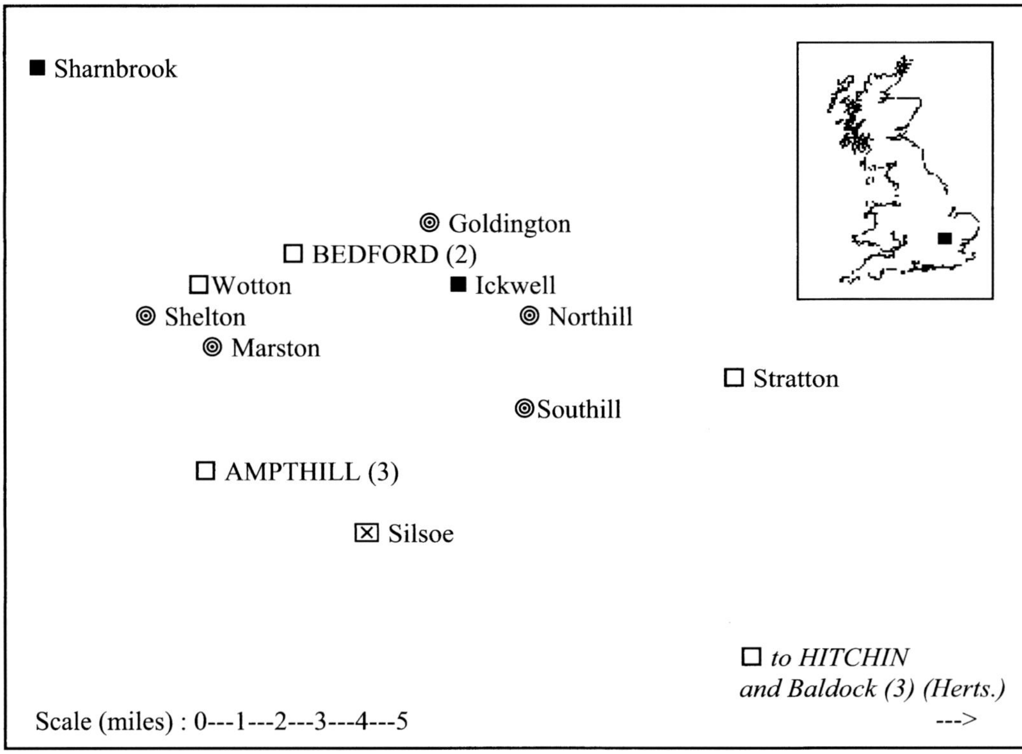

■ – plaintiffs identifiable in 1332 lay subsidy by name and location.
◎ – plaintiffs identifiable by name and proximate location.
☒ – plaintiffs identified by local family name only.
□ – unidentified plaintiff.
TOWNS in capitals.

Figure 5.2 Location of plaintiffs in Bedfordshire County Court, 1332/3. Pleas of debt.

of the subsidy lists to draw some limited conclusions regarding the clientele of the Bedfordshire county court, its wealth and its regionality, we need to draw on additional information, regarding both the individual litigants identifiable in the subsidy lists and those who cannot be identified, to supplement this material and to provide a check upon it and, most importantly, to attempt to identify local men of moderate wealth. Important in this respect is information ancillary to the pleas of debt in the county court, most especially information on size of debt and the process of attachment.

Size of debts and distraints, where recorded in the county rolls, do emphasise the relative, though not extreme, wealth of the defendants. There is relatively little information on the size of debts; while the debts owed to Richard Wariner of Sharnbrook remained within the 40s. jurisdictional limit,[41] the two other debts for which we have details were substantially larger (*Mareschall v. Flitwick*: 61s.; *Studham v. Baldok*: £12).[42] John Baldok of Stanbridge owed money for the purchase of two horses.[43]

Information on distraints is slightly more revealing as to the wealth of the defendants. John Potton, the third wealthiest of the defendants according to the subsidy listing, was distrained by four horses.[44] John Bishop of Cranfield, who can be identified in the Cranfield court rolls as a manorial office-holder, was distrained by a single horse.[45] Of the other defendants, three were distrained by one horse, two by a cow, one by two sheep, one by two quarters of wheat and rye and a cow, one by two horses, whilst amongst the unidentified or weakly identified defendants, three individuals could not be distrained because they possessed insufficient goods.[46] One of these, Thomas Hayroun, a butcher, from Riseley, may have been assessed at only 22d. in the 1332 subsidy list whilst the other, Nigel son of Eustace of Bletsoe, cannot be clearly identified at all.[47] Further, one of the defendants who clearly features in the lay subsidy list also had insufficient goods against which distraint could be made; as in the previous cases, this individual, Michael Warde, also of Bletsoe, was assessed at the lower end of the payors of the 1332 lay subsidy, 2s. 1d.[48] In fact, he was assessed at one of the three lowest discoverable amounts of all of the defendants in pleas of debt. The impression, therefore remains one of relative wealth with the further indication that plaintiffs could not easily pursue the poorest of the defendants.

A similar impression is gained if we consider the process of attachment in the county court. Attachment was employed in nine debt cases in the county court. In five of eight cases, the defendants who were attached by mainpernors were to be counted amongst the poorest of the litigants, involving individuals who, in 1332, paid between 12½d and 3s. 3¾d.[49] In one case, that of John Smyth of Sharnbrook, the defendant, who was attached, cannot be identified in the subsidy list which might suggest that he fell below the property qualification for the subsidy. Importantly, for this analysis, the information on mainpernors looks to confirm the impression that some defendant debtors were relatively poor men but also villagers. Mainpernors, who were named in the county rolls, can frequently be identified in the subsidy lists: they tended to be men of a similar economic standing to the defendants for whom they were responsible, if sometimes slightly poorer. To quote one example, Geoffrey Joye of Ickwell, who paid 16d. in 1332 and was in the debt of a Richard Bazeley of Baldock (Herts.), a creditor in two other instances, was attached by two local men, Henry Chapman and John Draggeberd, who paid 18d. and 2s. 1d. in 1332.[50]

These poorer defendants stand in some contrast to other litigants in the Bedfordshire county court. The names of minor gentry, such as David Flitwick, described as chevalier, appear amongst both plaintiffs and defendants.[51] Thomas de Stodleye, the wealthiest of the creditors according to the subsidy listings, was a knight of the shire, a close friend of the deputy Justiciar of Ireland and a prominent figure in the Bedfordshire county community.[52] Plaintiff creditors and defendant debtors include individuals identified by occupation or office, including a chaplain and the prior of Chicksand. Guy Test, a debtor who paid 16s. 3d. to the 1332 lay subsidy at Thamesford, was described in the county roll as 'Lombard'.[53] At least two other individuals, neither of whom appears in the 1332 subsidy list, Richard Exmouth and Philip de Aylesbury, are identifiable as, respectively, an attorney-at-law and the sheriff of Bedfordshire and Buckinghamshire.[54] Undoubtedly, some of the debts were contracted between men of elevated social and economic status. Test, the Lombard, was debtor to Thomas Stodleye, knight of the shire; similarly, Robert Gobyoun was in the debt of Thomas Rous, and both men were members of the Bedfordshire gentry.[55] Despite the existence of litigants of such status, the above analysis, inexact and limited as it undoubtedly is, does suggest that there were, amongst the Bedfordshire county court litigants, some debtors, perhaps as many as six, who can be identified by location, were attached by local men, and/or paid relatively sums low to the 1332 lay subsidy. These men may well have been villagers.[56]

Since, however, we have very little information on the size of the debt and almost no local records for early fourteenth Bedfordshire against which to compare the information of the lay subsidy and the county court roll, it is impossible, in this particular, context either to follow these defendants into their own communities or, consequently, to provide meaningful comment on the employment of external capital at the village level. Most importantly, we cannot here gain any sense of the extent of the credit-debt relationship; whilst we can be reasonably certain that poorer individuals from Bedfordshire villages were in the debt of wealthier individuals from other communities, we do not know, in the vast majority of cases, whether the debts involved large cash loans or were simply credit sales. Further investigation which attempts linkage of individuals using a range of contemporary records, both manorial and local/regional/national, will certainly help to define this picture and allow some assessment of the size and impact of external capital at the local level. For the present, in order to support the contention that wealthier villagers engaged in credit markets beyond their vills and to discuss the role of that credit in a local context, we will need to return to manorial sources.

Village credit

Historians are already aware that a good deal of credit was available at the manorial level and that villagers did not necessarily need to move beyond the boundaries of their villages in order to borrow.[57] A large amount of very simple credit would never have found its way into the court rolls at all. Thus, borrowing of an everyday kind between those in the same social group, mostly kin or neighbours, is unlikely to have ended in pleas of debt and certainly would not have been initiated with a court roll recognisance.[58] Illegal distraints, house-breakings and assaults, many examples of which can be found in the court rolls, may, at least in part, be explained in terms of recovery of or disputes over small loans.[59] It seems likely, therefore, that borrowing on this rather personal level will be under-represented relative to the larger and, perhaps, less typical credit arrangments which are more likely to have taken place outside of the kin group or the circle of a villager's immediate peers and with a villager who was socially and economically superior.

If we confine ourselves to recorded credit – and what choice do we have? – most peasant credit at the village level seems to have been fairly small scale. Even on royal manors where the 40s. limit for litigation did not apply, debts seldom exceeded this amount and were quite often much less.[60] At Writtle, in the fifteenth century, Clark discovered a considerable range of goods and services for which payment could be deferred or which could be available for loan.[61] However, about 50 *per cent* of all debt categories involved credit sales – deferred payments on goods, usually of animals or cereals – rather than loans. Deferred payments for services comprised on average about 20 *per cent*, as did leases, most often of land but also of animals; finally, loans of cash or chattels made up the additional 10 *per cent*.[62] Elsewhere, on manors which were not ancient demesne, claims usually fell well below the 40s limit.[63] At Hinderclay (Suffolk), in the late thirteenth and early fourteenth centuries, with population at its medieval maximum and most villagers holding very small parcels of land, the majority of debts were for cash or, most typically, grain[64] and most were worth substantially less than 5s.[65]

Further, the majority of credit relationships recorded in the manor courts are, unsurprisingly, local but they were not necessarily lateral. Who lent to whom? Commentators on debt in the early modern period have often noted that debt relationships tended to be horizontal rather than vertical.[66] However, in the medieval village, credit relationships involving larger loans tended to be vertical rather than horizontal. Within the village community, the wealthiest landholders acted as creditors more than most because they, inevitably, possessed a saleable surplus; local gentry and clergy may also have fulfilled this function. It is difficult to see how poorer villagers, at least in some parts of the medieval English countryside, could have ever found themselves in a position to act as creditors for the simple reason that they may never have produced more than their immediate needs and, thus, less than could be extended as credit.[67] At Halesowen, the richest peasants frequently acted as lenders of money, grain and livestock whilst the poor families were often in debt.[68] At Hinderclay, again, in the late thirteenth century, individuals tended to appear either as creditors or debtors and seldom as both; furthermore, the poorest villagers do not seem to have been involved in credit transactions at all, or, at least, not in those recorded in the court rolls.[69]

How should we characterise this local credit? Predominance of horizontal lines of credit is suggestive of commercial confidence in the same way that a clear majority of vertical credit arrangements is not.[70] If the bulk of individuals in the medieval village, as seems likely, borrowed predominantly small items and sums of grain or money from their neighbours and other family members, in lateral and largely invisible relationships, then it seems reasonable to see credit as, to use the terminology of economic anthropology, sought for *consumption* rather than *investment*.[71] However, it is clearly also the case that some credit was extended in vertical relationships which included a significant component, at least on the part of creditors, of *investment*. In these relationships concepts of mutual dependency and moral economy do not easily apply.[72]

To glance at any number of manorial court rolls from the early fourteenth century is to discover tensions and rivalries. Inter-peasant litigation at, for instance, Blunham (Beds.) reflects this tension. Litigation is strongly in evidence in the Blunham manorial court rolls from the early- to mid-fourteenth century, with an average of one new plea of debt or trespass recorded in each of the surviving courts from the second and third decades of the fourteenth century. The debt and trespass cases recorded at Blunham are strongly suggestive of fairly intense local competition, verging on the private feud, as, for instance, the long-term quarrel between the Bernards and the Passelewes. In

1318 William Bernard successfully attempted to sue Robert Passelewe, impleading Robert in a debt of 2s. 10d. for sale of sheep and drage. Interestingly, also in this court, it was recorded that a Hugo Passelewe had burned down the house (*comburit domum*) of Peter Bernard. The lord seized Hugo's moveable goods (details of which were listed) and handed them to Peter.[73] At a later court, in 1321, Robert Passelewe failed to defend himself against the allegation of Peter Bernard that he had defamed Peter to his damage, the cost of the defamation valued at 2s.[74] In the next court in Blunham, held in November 1321, during a period of real hardship in the countryside, the same Robert called in two debts, each owed by members of the Bernard family, one of whom was Peter. William and Peter Bernard both acknowledged separate debts of, respectively, 5s. plus interest of 12d. and 2 quarters of barley.[75] We sense that this dispute was conducted between two fairly wealthy village families with the probability that the Passelewes were the stronger, more financially secure, party. Robert Passelewe appeared in the 1332 lay subsidy for Bedfordshire as one of the six wealthiest villagers; unlike Passelewe, none of the Bernard Blunhams appears in the subsidy, although the surname does appear locally in other vills and a William Bernard paid 2s. 4¼d. at nearby Eastcotts.[76]

The calling in of debts at particular moments, their actions seemingly set against a backdrop of petty assaults and other acts of violence, defamations, other pleas and counter pleas, was an integral part of village politics. Disputes such as these, familiar in the manorial court rolls from this period, are also distinguished by the inequality of the parties. Razi's investigation of Halesowen, for instance, shows that the alignment of inter-peasant dispute was reflective of economic relations: poorer peasants at Halesowen were the victims of the wealthier.[77] However, if village society in the early fourteenth century was clearly stratified it was still not intensely polarised. In other words, there was sufficient difference to matter in the medieval village but insufficient difference to make even the wealthiest of the peasantry feel wholly secure. This, of course, is a situation that would vary from manor to manor and from vill to vill. But on those vills where we can find evidence of a competitive land market by the early fourteenth century, there really is little likelihood that the wealthier peasantry were economically able or sufficiently inclined to provide their poorer neighbours with the capital necessary to turn them into competitors. Instead, what those few examinations of peasant credit at the village level have so far discovered is that peasant credit reflected stratification and helped promote polarisation. There is, for instance, clear evidence that larger loans required the security of land and that peasant creditors were not averse to calling in debts of neighbours and foreclosing on their gages. This raises questions relevant to the theme of this chapter: could poorer villages seek credit beyond the manor or, alternatively, did extrinsic credit supplies permit wealthier villagers to reinforce their security and their role within village society? Further to this, did wealthier villagers effectively enjoy an exclusive access to external supplies of credit and, thereby, control the credit markets of manors and villages or could they be by-passed by their poorer peers?

External credit within the village: the evidence of the manor court

Examination of series of manorial court rolls can produce information highly suggestive of a polarised external credit market, indicating that, while pleas of debt for small sums of money or other minor loans were frequently conducted between villagers, the litigants in larger pleas frequently involved a plaintiff from beyond the village. A fine example of this comes from early fourteenth-century Walsham le Willows (Suffolk). In December 1321 John Bande ('Baude' where he appears in other published sources and hereafter) of Ipswich made his only court roll appearance in the Walsham manorial rolls when he pursued William Wodebite, a villein of the manor who appeared in the manorial records on numerous occasions, into the manor court of Walsham in a plea of debt. William was attached to respond to John. The jurors of the manor court, seemingly attesting to events beyond their immediate cognizance,[78] agreed with John that he had delivered 12 marks of silver to William, in 1319 at Ipswich 'to trade and profit for John's benefit, and William was required to render faithfully a true account thereof quarterly, in accordance with the Law Merchant and by a certain written agreement'. William had refused on numerous previous occasions to render his account but continued to withhold the debt 'and the profits therefrom'.[79] It was ordered that John should recover. We will return to William a little later when we consider the implications of external borrowing. The important point, for now, is that no plea of debt in this period at Walsham was comparable in size, a feature that must have reflected the external source of the capital. John Baude was a merchant of some standing beyond the manor. He is recorded in the Ipswich lay subsidy returns for 1327, paying 10s., the sixth highest of 210 individual payments for the town in that year.[80] Baude can also be found in the Ipswich recognisance rolls: in 1322 a John Baude the elder acted as co-executor to the testament of a Richard Salwe, whose property included four messuages and a barn, while, by the 1330s, a John Baude, miller, had erected his own mill at Ipswich.[81]

Examination of the debt pleas for the manor of Downham (Cambs.) is similarly revealing of supplies of external credit.[82] The published court rolls for Downham, 1310–1327 contain twenty-five pleas of debt or unjust detention. Of these twenty-five, sixteen include mention of sums of money. The sums range from 1/2d. to 35s. and a bushel of wheat. Although the rolls are in such broken series that the construction of biographies of most of the villagers is not possible, it is clear that the defendants in the larger debt pleas were some of the most prominent villagers and that, moreover, their creditors, the plaintiffs, hardly feature in the court rolls at all. Of the four largest pleas – those for 20s.; 29s. 41/2d., 33s. 6d. and 35s. plus a bushel – the defendants appeared between 48 and 62 times in the rolls (William Stoneye, 48 times; William Persoun (two debt pleas), 62 times; Simon Cardinal the elder, 58 times) while the four plaintiffs – Ralph Valentyn, John le Fisher, Robert de la Grene and Stephen Gleys, a miller – each appeared only once. This pattern is less evident when we move to the smaller pleas. The seven smallest pleas of debt – for 1/2d., 8d., 11d., 12d., 13d., 18d., 2s. 1d., 40d. – involved plaintiffs and defendants who both, with two exceptions (both female creditors, one the widow of a peasant frequently named in the rolls[83]) made more than single appearances in the manor court rolls. Here we would also expect the total number of appearances to be smaller, as indeed they mostly are, since the poorer villagers appeared less frequently in the manor court rolls anyway.[84] At this, the lower end of the village credit market, we are in a world of small loans for consumption, not for investment. This world also appears to have been local and desperate: John Man, described as a pauper, unjustly detained 1/2d. from Robert Aleyn but 'nevertheless attacked the same Robert with malicious words' while, when, on the death of her husband, Amicia, the widow of Adam the son of Philip, called in debts owed to her by seven villagers, the total of the seven debts came to only 2s. 1d. (approximately 3 1/2d. per debtor).[85] Finally, the four pleas of middling size at Downham – 6s.; 6s. 61/2d. [reduced to 10d. on plea]; 8s.; 12s. 10d. – involved plaintiffs and defendants who both, for the most part, made regular appearance in the court rolls. In this middle strata of debt pleas, individuals who appear as creditors amongst the poorer villagers here appear in the role of debtors. Adam the son of Philip, for instance, whose widow called in a number of small debts as we have seen, was a debtor to one Nicholas Prat for the sum of 12s. 10d.[86] The impression is, again, that we are witnessing an intra-village credit market, with an enhanced degree of reciprocity at the lower end of the economic scale. Importantly, credit, as is better evidenced elsewhere than in the Downham manorial rolls but is certainly suggested even there, was extended downwards and that the poorer villagers were almost exclusively consumers of credit. This made the poorer peasantry vulnerable both to the rapacity of wealthier villagers and to the dictates of external markets, a point to which some brief return will be made. Above all, this brief examination appears to indicate that the larger debts were accumulated beyond the vill. In some cases, these were long-standing accounts with traders and merchants but in others, as in the case of Wodebite discussed above, they could be single large loans. Whether a long-term series of credit sales or a single lump sum loan, such facility provided wealthier villages with a flexibility and credit surplus which their poorer neighbours could not hope to match.

A range of factors will have aided the endeavours of wealthier villagers beyond the manor and militated against similar activity on the part of poorer villagers. As we have already discussed, the wealthier villagers frequently operated beyond the manor in official roles and were cognizant of modes of dealing both in law and in commerce. The two villagers who appear to have owed the largest debts to outsiders at Downham, were or had been reeves, as was William Wodebite at Walsham. While not discounting the possibility that external creditors were sometimes pursuing such individuals in their official capacities – offices for which they were, of course, personally liable – it is clear that medieval office-holders made no clear distinction between performance of office for the advantage of their lord and for themselves. One of the reeves at Downham, William Persoun, was ejected from office for a list of misdemeanours, mostly involving misappropriation of the lord's property. This included using the lord's horse and cart on trips to and from Ely.[87] But the normal everyday performance of manorial business would also have drawn them into markets and opportunity to trade with more substantial merchants. Furthermore, in such circumstances, with trade at a relative distance, formal securities must have played a significant role. The use of proofs and specialties are evident in such contracts, as, again, the Wodebite example, clearly shows.[88] Again, awareness of normal business dealing and a familiarity with the mechanisms of trade and law must have served the wealthier peasantry well in this regard.

Most importantly, wealthier villagers possessed security against which credit could be raised. In the case of reeves and other manorial officials, the security could also have been the lord of the manor's. For the most part, though, their landholding and, most importantly, the produce of their holdings would serve. The relative wealth of villagers was, self-evidently, a crucial determinant of the ability of villagers to raise cash beyond their manors and vills. A 1311 presentment in the Downham manor court of those villagers who kept sheep beyond the lord's fald, named five individuals, three of whom were William de Stoneye, Simon Cardinal and William de Persoun, the three villagers earlier identified as raising credit beyond the vill.[89] Robert son of Adam was one of the wealthiest villagers on the Bury St Edmunds manor of Hinderclay (Suffolk). He and his brother, William, dominated the land market in the late thirteenth century and were both important creditors in the village.[90] The lay subsidy assessment for 1283 indicates that Robert was a trader in grain. While the majority of the peasantry assessed in 1283 spread their resources amongst a range of crops and livestock, Robert's possessions were valued at £4 and were composed solely of barley – 20 quarters of it – a sum incompatible with his landholding.[91] Individuals with such a proportion of their wealth tied up in movables would not have found it difficult to raise capital which could be re-employed in the village or elsewhere. The same was almost certainly true for villagers such as the significant peasant players at Downham or William Wodebite at Walsham. As Biddick has pointed out, concentration of single assets in grain or livestock reflects ways in which 'wealthier peasants...put themselves in marketing chains different from peasants who circulated their surplus in local markets'.[92]

Important also in this regard is the fact that security based on produce removed any constraints associated with unfree land – whilst creditors may not have wished to accept customary or servile land as security for loans, money lent on future sales or harvests or on the security of existing produce was relatively free of the taint of servility.[93] Where an individual did not have security in movables, he or she could only offer land as security. If the individual was a villein, then their potential creditors – those prepared to accept villein land as security – were also likely to be villeins from the same manor. The same, of course, did not apply to free tenants but what is interesting about the court roll examples gathered here is that the wealthier villagers who raised credit beyond the vill were villeins, not free tenants.

Implications and conclusions

Evidence for the peasantry raising credit beyond the manor has, of course, implications for the ways in which we see the local community and the village economy operating.[94] In particular it has implications for the study of the local land market since, if credit could be raised in large sums beyond the village, these wealthy peasants could dominate economic life within their own communities, a point emphasised by Paul Hyams three decades ago.[95]

If we return to William Wodebite at Walsham-le-Willows, an individual who, as we have already seen, entered into extensive credit agreements beyond the manor, his activity within the village can, in part, be explained in terms of that external activity.[96] Wodebite, who died *c.* 1345,[97] makes early appearance in the rolls from the 1310s; from that decade we see him behaving as a successful player in the local economy but his elder brother, John, was clearly already fulfilling that role. Although William Wodebite does not appear in the published lay subsidy list for Suffolk from 1327, a feature perhaps of his indebtedness by that time but, possibly, given his forceful presence in the contemporary surviving manorial records, his ability to evade assessment, he was, nevertheless a significant individual in the village. In the 1320s and 1330s, the two brothers were amongst the most dominant villagers within the community. John, for instance, appeared as pledge for the prior of Ixworth in 1319.[98] William was actively involved in the land market, always as a purchaser in this period. In 1317 he entered a half messuage and five acres plus a reversion of the other half as well as an additional five acres;[99] in 1319, Margaret of Angerhale quitclaimed all lands and tenements to him.[100] When, in 1325, Nicholas de Walsham inherited the manor of High Hall, a number of previous, undisclosed land transfers 'from the time of Alice de Walsham' were to be licenced. Three of these involved separate purchases by William, totalling 17a. of land in all.[101] As well as an active purchaser of land, William, as his brother, was an energetic litigant and a holder of office, though he avoided in so far as he could performance of customary dues and, on at least one occasion, paid other villagers to fulfill his labour rent. He was also a frequent pledge to other villagers.[102]

If, as the example of Wodebite suggests, the more important villagers – politically and economically – served as creditors and major purchasers amongst the poorer tenantry/peasantry, any effective attempt to withdraw credit or restrict the capital of the wealthier villagers by outsiders, as in the example of the plea initiated by John Baude of Ipswich, is likely to have had a deleterious effect on the less substantial members of village communities. I have suggested in an earlier article that taxation in the late thirteenth century encouraged those who were frequently creditors in the medieval village to withdraw their credit – potentially, a taxable movable – and reinvest in the land market.[103] There, the withdrawal of creditors and, thereby credit, from local economies was represented as a choice imposed by central authority. Here, in discussing the actions of creditors at the level of urban and regional trade, we are reflecting a further choice, one informed perhaps by shifts in trade or government policy, warfare or weather, individual triumph or disaster. Both instances, however, remind us that the economy of the village was subject to the vicissitudes of political and commercial shifts and that we need to be constantly alive to what Chris Dyer, in a slightly different context, has termed the 'hidden trade of the middle ages'.[104]

Finally, it is also evident that these patterns cannot have applied universally amongst the peasantry and that they will have differed temporally as well as spatially. Small-scale lending and borrowing was, undoubtedly, carried out in all communities but larger-scale, investment credit may not have been so ubiquitous. The demands of a credit market and the availability of external credit will have been subject to a wide range of variables including, proximity of significant urban centres and polarisation of landholding, the latter itself a consequence of a further tranche of determinants including seigneurial policy, village custom and practices of inheritance. Investment credit may well have played a more significant role in the lives of villagers where landholding was partially polarised, a large proportion of villagers lived on small-holdings insufficient to provide them with their daily food intake, and there was limited access to external supplies of credit. The extent to which this access was also capable of being controlled will have been especially significant.

Notes

1 See, for example, M. M. Postan, *The medieval economy and society* (Harmondsworth, 1972), p. 137; R.H. Hilton, 'Introduction', in *The transition from feudalism to capitalism* (London, 1978), p. 18.

2 R. H. Hilton, 'Small town society in England before the Black Death', *Past and Present*, 109 (1984); C. Dyer, 'The consumer and the market in the later middle ages', *Economic History Review*, 2nd ser., 43 (1990), reprinted in *idem*, *Everyday life in medieval England* (London, 1994) (from which subsequent references are taken); C. Dyer, 'The hidden trade of the middle ages: evidence from the west midlands', *Journal of Historical Geography*, 18 (1992), repr. in *idem*, *Everyday life in medieval England* (from which subsequent references are taken); R. M. Smith, 'A periodic market and its impact upon a manorial community: Botesdale, Suffolk, and the manor of Redgrave, 1280–1300', in Z. Razi and R. M. Smith, eds, *Medieval society and the manor court* (Oxford, 1996).

3 Dyer, 'Hidden trade of the middle ages'; *idem*, 'Consumer and the market'.

4 Kowaleski, *Medieval Exeter*.

5 Masschaele, *Peasants, merchants and markets*.

6 Maddicott, 'English peasantry and the demands of the crown'. See also, for earlier work, *A Lincolnshire Assize Roll*, ed. Thomson.

7 For instance, K. Biddick, 'Medieval English peasants and market involvement', *Journal of Economic History*, xlv (1985); *idem*, 'Missing links: taxable wealth, markets and stratification among medieval English peasants', *Journal of Interdisciplinary History*, xviii (1987).

8 Raftis, *Peasant economic development*; Masschaele, *Peasants, merchants and markets*.

9 Kowaleski, *Medieval Exeter*, pp. .280ff.

10 see above, 57–9; also, Mundill, *England's Jewish solution*, c. 7; see also the comments re. the necessary security of debtors, *ibid.*, pp. 217–8; *idem*, 'Lumbard and son'; *idem*, 'Rabbi Elias'.

11 McIntosh, *Autonomy and community*, pp. 167–8; *idem*, 'Money lending', 563–4.

12 Though McIntosh does make some brief observations in this respect, 'Money lending', 564. Hyams, 'Origins of a peasant land market', 20, raises similar questions.

13 Postan, 'Credit in medieval trade'.

14 For example, the recent work of Kermode, *Medieval merchants*; Nightingale, *Mercantile community*; Keene, 'Changes in London's economic hinterland'. See also the chapters by McNall and Nightingale in this volume.

15 Postan, 'Credit in medieval trade', p. 3.

16 Kowaleski, *Medieval Exeter*; Dyer, 'Consumer and the market'; D. Farmer, 'Marketing the produce of the medieval countryside, 1200–1500', in E. Miller, ed., *The agrarian history of England and Wales. Volume iii. 1348–1500* (Cambridge, 1991), p. 424.

17 *Two Bedfordshire Subsidy Lists 1309 and 1332* (Suffolk Green Books, xviii, 1925) [hereafter *Subsidy*]; *Early taxation returns. Taxation of personal property in 1332 and later* (Buckinghamshire Record Society, 14, 1966).

18 Manorial court rolls: Blunham, B.R.O. L26/50; Cranfield, P.R.O. SC 2/179/26, 32; Eggington, 'Eggington court rolls (1297–1572)', in *Hundreds, manors, parishes and the church. A selection of early documents for Bedfordshire*, ed. J. S. Thompson (Bedfordshire Historical Record Society, 69, 1990), pp. 200–1. Rentals and lists of tenants: Stanbridge, P.R.O. SC 2/11/586; Wilden, P.R.O. SC 12/40/1.

19 *Rolls from the Office of the Sheriff of Bedfordshire and Buckinghamshire, 1332–1334*, ed. G. H. Fowler (Bedfordshire Historical Record Society, 4to, 1929) [hereafter *Rolls*]. Fowler's transcript of the sheriff's returns has not been published in full but his full transcript and analysis survive, Bedfordshire

Record Office [hereafter B.R.O.] X364/36/1. The 1327 roll, Public Record Office SC 2/153/7, Bedfordshire County Court, 1 Edward III, was also published by Fowler, *Rolls*, p. 77. See also, H. C. Jenskinson and M. H. Mills, 'Rolls from a sheriff's office of the fourteenth century', *English Historical Review*, 43 (1928).

20 Compare figues in Palmer, *County courts of medieval England*, p. 227.

21 Richard Wariner of Sharnbrook, a plaintiff in two pleas of debt; *Rolls*, p. 71, *Subsidy*, p. 132; John Budnoe [de Buddenhoe] of Bedford, *Rolls*, p. 73, *Subsidy*, p. 187.

22 Thomas Rous of Wootton Bourne, *Rolls*, p. 69, *Subsidy*, p. 182; Ralf Mareschall of Ampthill, *Rolls*, p. 72; *Subsidy*, p. 187; William Blundell of Caldecote, *Rolls*, p. 70, *Subsidy*, pp. 139, 157.

23 Richard Bazeley of Baldock; Robert Felmersham of Hitchin, *Rolls*, pp. 69–70, 71.

24 William Baxtere of Ampthill, *Rolls*, p. 72; John le Baxtere, *Subsidy*, p. 176. Ralph son Ralph son of Richard of Silsoe, *Rolls*, p. 72; Ralph son of Richard, *Subsidy*, p. 159.

25 William May of Bedford, *Rolls*, p. 69, *Subsidy*, numerous references; Robert Felmsersham, vicar of Hitchin, *Rolls*, pp. 69–70, *Subsidy*, p. 166; Henry Taillour of Ampthill, *Rolls*, p. 70, *Subsidy*, numerous references.

26 Names not found in the subsidy list: William Digne, *Rolls*, p. 69; Richard Exmouth, *Rolls*, p. 70; Richard Bazeley of Baldock, *Rolls*, pp. 70, 71; Roger de Baynhale, *Rolls*, p. 72; Nicholas de Studham, *Rolls*, p. 73; Ambrose de Chawston, *Rolls*, pp. 73, 74; Walter Haudlo, *Rolls*, p. 73; Ralph de Marston, *Rolls*, p. 74; Roger Beauchamp, *Rolls*, p. 73; Walter Boneys, *Rolls*, p. 75; Adam de Polhanger, *Rolls*, p. 75; Richard Latoun, *Rolls*, p. 75; John prior of Dunstable, *Rolls*, p. 75; Laurence Hery, *Rolls*, p. 75. Individuals with same full name in both county roll and subsidy list: Simon Cranfield, *Rolls*, p. 72, *Subsidy*, pp. 121, 135; John Osemond, *Rolls*, p. 73, *Subsidy*, p. 173; Thomas de Stodleye, *Rolls*, p. 74, *Subsidy*, p. 174. In addition, the prior of Chicksand appears as a principal payor of the lay subsidy in a number of vills, Simon Gousehulle, prior of Chicksand, *Rolls*, p. 70, *Subsidy*, pp. 134, 156, 184.

27 Shared surname: Philip de Aylesbury, *Rolls*, p. 73, *Subsidy*, p. 163.

28 John Potton of Cople, *Rolls*, p. 69, *Subsidy*, p. 110, 134; Robert Gobioun of Wootton Bourne, *Rolls*, p. 69, *Subsidy*, p. 174; Michael Warde of Bolnho, *Rolls*, p. 70, *Subsidy*, p. 123; William Bonseriaunt of Shefford, *Rolls*, p. 70, *Subsidy*, p. 156; Peter Dallyng of Potton, *Rolls*, p. 71, *Subsidy*, p. 110; John Baldok of Stanbridge, *Rolls*, p. 73, *Subsidy*, p. 146; John Bishop of Cranfield, *Rolls*, p. 73, *Subsidy*, pp. 132, 173; Richard Kempson of Wilden, *Rolls*, p. 74, *Subsidy*, pp. 118, 119; Nicholas Dyme of Shefford, *Rolls*, p. 75, *Subsidy*, p. 156.

29 Roger Pertsoyl of Hargrave (Riseley), *Rolls*, p. 70, *Subsidy*, p. 180; John Maheu of Hargrave (Kempston/Shelton), *Rolls*, p. 70, *Subsidy*, p. 177, 182; Geoffrey Joye of Ickwell (Northill), *Rolls*, p. 70, *Subsidy*, p. 138; John Sharman of Stanford (Arlesey), *Rolls*, p. 75, *Subsidy*, pp. 154, 156.

30 unfound: William son of Roger of Eggington; Juliana widow of Roger of Millo; John Smyth of Sharnbrook; Richard son of Walter Skernyng of Sharnbrook and his wife Matilda; John Jessop of Stopsley, *Rolls*, pp. 69, 70, 71, 72. Individuals not appearing in the subsidy list but whose surnames do appear in both county roll and subsidy list: Eustache son of Nigel of Marston [Morteyne], *Rolls*, p. 69, *Subsidy*, pp. 146, 173; Roger Babbe of Hargrave, *Rolls*, p. 70, *Subsidy*, p. 183; Alice Bolle, *Rolls*, p. 72, *Subsidy*, pp. 168, 183; John Flexhewer, *Rolls*, p. 73, *Subsidy*, p. 132.

31 Thomas Hayroun, *Rolls*, p. 70, *Subsidy*, p. 180; John Daye, *Rolls*, p. 75, *Subsidy*, p. 140.

32 Individuals not found in the subsidy list: Ralph Bronewyne; Henry Blundel; Reginald Blundel, *Rolls*, pp. 72, 73. Individuals with same full name in both county roll and subsidy list: John Toller, *Rolls*, p. 72, *Subsidy*, pp. 186, 187; David Flitwick, *Rolls*, p. 72, *Subsidy*, p. 169; Walter de Huntyngfeld, *Rolls*, p. 73, *Subsidy*, p. 136; Roger Asplon, *Rolls*, p. 73, *Subsidy*, p. 174; Guy Test, *Rolls*, p. 74, *Subsidy*, p. 114; Thomas Fotyng, *Rolls*, p. 75, *Subsidy*, p. 156; Thomas le Tanner, *Rolls*, p. 75, *Subsidy*, p. 156; Edmund Wedon, *Rolls*, p. 75, *Subsidy*, p.169; Simon le Revessone, *Rolls*, p. 75, *Subsidy*, p. 177; John Wymund, *Rolls*, p. 75, *Subsidy*, p. 124, 134, 187. Shared surname only: Thomas Baroun, *Rolls*, p. 72, *Subsidy*, p. 109.

33 For a partial list of Bedfordshire markets, see *Victoria County History, Bedfordshire*, ii, p. 88.

34 Two of these four instances relate to debts owed to Richard Wariner of Sharnbrook; both of his debtors, neither identifiable in the lay subsidy lists, were described, in the county roll, as coming from Sharnbrook, *Rolls*, p. 71.

35 *Rolls*, pp. 70–1.

36 Thomas de Stodleye, *Rolls*, p. 74, *Subsidy*, p. 174; Walter de Huntyngfeld, *Rolls*, p. 73, *Subsidy*, p. 136. A William Blundel, described as coming from Caldecote in the county roll (*Roll*, p. 70 – presumably Upper Caldecote in eastern Bedfordshire), may have been wealthier still, although, equally, he could have been one of the poorest creditors: William Blundel paid 10s. 2d. at nearby Clifton, but was he also the William Blundel who paid 12d. at Northill, a village as near to Upper Caldecote (*Subsidy*, pp. 139, 157)? For the purposes of this examination, neither payment was employed in the calculation of the average.

37 *Rolls*, p. 73, *Subsidy*, p. 173.

38 Geoffrey Joye of Ickwell, *Rolls*, p. 70, *Subsidy*, p. 138; William Bonseriaunt of Shefford, *Rolls*, p. 70, *Subsidy*, p. 156;.

39 There are very few cases (4) where information on 'wealth' of both the creditor and the debtor survives. There is little consistency in the information afforded by them; *Rous* (9s. 4d.) v. *Gobyoun* (3s. 2½d.); *Mareschall* (5s.) v. *Flitwick* (5s. ½d.); *Osemond* (16d.) v. *Asplon* (6s. 7¼d.); *Stodleye* (9s. 6½d.) v. *Test* (16s. 3d.). Figures in brackets are 1332 lay subsidy payments. In the case of *Stodleye v. Test* and *Mareschall v. Flitwick*, both plaintiff and defendant were clearly substantial individuals. See also the comments of Briggs, below, p. 139.

40 Simon Cranfield, *Rolls*, p. 72, *Subsidy*, pp. 121, 135. See also, John Potton of Cople, *Rolls*, p. 69, *Subsidy*, p. 110, 134; John Maheu of Hargrave (Kempston/Shelton), *Rolls*, p. 70, *Subsidy*, p. 177, 182; John Toller, *Rolls*, p. 72, *Subsidy*, pp. 186, 187; John Sharman of Stanford (Arlesey), *Rolls*, p. 75, *Subsidy*, pp. 154, 156; John Wymund, *Rolls*, p. 75, *Subsidy*, p. 124, 134, 187; also, Simon Gousehulle, prior of Chicksand, *Rolls*, p. 70, *Subsidy*, pp. 134, 156, 184. See also J. F. Willard, *Parliamentary taxes on personal property, 1290 to 1334* (Cambs., Mass., 1934), p. 154, for brief discussion of taxation of individuals in more than one vill.

41 9s. and 39s. 11d. – both of which were owed by John the son of Walter le Smyth of Sharnbrook to Richard, the money changing hands in his house at Sharnbook, *Rolls*, p. 67.

42 *Rolls*, pp. 72, 73; cf. J. S. Beckerman, 'The forty-shilling jurisdictional limit in medieval English personal actions', in D. Jenkins, ed., *Legal History Studies* (Cardiff, 1975), p. 111.

43 *Rolls*, p. 73. John Baldok may be the John Baldon who is recorded in the Stanbridge rental for 5 Edward III (1331/2) holding a cottage and croft plus 1 acre for 4d quarter, P.R.O. SC 11/586. He may also, of course, have been a freeholder who held land elsewhere.

44 *Rolls*, p. 69.

45 P.R.O. SC 2/179/26, 1333?, *de Johanne Bysshop dum utitur officio Tannator' ii capones.*

46 *Rolls*, pp. 69–75.

47 *Subsidy*, p. 180.

48 *Subsidy*, p. 123

49 Roger Asplon of Marston, who was attached by local mainpernors, paid a larger sum in the 1332 lay subsidy (6s. 7¼d.), *Rolls*, p. 73, *Subsidy*, p. 174; John de Potton, appears also to have been mainperned by local men, he paid at least 12s. 10¾d. to the 1332 subsidy, *Rolls*, p. 69, *Subsidy*, p. 134. Whilst David Flitwick, a member of the Bedfordshire gentry and a substantial tax-payer in 1332, was also mainperned, the names of his mainpernors are not identifiable in the subsidy lists, *Rolls*, p. 72–3, *Subsidy*, p. 169.

50 Geoffrey Joye, *Rolls*, p. 70, *Subsidy*, p. 138, who looks to have paid only 16d in 1332 (Northgivel) was attached by two local men, Henry le Chapman and John Draggeberd, who also appear in the 1332 subsidy and paid similarly small sums (Draggeberd – 18d; Chapman – 2s 1d; William Bonseriant, *Rolls*, p. 70, *Subsidy*, p. 156 – one of the mainpernors and pledge, John Euer, was a local man, from Shefford (pays 12½d in 1332) while the two other mainpernors, John de Bernestede and Roger Baly, do not appear in the subsidy list and may have been poorer still; Peter Dallyng, *Rolls*, p. 71, *Subsidy*, p. 110 – mainpernors at Potton are John Robyn (18¾d) and John Colyn (19¾d) while Henry Richeman from nearby Saundeye, who paid 12d in 1332, *Subsidy*, p. 108, stood as pledge; John Smyth, *Rolls*, p. 67 – mainpernors at Sharnbrook (*Subsidy*, pp. 131–2) are Simon Hardy (no entry), Henry Gery (no entry), John Chaundeler (18d), John Mainpeny (12d); Roger Asplon, *Rolls*, p. 73, *Subsidy*, p. 174 – mainpernors at Marston (*Subsidy*, pp. 173–4) are Matthew Aleyn (3s 5¼d) and William Page (16¾d) and distrained by two horses; the mainpernors were amerced – new mainpernors were Simon Page (13¾d), Guy Love (no entry), William Page (16¾d); Simon le Revessone, *Rolls*, p. 75, *Subsidy*, p. 177,

attached by Gilbert Archer (3s 6½d) and William Archer (no entry); John Wymund at Blunham, *Rolls*, p. 75, *Subsidy*, p. 134 – attached by William Lightfoot (Coupol, 16¼d), *Subsidy*, p.134, and John Bonum (no entry but Bonums also listed at neighbouring Coupol).

51 For example, Flitwick, Gobyoun, Rous, for which see K. S. Naughton, *The gentry of Bedfordshire in the thirteenth and fourteenth centuries* (Department of English Local History Occasional Papers, Leicester, 3rd ser., 2, 1976), pp. 71–5; also M. Bassett, *Knights of the shire for Bedfordshire during the middle ages* (Bedfordshire Historical Record Society, xxix, 1947), pp. 42, 44, 85–6.

52 Bassett, *Knights of the shire for Bedfordshire*, p. 90.

53 *Rolls*, p. 74, *Subsidy*, p. 114. A Guy Test also appears in the Close Rolls for 1331 as creditor in 100d owed to him by one Hugh de Brey of Thamesford, the amount to be levied on lands and chattels in Bedfordshire. Test is here described as merchant and citizen of London, CCR, 1330–1333, p. 411.

54 Richard Exmouth, *Rolls*, pp. 70, 79; Philip de Aylesbury, *Rolls*, pp. 3, 73; also P.R.O., *Lists and Indexes*, ix, p. 1.

55 *Rolls*, pp. 69, 74.

56 No plaintiff-creditors, with the sole exception of John Osemond, shepherd, who paid 16d. in 1332, *Rolls*, p. 73, *Subsidy*, p. 173, have been identified as probable villagers.

57 Clark, 'Debt litigation'; Schofield, 'Dearth, debt and the local land market'; also, Briggs, this volume.

58 Spufford, *Money and its uses*, p. 336, terms this "black credit" in his tripartite definition of medieval credit as black, white and gold.

59 For discussions of violence in the village comunity, see, for example, Dewindt, *Land and people in Holywell-cum-Needingworth*, pp. 272–3; Britton, *Community of the vill*, pp. 38–43; Razi, 'Family, land and the village community', pp. 370–1, 386, 390–1.

60 Clark, 'Debt litigation', p. 263; McIntosh, *Autonomy and Community*, p. 194; see also, Britnell, *Colchester*, pp. 107–8.

61 Clark, 'Debt litigation', *passim*; see also McIntosh, *Autonomy and Community*, p. 194, 'The number and types of suits were shaped by the commercialised local economy.'

62 Clark, 'Debt litigation', p. 254, Tables 8.5 and 8.6.

63 Hilton, *English peasantry*, p. 47; *The court rolls of Ramsey, Hepmansgrove and Bury, 1268–1600*, ed. E.B. DeWindt (Toronto, 1990), p. 51.

64 mostly, barley; note also M. Bailey, *A marginal economy? East Anglian Breckland in the later middle ages* (Cambridge, 1989), p. 168; cf. Hilton, *English peasantry*, p. 46, where he calculates that 'out of over a hundred unexplained pleas of debt in our court rolls [from the West Midlands] only 7 or 8 *per cent* concern loans in kind, that is, in grain'. The situation in East Anglia may have been rather different.

65 Details are set out in Schofield, 'L'endettement et le crédit', p. 87.

66 Clark, 'Debt litigation', p. 265; for an early modern example, see C. Muldrew, 'Credit and the courts: debt litigation in a seventeenth-century urban community', *Economic History Review*, xlvi (1993), pp. 23–38.

67 Postan, 'Medieval agrarian society in its prime: England', pp. 627–8; also, Spufford, *Money and its uses*, p. 337. Undoubtedly, this distinction is dependent upon a rigid definition of credit. Poorer villagers could also act as 'creditors' in the sense that they were 'owed' for services rendered or goods loaned to other, perhaps wealthier villagers. The same applied to outright sales for which the purchase price remained unpaid. Characterising these exchanges as 'creditor-debtor' relationships does, however, appear to omit considerations of inequalities of power.

68 Razi, *Life, marriage and death*, pp. 76, 78; *idem*, 'Family, land and the village community', pp. 367–8.

69 Schofield, 'Dearth, debt and the local land market', 13–14; for evidence of poor creditor litigants, cf. Muldrew, 'Credit and the courts'.

70 Clark, 'Debt litigation', p. 267.

71 R. Firth, 'Capital, saving and credit in peasant societies: a viewpoint from economic anthropology' in R. Firth and B. S. Yamey, eds, *Capital, saving and credit in peasant societies. Studies from Asia, Oceania, the Caribbean and Middle America* (London, 1964), pp. 29–33. It is, of course, possible that peasants borrowed basic goods from their neighbours in order to buy less available services or goods further afield in local markets and towns, Dyer, 'The consumer and the market', p. 276; Kowaleski, *Medieval Exeter*, pp. 203–4, 286–8.

72 Schofield, 'Dearth, debt and the local land market'.

73 B.R.O. L26/50, court of 24 Mar. 1318.
74 B.R.O. L26/50, 23 Jun. 1321.
75 B.R.O. L26/50, court of 7 Nov. 1321.
76 Five villagers including Robert were assessed at 3s., one was assessed at 3s. 6d, *Subsidy*, pp. 134, 138.
77 Razi, *Life, marriage and death*, pp. 77, 83 n.; cf. DeWindt, *Land and people in Holywell-cum-Needingworth*, pp. 262–3.
78 Since, however, the debt appears to have been secured by bond, they may have had sight of this. Although manorial courts were not considered appropriate fora for the employment of specialties as proof, it is clear that this did occur, and not infrequently, Beckerman, 'Procedural innovation and institutional change', 208–9; Schofield, 'L'endettement et le crédit', p. 81.
79 *Court rolls of Walsham-le-Willows*, ed. Lock, p. 92; for William Wodebite's villein status, see *ibid.*, p. 96 and the early fourteenth-century list of unfree tenants recorded by E. Powell amongst his earlier material, *A Suffolk hundred in the year 1283* (Cambridge, 1910), p. 91.
80 *Suffolk in 1327 being a subsidy return* (Suffolk Green Books, ix, 1906), p. 218.
81 *The Ipswich recognizance rolls, 1294–1327. A calendar*, ed. G. H. Martin (Suffolk Record Society, 1973), pp. 99–100; 'Ipswich borough records. No. 3 (Part 2, the borough). Reign of Edward III, 1327–1377', *East Anglian Daily Times*, Feb. 17th, 1927, 2.
82 *Court roll of the manor of Downham, 1310–1327*, ed. M. C. Coleman (Cambridgeshire Records Society, ii, 1996).
83 Isabella Queu, *Downham, 1310–1327*, ed. Coleman, p. 45; Amicia widow of Adam the son of Philip, *Downham, 1310–1327*, ed. Coleman, p. 133.
84 L. R. Poos, Z. Razi, R. M. Smith, 'The population history of medieval English villages: a debate on the use of manor court records', in Z. Razi and R. M. Smith, eds, *Medieval society and the manor court* (Oxford, 1996), pp. 305–7.
85 *Downham, 1310–1327*, ed. Coleman, pp. 42, 49.
86 *Downham, 1310–1327*, ed. Coleman, pp. 19, 23.
87 *Downham, 1310–1327*, ed. Coleman, pp. 65–7.
88 above, p. 117.
89 *Downham, 1310–1327*, ed. Coleman. p. 31.
90 Schofield, 'Dearth, debt and the local land market', 11–14; Schofield, 'Peasants and the manor court', 18–20.
91 *Suffolk hundred in 1283*, ed. Powell, Table 12.
92 Biddick, 'Missing links', p. 297.
93 P. R. Hyams, *Kings, lords and peasants. The common law of villeinage in the twelfth and thirteenth centuries* (Oxford, 1980), c. 6; but see also the interesting case where a creditor attempted to employ the servile status of gaged land to his advantage, *ibid.*, p. 53; cf., also, P. Vinogradoff, *Villainage in England* (Oxford, 1892), pp. 80–1.
94 As noted by Biddick, 'Missing links', p. 297, 'During the thirteenth century, when peasants both traded part-time and produced, those who traded in regional markets could better control the distribution of their products through greater opportunities for credit and better information on prices. With such advantages they could easily broker between village and regional markets, thus gaining more social and economic power within their own communities'.
95 Hyams, 'Origins of a peasant land market'.
96 above, p. 117.
97 *Court rolls of Walsham-le-Willows*, ed. Lock , p. 283.
98 *Court rolls of Walsham-le-Willows*, ed. Lock, p. 87.
99 *Court rolls of Walsham-le-Willows*, ed. Lock , p. 49.
100 *Court rolls of Walsham-le-Willows*, ed. Lock , p. 87.
101 *Court rolls of Walsham-le-Willows*, ed. Lock, pp. 96–7. The Walsham examples also raises the important issue that local courts records are partial records, capable of being manipulated by the most persuasive and aggressive villagers. But for the change of lordship in 1325, a good deal of William de Wodebite's land market activity in the previous decade would have gone unnoticed. Seigneurial expectations regarding the licencing of land transfers and, importantly, leases (which may have been gages for debts) may have hidden debtor-creditor relations.

102 Litigation – *Court rolls of Walsham-le-Willows*, ed. Lock, pp. 63, 91, 96; examples of pledging, *ibid*. pp. 64, 88, 93; non-performance of labour services/paying individuals to perform his services for him, *ibid*., pp. 74, 87, 98; manorial office – elected reeve, also affeerer, *ibid*., p. 88; collector, *ibid*., p. 91. Disappointingly, the courts between 1319 and that of Jan. 1324 are missing so we cannot know the immediate impact of John Bande's successful recovery upon William or upon those with whom he dealt in the village.

103 Schofield, 'Dearth, debt and the local land market', 16.

104 Dyer, 'Hidden trade of the middle ages'.

Chapter 6

Creditors and debtors and their relationships at Oakington, Cottenham and Dry Drayton (Cambridgeshire), 1291–1350[1]

Chris Briggs

Existing research dealing directly with the subject of credit and its uses among the English peasantry between about 1200 and 1500 is far from extensive.[2] Like other aspects of the study of rural credit, the task of identifying those most heavily involved as lenders and borrowers in the village has suffered from a shortage of detailed local studies. This essay is concerned with the relationship between socio-economic status and involvement in credit networks. It examines some of the individuals who entered into credit relationships in three Cambridgeshire villages in the period before the Black Death, and asks how often and in what capacity they became involved in the market for credit. Consideration will also be given to the closely related issue of why these people became creditors and debtors.

The discussion that follows is based on 376 plaints or 'civil actions' of debt recorded in the manorial court rolls of Oakington in Cambridgeshire, a manor belonging to Crowland Abbey. The abbey held three manors very close to one another in Cambridgeshire, in the parishes of Oakington, Cottenham and Dry Drayton. These parishes lie to the north and west of Cambridge at distances of between four and six miles from the town. They are located in the upland part of the county, between the southernmost extent of the medieval fenland and the chalk and clay regions to the south.[3] Only one court was held for the abbot's tenants from all three places, rather than three separate courts, presumably because the manors were so close together.[4] A particular advantage of these court rolls is that they form a relatively continuous series, and for the periods when coverage is good there are few signs that court sessions were held of which the records are now lost. The Oakington rolls are almost entirely unbroken from 1291 to about 1390. Figure 6.1 shows the number of new debt plaints begun in the court each year between 1291 and 1350. The most noticeable feature, to be considered further below, is the striking increase from the late 1330s in the number of new plaints per annum.[5]

The essay consists of two main sections. Firstly, all the creditor-debtor ties recorded for the period 1291–1350 are considered in aggregate in an attempt to assess the overall structure of debt relationships. The second section examines some of the most prolific participants in debt litigation in greater depth. Although it has been possible to study only a very small group of litigants, it is hoped that a clearer perspective on these individuals and their characteristics will be gained through a discussion of the court

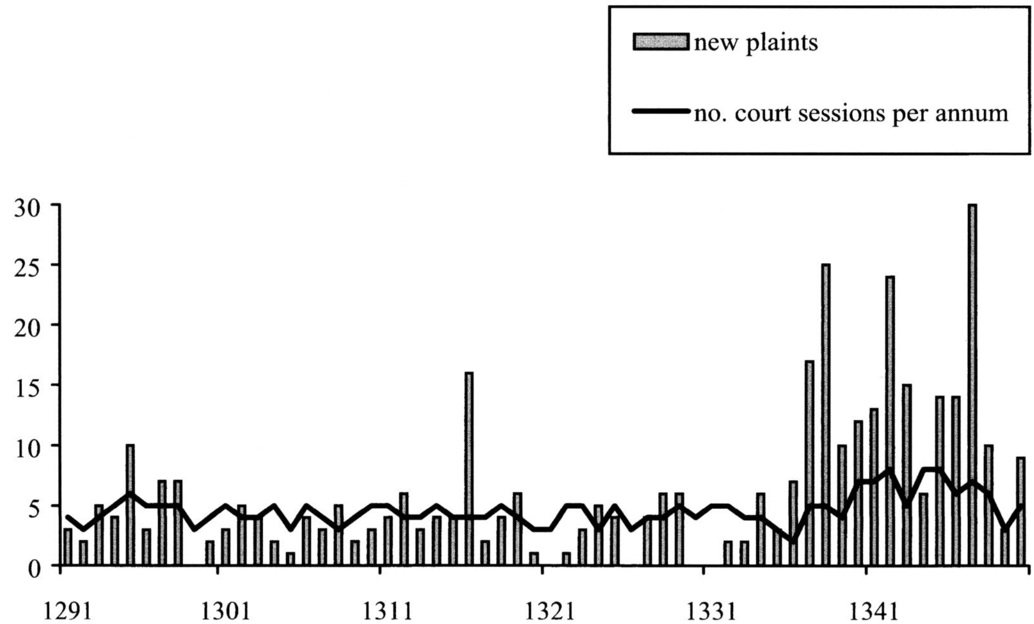

Source: Cambridge University Library, Queens' College Muniments, Boxes 3 and 4

Figure 6.1 Oakington: new plaints of debt/detinue per annum, 1291–1350

roll material relating to them.[6] Some of the conclusions suggested by the first part of the analysis will also be examined more closely in the light of this more detailed assessment.

First, however, some remarks are required concerning the limitations of the sources for the purposes in hand. There are various reasons why it would be unrealistic to suppose that by using these court rolls alone evidence can be found about all the creditors and debtors active in Oakington, Cottenham and Drayton before the Black Death. An unknown number of those involved in credit networks in these villages inevitably remain invisible. A brief consideration of the reasons for this is worthwhile, as it gives us some impression at least of the size and composition of that group about which the sources used here provide no information. In the first place, an unknown but possibly substantial proportion of debts involving residents of these villages were the subject of litigation in courts other than that of the abbot of Crowland at Oakington. It would be excessively optimistic even to suppose that the Oakington rolls are necessarily representative of debt relations involving the abbot's own tenants, as many of them undoubtedly engaged in credit transactions with residents of other manors and villages, thereby increasing the range of different courts that might be used when enforcing repayment. There were certainly various competing courts in these villages and in the surrounding area as well as further afield, all of which were potentially available to peasants who wished to sue for debt.[7] All three vills under scrutiny contained land held by more than one lord, and although no contemporary rolls relating to the courts of manors other than that of Crowland Abbey are known to be extant, there is little reason to believe that sessions of such courts were not in fact held. In Cottenham, five other lords held manors in the vill, all of whom presumably held courts for their tenants in this period.[8] At Drayton, three other manors can be identified, two of which were monastic properties.[9] In Oakington itself, the situation was more complex. The Hundred Rolls of 1279–80 and other sources reveal that landholding there, with the exception of the Crowland manor, was highly fragmented, and much of the freehold land was held in very small units from a complex combination of chief and mesne lords.[10] Although a few relatively well-defined manorial units can be identified in Oakington at this period, it is difficult to say which if any of these smaller lordships would have held courts for their tenants. One effect of the Oakington tenurial structure must have been that for a substantial proportion of the population there was no single obvious court of first resort where debt litigation was concerned.

As well as the various seigneurial courts in these and neighbouring villages, there were other jurisdictions in which small debt cases involving residents of Oakington, Cottenham and Drayton were heard from time to time. That the abbot's tenants were familiar with the legal world of various royal and ecclesiastical courts is demonstrated by references in the court rolls to persons amerced for breaching seigneurial prohibitions against pleading in 'alien courts'. The right of a lord to impose an amercement where a tenant suffered a financial penalty in a jurisdiction other than that of his lord was based on the theory that a villein had no chattels of his own. The lord therefore required compensation for the loss of what was in principle seigneurial property.[11] The entries in the Oakington rolls arising from this doctrine do not all concern debt litigation or other forms of civil action; those that do, however, provide evidence that some at least of the creditors and debtors in these villages settled their disputes in jurisdictions other than the Oakington manor court.[12] Although legal status clearly formed a potential obstacle to extra-manorial litigation by villagers, the amercements resulting from transgressions of seigneurial prerogative are themselves evidence that the rules were broken, and it is clear that in certain circumstances a lawsuit might enjoy immunity from the adverse seigneurial attention associated with the disabilities of villeinage even if one of the parties was of unfree status.[13] The court roll references to appearances in 'alien courts' therefore probably understate considerably the frequency with which villagers litigated beyond the manor, although the practical difficulties of time and cost facing such litigation, if difficult to assess, cannot be ignored. At the same time, the extent to which local debt disputes ended up in courts other than that of the abbot of Crowland should not be exaggerated. The Oakington court was itself an important focus of the legal 'microgeography' of the locality, and it is likely to have attracted litigation begun by plaintiffs from other lordships just as frequently as its own suitors chose to use 'alien courts' to obtain legal remedies.

A second set of reasons for the undoubtedly incomplete picture of creditors and debtors provided by the court rolls concerns the fact that many of the credit transactions in which they were involved did not result in legal actions in this or any other court. Obviously, most credit relationships concluded successfully and did not require enforcement. In addition, not all those who extended or received credit were equally likely to appear in manor court litigation. It is well attested that lower status groups such as subtenants, cottagers and landless individuals appeared only infrequently in the manor court in connection with all aspects of its business.[14] On the whole, it seems safe to assume that such people were less likely than substantial manorial tenants to initiate personal plaints because they did not possess the social standing or the time and money required to be successful. Similar circumstances appear also to have affected women who, particularly where married, were less likely to appear than men; less than one fifth of all Oakington debt plaints in this period involved female parties. This does not necessarily mean that poorer peasants and women were not involved in lending, however; indeed, many smaller loans may have been advanced on the understanding that they would not be enforced by formal means. It should be remembered, then, that even when a full body of manorial court records is used it is possible to obtain only a restricted impression of the potential range of participants in local credit networks. Certain types of credit relationship, and certain types of creditor and debtor, are more likely than others to remain hidden from view.

I

'Debt accumulation' and 'reciprocal indebtedness'

A good starting point for a discussion of the structure of debt relations in medieval rural society is to consider how far they were socially 'vertical' or 'horizontal'. Here the two fullest existing local studies of debt provide opportunities for comparison. Firstly, Clark's work on fifteenth-century Writtle (Essex) employs the useful concepts of 'debt accumulation' and 'reciprocal indebtedness'. Clark acknowledged that the repeated extension of credit in one direction only between a particular pair of individuals often led to ties of dependence ('debt accumulation'). However, she also placed considerable emphasis on those instances where an ongoing series of credit-based transactions between two individuals was evident, in which each party acted from time to time as both creditor and debtor ('reciprocal indebtedness'). At Writtle, Clark found that 12 per cent of cash loans and 17 per cent of deferred payments for goods and services entailed reciprocal indebtedness. In her account, relationships involving reciprocal indebtedness arose primarily as a means of satisfying the recurrent material needs of households through mutual exchange. Trust was an important feature of such relationships, which might continue indefinitely until one party did something to upset the arrangement. Even debt accumulation is not depicted by Clark as being in any sense necessarily exploitative, as the willingness of lenders to extend credit repeatedly on fairly easy terms to particular borrowers is interpreted as arising partly out of a desire to cultivate personal ties with clients with a view to future trading, rather than simply as a form of straightforward economic opportunism. Finally, although Clark suggests that lending by wealthier villagers to poorer tended to predominate in some aspects of Writtle's credit activity, such as the provision of labour and agricultural services, most other credit tended to be extended between persons who were relative equals in socio-economic terms.[15]

In contrast to this, more recent research on rural debt by Schofield has pointed to the existence of credit-debtor ties in the late thirteenth century of a markedly vertical character.[16] Concerned specifically with the effect of high grain prices in the 1290s on indebtedness and the land market at Hinderclay in Suffolk, this research suggests that the most regular buyers of land tended also to be the most frequent creditors, while the sellers mainly appeared as debtors. Debt obligations and land sales stimulated by need were linked, it is argued, in an economic climate that produced only 'winners and losers'.[17] The evidence used by Schofield gives little indication of the reciprocal indebtedness found by Clark, and there are few signs that credit relationships could be maintained for long on a basis that was mutually advantageous for both parties.

There is little doubt that these contrasting interpretations of the social character of debt relationships can partly be explained by substantial differences between late thirteenth-century Hinderclay and fifteenth-century Writtle in such matters as the distribution and size of landholdings, the importance of crafts and trades, and the intensity of market exchanges. In addition, considerable institutional differences between the manor courts of Hinderclay and Writtle may have given rise to very different patterns of litigation and levels of participation in debt cases by members of particular social groups in the two places. The manor of Writtle can be regarded as untypical due to its ancient demesne status, and this impression of the exceptional nature of the Writtle evidence is reinforced by its court rolls, which by comparison with many fifteenth-century examples are unusually full, particularly where the material relating to interpersonal litigation is concerned. It is probable that a court like that of Writtle would have had only the broadest institutional features in common with a tribunal such as that held for the tenants of the abbot of Bury St Edmunds at Hinderclay at the end of the thirteenth century.[18] An additional effect of such differences in the institutional character of the two manor courts and in the nature and detail of the documentary information they produced is to make effective comparison problematic for the historian. Furthermore, information on important issues such as the charging of interest is scarce or nonexistent, making it very difficult to assess properly the incentives and objectives weighed up by lenders in deciding to whom they would lend and on what conditions. However, it does seem clear that there were genuine contrasts between Hinderclay and Writtle in the extent to which credit relationships were socially vertical or horizontal.[19] One aim of this essay is to assess how far these accounts of local debt ties compare with findings from Oakington.

In this first section of the essay, the use of the terms 'horizontal' and 'vertical' in the context of rural debt relations does not necessarily imply any judgement about the relative social status or wealth of the parties, since the additional court roll evidence about every individual involved has not been exhaustively studied. Instead, it can only really be asked whether or not villagers engaged in reciprocal litigious relationships. The evidence suggests that they did not. Debt accumulation, rather than reciprocal indebtedness, was the more prominent feature of credit activity among the sample of litigants. Table 6.1 gives details of multiple cases recorded between the same plaintiff and defendant within a period of twenty years or less. (Some of the well-known pitfalls associated with identifying individuals in court rolls caused by such matters as unstable and shared surnames have, it is hoped, been avoided here as elsewhere in this essay, although without a full reconstruction of family linkages a few incorrect identifications are inevitable.)[20] The 52 cases that made up the relationships in Table 6.1 certainly represent a substantial proportion of the total (14 per cent), yet there is a possibility

Table 6.1 Debt accumulation relationships at Oakington, 1291–1350

Creditor	Debtor	First case	Last case	Interval[a]
Henry Carter	William France	1294 (Feb.)	1312 (Nov.)	214
Henry Kyle	Roger Court	1295 (Feb.)	1295 (Nov.)	8
Ralph Atpond	Roger Reeveson	1301 (Sept.)	1303 (Oct.)	24
Henry Wyot	John Osborn	1302 (Nov.)	1317 (Oct.)	178
Ralph Atpond	Thomas de Elsworth	1308 (Oct.)	1309 (Apr.)	5
John Wyot[b]	William France	1311 (Dec.)	1314 (Dec.)	35
John Alberd	Walter Harger	1317 (Mar.)	1328 (Apr.)	132
William Chapman	William Brown	1329 (Mar.)	1329 (Aug.)	4
William Chapman	Thomas Bass	1329 (Mar.)	1329 (Aug.)	4
Thomas Dobyn	John Burman	1336 (Oct.)	1340 (Nov.)	49
Henry Tailor	William son of Roger Smith	1336 (Oct.)	1343 (Jan.)	74
Geoffrey serviens of John Rous	Andrew Noteman	1337 (Mar.)	1342 (Oct.)	66
Alice Page	John Tankred	1337 (Dec.)	1338 (Jul.)	6
Will Danewell	John Kyle	1337 (Dec.)	1342 (Jun.)	53
John Noteman	John Sebely	1338 (Mar.)	1346 (Jan.)	93
William Kyle jr.	Geoffrey King	1339 (Oct.)	1341 (Dec.)	35
John Sebely	Geoffrey King	1341 (Jan.)	1342 (Oct.)	20
John Noteman	Geoffrey King	1341 (Jul.)	1346 (May)	57
John Ashman[b]	Andrew Noteman	1342 (Nov.)	1346 (May)	41
John Gerard	William Kyle sr.	1344 (Jan.)	1347 (Feb.)	36
Roger Bate	John de Cottenham	1345 (Nov.)	1348 (Oct.)	57
William Noteman	Andrew Noteman	1346 (Nov.)	1347 (Dec.)	12
John Gerard	Andrew Noteman	1347 (Nov.)	1347 (Dec.)	1
Thomas Kyle	John de Cottenham	1347 (Nov.)	1348 (Mar.)	3
Juliana Colin	Walter Makehate	1348 (Mar.)	1348 (Nov.)	8

Source: Cambridge University Library, Queens' College Muniments, Boxes 3 and 4
a between first and last case, in complete months
b relationships featuring three cases rather than two

that they may overstate the role of accumulated indebtedness, as some of these multiple cases probably represent repeated attempts at recovery of the same debt. It should also be noted that most relationships featuring debt accumulation gave rise to two court cases only.

Reciprocal indebtedness, however, appears to have been virtually non-existent at Oakington between 1291 and 1350. The only instance where it can be shown with any certainty that a plaintiff and a defendant later reversed their roles was Geoffrey King's 'false plea' against John Noteman in 1346, a response to Noteman's successful plaints against King of 1341 and 1346.[21] When considered purely as a collection of names and cases, therefore, the Oakington records show little evidence of the mutuality associated with indebtedness at Writtle in the fifteenth century. Instead, they suggest that vertical ties of credit were dominant, as in socially-polarized Hinderclay at the end of the thirteenth century.

The ratio of debt plaints to debt litigants

By examining the names of individual plaintiffs and defendants and counting their appearances in litigation, it is possible to seek answers to various questions about the nature of participation in the credit market that lay behind the surviving record of court cases. For instance, was lending and borrowing limited to a few individuals, or were these activities engaged in quite widely in society? Was it typical to enter the credit market only occasionally, or was there a substantial population of recurrent creditors and debtors? And did particular individuals tend only to act as either creditor or debtor, but never both? Although such questions can be considered only briefly here, some fairly clear developments in the patterns of participation in litigation can nonetheless be identified.

In Table 6.2 data are presented concerning the appearances of named individuals as plaintiffs and defendants in the 376 debt plaints. Each decadal sub-period is treated as a self-contained unit, so that an individual's appearances in more than one sub-period are counted separately. Although this approach may seem artificial, because the boundaries of each sub-period are arbitrarily chosen, a secondary check on litigious behaviour across the period 1291–1350 as a whole has shown that individuals who did not appear more than once within a particular sub-period rarely featured more than once across different sub-periods. In addition to this, considering each decadal division in isolation tends to reduce the number of incorrect associations of names appearing more than 10 years apart. In arriving at the totals, all joint plaintiffs and defendants are counted as separate individuals.

Table 6.2 reveals that a significant change occurred in the 1330s and 1340s in the relationship between the number of plaints that came into the court and the number of individuals involved in those plaints. It indicates that the substantial rise in the annual number of new plaints witnessed in the 1330s and 1340s was produced not simply by an increase in the number of different people bringing plaints, but also by a growing tendency for plaintiffs to bring more than one action. It is clear too that in the last two decades of the period recurrent appearances by particular defendants were also somewhat more common than they had been in earlier years. In terms of the proportion

Table 6.2 Numbers of litigants participating in Oakington debt cases 1291–1350, by decade

	Decade											
	1291-1300		1301-1310		1311 -1320		1321-1330		1331-1340		1341-1350	
No. court sessions	44		42		42		41		42		63	
No. cases	43		32		50		29		84		138	
Cases with joint parties[a]	6	(14.0)	4	(12.5)	10	(20.0)	3	(10.3)	10	(11.9)	14	(10.1)
Total individual plaintiffs	38		27		31		25		60		78	
Individuals acting as plaintiff more than once[b]	4	(10.5)	2	(7.4)	10	(32.3)	3	(12.0)	17	(28.3)	28	(35.9)
Total individual defendants	35		29		40		21		51		69	
Individuals acting as defendant more than once[c]	10	(28.6)	6	(20.7)	7	(17.5)	6	(28.6)	18	(35.3)	23	(33.3)
Total individual litigants	72		53		65		46		95		130	

Source: Cambridge University Library, Queens' College Muniments, Boxes 3 and 4
a in brackets: cases with joint parties as percentage of all cases in decade
b in brackets: individuals acting as plaintiff more than once as percentage of all individual plaintiffs
c in brackets: individuals acting as defendant more than once as percentage of all individual defendants

of plaintiffs acting in more than one case, the decade of the Great Famine and agrarian crisis (1311–20) shares characteristics with the 1330s and 1340s. By contrast with the later decades, however, multiple appearances by particular defendants were at their lowest in the second decade of the century. It might be argued that the changes that occurred in the 1330s and 1340s are perhaps an illusion created by a greater stability of surnames in those decades, but against this it should be noted that a fairly balanced mix of occupational/locational surnames and more well-known family surnames is evident across the entire period.

More likely is that the decades 1311–1320, 1331–40 and 1341–50 show a pattern of participation in debt litigation that is different from that of the other sub-periods because these decades witnessed what, for varying reasons, were some of the more difficult phases of the whole period 1291–1350 in terms of the economic circumstances of the peasantry.[22] One interpretation of the evidence in Table 6.2 is that it is indicative of the considerable impact of exceptionally adverse conditions on existing credit relationships, as important creditors litigated more often in order to collect debts that at other times would have been successfully discharged or left uncollected for longer, and, in the 1330s and 1340s at least, persistent debtors were brought to book more regularly than would have been the case in better years.[23] At the same time, the role of institutional change should not be ignored. A further plausible explanation for the changes that occurred in the last two decades of the period under consideration is that debt litigation became increasingly dominated by 'repeat' plaintiffs from a particular social group as a result of the control exercised by the members of that group over matters such as jury trial and other litigation procedures, though this is a possibility that has yet to be fully explored.[24]

In many respects, therefore, the findings so far suggest that vertical links predominated in debt relations at Oakington before the Black Death. Most significantly, debt accumulation was much more prevalent than reciprocal indebtedness. It is also tempting to see in the evidence of Table 6.2 the emergence in the 1330s and 1340s of two socially distinct groups, one containing a core of those richer peasants who

Table 6.3 Individuals appearing as both plaintiff and defendant in Oakington debt plaints, by decade

Decade	No. individuals appearing as both plaintiff and defendant (in brackets: as percentage of total individual litigants in that decade)	
1291–1300	1	(1.4)
1301–1310	3	(5.7)
1311–1320	6	(9.2)
1321–1330	0	(0.0)
1331–1340	16	(16.8)
1341–1350	17	(13.1)

Source: Cambridge University Library, Queens' College Muniments, Boxes 3 and 4

possessed the resources to lend to a number of different borrowers, the other containing a class of recurrent debtors. However, certain contradictions in such a picture of debt relations are quickly noticed. For example, one might assume that at Oakington, as at Hinderclay in the crisis years of the 1290s, a person tended to act as either plaintiff or defendant, and therefore as either creditor or debtor, but never as both. If this was the case, however, why were the highest proportions of litigants who acted in both capacities recorded in the decade 1311–1320 and in the last two decades of the period, just when relations might be expected to be at their most polarized (Table 6.3)? To address such questions a more qualitative examination of some of the creditors and debtors is required.

II

An investigation into the most prominent Oakington creditors and debtors reveals some features in common with the situation at Hinderclay in the late thirteenth century as described by Schofield. For instance, a small body of prominent villagers possessing considerable capital resources is identifiable in the Oakington rolls as a frequent source of local credit, although Oakington was different to Hinderclay in that the most important figure in this category from the Cambridgeshire villages was a member of the parochial clergy. At the same time, however, certain tendencies that were not pronounced at Hinderclay in the 1280s and 1290s are observable among Oakington suitors documented for the period 1291–1350. These differences are probably due partly to the fact that Schofield's study is essentially concerned with the effects of crisis years on debt and the land market, while this research on Oakington also takes note of debt relationships outside the worst periods of dearth, when, as Schofield implies, the 'context of indebtedness' could change.[25] Most importantly, one finds at Oakington that repeated appearance as a debtor was not invariably the result of short-term borrowing to make up a shortfall in the subsistence resources of an individual and his household, but could also be the product of a positive attempt to consolidate or improve one's economic position by seeking credit to buy land. This finding has important implications for our assessment of how 'vertical' credit relations in these Cambridgeshire villages really were, particularly when considered alongside some further evidence, to be presented below, which points in the direction of relative equality in socio-economic status among some of the most frequent creditors and debtors.

Table 6.4 presents information on some of the most frequent creditors and debtors, or, more accurately, the most frequent debt litigants. As might be imagined from the evidence already presented, the majority of those who came repeatedly to court in connection with debt cases did so in the 1330s and 1340s. However, in order to avoid exclusive concentration on that part of the period, the three most frequent creditors and debtors from each of the two broad phases of debt litigation activity – that is, before and after 1320 – have been subjected to closer study. Although these individuals acted predominantly as either plaintiff or defendant, both John Noteman and John Gerard, who were mainly plaintiffs, appeared on eight and four occasions respectively as defendant, while John Cousin, Geoffrey King, Andrew Noteman and William Kyle senior, who are recorded mainly as defendants, each brought between one and three actions as plaintiff.[26] Although little supplementary information can be obtained concerning William Porter, discussion will be offered below of some of the court roll entries that mention the eleven remaining debt litigants and their relationships. In some cases it is possible to discern the context of indebtedness by examining the full range of contacts between the parties to the debt. However, caution is required as there are basic problems facing any attempt to use court rolls to investigate experience at the level of the individual. The surviving information pertaining to the persons involved in particular debt cases is selective and incomplete, and using it to explain the possible motivations and causative factors at work in their relationships runs the risk of constructing an attractive and superficially coherent but potentially mistaken account on the basis of pieces of evidence that are susceptible to a variety of different interpretations depending on one's prior assumptions. In many respects, aggregative analysis of the entire body of Oakington debt litigants would have been preferable to the study of a few notable individuals as a way of proceeding. At present, however, that analysis is not yet complete. When it is, it will be possible to reassess the significance and typicality of the individual circumstances presented here, as well as the interpretation of them that is offered.

With one or two important exceptions, it is very difficult to distinguish between the creditors and debtors as far as their standing as tenants or possessors of property is

Table 6.4 Frequent Oakington creditors and debtors

Creditors		
	Years	No. plaints
Ralph Atpond	1291–1309	6
William Porter	1293–1314	5
John Wyot	1298–1320	11
John Noteman	1334–1346	11
Geoffrey serviens of John Rous	1337–1347	9
John Gerard	1342–1347	7
Debtors		
	Years	No. plaints
William Fraunce	1294–1314	12
John Cousin/Athallgate	1298–1314	7
John Osborn/Hayward	1302–1319	7
William Kyle sr.	1327–1347	17
Andrew Noteman	1337–1348	16
Geoffrey King	1338–1350	22

Source: Cambridge University Library, Queens' College Muniments, Boxes 3 and 4

concerned. Of course, relative equality of wealth and status among litigants is perhaps to be expected, as lenders would have been unlikely to extend credit to those without sufficient resources and reputation to guarantee at least the possibility of repayment.[27] All six individuals in the pre-1320 group appear to have lived in Dry Drayton. The evidence suggests Osborn, Fraunce, Atpond and Cousin were all customary tenants of the abbot. Unfortunately, it is difficult to be specific about the size of the landed holdings of each at any one time as the relevant details are supplied only inconsistently in the court rolls. Further evidence for the wealth of these litigants on the eve of the Great Famine is provided by the Dry Drayton lay subsidy assessment of 1315.[28] The tax charges on the 124 taxpayers who contributed to this subsidy ranged from 7*s* 2¾*d* to 6*d*, with a median tax charge of 18*d*. Two creditors and two debtors of the group of six pre-1320 litigants can be traced on the roll. The names of Ralph Atpond and John Cousin cannot be traced and may be among the 22 names that have been wholly or partially lost from this document. The tax charges on the remaining four men were: William Porter 22*d*, John Wyot 29½*d*, John Osborn 25*d* and William Fraunce 7*d*. In this subsidy, none of the litigants figured among the top 20 *per cent* of taxpayers. Although William Fraunce's tax charge was relatively low, this does not necessarily place him among the poorest in the village, as it is usually understood that such persons were exempted from contribution to lay subsidies, either through fixed minimum assessments or concessions made by the local taxers. On the other hand, the number of Drayton taxpayers appears suspiciously high, which raises the possibility that the Cambridgeshire assessors chose in 1315 to tax a relatively large proportion of the local population, including some individuals who might in other levies have been considered insufficiently wealthy to pay. This uncertainty about the proportion of the village's wealth hierachy captured in the lay subsidy assessment makes interpretation difficult. However, one can say rather imprecisely that as far as movable wealth is concerned, two of the most frequent creditors and one of the most frequent debtors of the years before 1320 occupied the middling ranks of village society in 1315, while a further debtor, William Fraunce, was relatively poor by comparison with the other taxpayers and possibly also in absolute terms within the village as a whole.[29]

The exceptional figure in the pre-1320 group was John Wyot, called chaplain of Drayton, and then vicar of Comberton by 1316. Wyot was responsible for lending some of the largest sums of cash reported owing in the Oakington court before the plague. The most notable of these debts was one of 44*s* 6*d* recognized by Robert Kynneson in 1311.[30] Wyot evidently farmed arable land, but he seems also to have had an unusually specialized sideline as a provider of credit. His movable wealth must have grown considerably in the years after 1315 as he appears in the Drayton lay subsidy list of 1327, by that time probably advanced in years, with a tax charge of 5*s* 4*d*, the largest in the vill.[31]

William Fraunce borrowed extensively from Wyot, and was pursued by him in the court in 1311 and 1313–14 on account of several debts. Yet there is evidence to suggest that Fraunce, John Cousin and John Osborn, all regular debtors, were borrowing from Wyot and other creditors not simply for purposes of survival, but rather as part of an attempt to augment their assets in the two decades either side of 1300, a strategy which subsequently encountered difficulties as each was faced with making repayments during an economic downturn. Most of Fraunce's debts were for large cash sums: for instance, he owed 21*s* to Henry Carter in 1294, 16*s* to Nicholas the Chaplain in 1297, and 24*s* to John Wyot in 1311.[32] It appears that Fraunce was using this money to enter the land market in order to try and add to his existing stock of land, a procedure that, as Ravensdale has shown with respect to the marriage of widows with land, could require the payment of large sums on the Crowland manors in Cambridgshire in this period.[33] A reference to land leased without seigneurial licence to Fraunce in 1296 gives a hint of the piecemeal way in which holdings could be enlarged,[34] but a more fundamental reason for his borrowing seems to have been the entry fine of 46*s* 8*d* paid for a tenement, possibly a virgate of 30 acres, which Fraunce received from the lord in 1303.[35] John Cousin pursued a strategy similar to that of Fraunce. As in the case of Fraunce, land was leased without licence to Cousin in 1296, which was followed by at least one and perhaps two purchases of whole tenements in 1307–8, with a possible total outlay in entry fines of nine marks (£6).[36] Most of Cousin's debts were expressed as volumes of grain, including one and a half quarters of wheat and half a quarter of barley owed to John Wyot, but there was also a debt of two marks in cash owed jointly by Cousin, William Fraunce and one other man to Henry Carter in 1312.[37] Finally, John Osborn provides a less striking example of the same pattern of borrowing for expansion. It is possible that some of Osborn's debts, which are concentrated in the years 1311–1317, originated in 1298 in his entry to a half-virgate formerly held by Peter Lemmer, although the fine for the land in this case was only half a mark.[38] This evidence is intriguing in the light of Postan's speculations as to how peasant land transactions were financed.[39] The problems of land shortage faced by non-inheriting offspring in the system of impartible inheritance that operated on these Cambridgeshire manors, and the inheritance customs intended to alleviate them, have been well documented by Page.[40] Perhaps Fraunce, Cousin and Osborn were themselves younger sons endowed through an 'allowance' with a limited number of customary acres,[41] or tenants hoping to increase a holding which might later be divided informally among sons and daughters. Whatever the case, the incentive for those who were able to enter the market for credit with purposes of expansion in mind is clear.

Judging by the evidence of the court roll, the three men were successful in satisfying most of their creditors, with the obvious exception of William Fraunce's obligations to John Wyot. Here Fraunce was unlucky in having become involved with a lender who was unusually persistent in pursuing his debtors in the manor court. Yet even Wyot, apparently, was prepared to exercise leniency towards Fraunce, since a concord between the two men concerning 'all contracts, plaints and demands from the beginning of the world up to this day' was made and recorded in the court roll in 1314, effectively writing off the greater part of Fraunce's debts to Wyot.[42] All three borrowers were additionally unfortunate to have found themselves owing sums at a time when most lenders would have felt a growing need for cash and grain as conditions worsened in the second decade of the century. Perhaps as a consequence of their numerous debt obligations, Cousin and Fraunce also leased small amounts of land on a handful of occasions in the years when they were debtors (further consideration of leasing and indebtedness is given below in the discussion of the post-1320 litigants). It should be noted, however, that both men made exchanges of land in this period as well as leases, which suggests they were interested in rationalizing the layout of holdings as well as simply raising money to repay debts.[43]

Whereas all the most frequent pre-1320 creditors and debtors were residents of Drayton, all those active in the latter part of the period appear to have lived in Oakington. Again, the evidence suggests a relative homogeneity of wealth and status among a number of the litigants. John Noteman, Andrew Noteman, John Gerard, William Kyle senior and Geoffrey King are all recorded on the Oakington rental of 1344 as 'full-landed men', that is, as customary tenants, probably of half-virgates of 15 acres.[44] Both Notemans, Kyle and King also appear on the list of Oakington tenants owing suit of court drawn up around 1346, although for reasons that are unclear John Gerard does not appear on this list.[45] Gerard was the only one of the six who served in manorial offices before the Black Death. He acted as a presentment juror in 1347–8, and was included in 1342 among members of the 'traversing jury' of freemen that swore to the veracity of the statements of each village's presentment jury at the view of frankpledge. He also served in the manorial offices of collector and hayward of Oakington.[46] The exceptional figure in this group is Geoffrey, *serviens* of John Rous (occasionally 'atte Rous'), otherwise undocumented in the court rolls, who was probably a more specialized lender. John Rous was one of the more important freeholders in the village,[47] and Geoffrey, who was perhaps his bailiff or estate manager rather than a domestic servant, may have been acting as an agent for his employer in providing a convenient source of loans for villagers encountering liquidity problems.

Many of the court roll entries relating to the six post-1320 litigants reinforce the view that recurrent appearances by particular creditors and debtors are indicative of ongoing ties of dependency in the village, caused by the inability of certain individuals to provide themselves with necessities without seeking the assistance of a privileged group controlling access to the greater part of the cash and grain available locally for lending. Important evidence of this dependency is the 'forced' leasing of land between known debtors and their creditors, which suggests land was used as a gage for debts, or as a form of repayment, making the obligations between debtor and creditor more profound as a consequence.[48] Thus, for instance, 25 leases of land are recorded as being made by Geoffrey King between 1336 and 1348, and it is highly probable, though not explicit, that most of these leases were somehow connected to his debts. Four of King's 21 creditors – John Noteman, John Gerard, Roger Bate and John Sebely – between them accounted for 17 of the 25 lessees benefiting from King's grants. A similar picture can be traced in the case of William Kyle senior, for whom 23 leases are documented between 1337 and 1348. The lessees in eight instances were creditors of Kyle. Six leases between 1339 and 1348 were also reported for Andrew Noteman, four of which were to his creditors. It is likely that more short-term subletting took place at Oakington than we are able to detect from payments for licences to let and presentments of illegal letting, however, and not all leases would have been connected to debts. No doubt many informal 'husbandry leases' were made which allowed widely scattered strips of land to yield an income to the lessor without the necessity of working them.[49] One would not wish to argue, of course, that the short leases of parcels of one or two acres at a time made by men like Geoffrey King were anything other than a way of maintaining an uneasy equilibrium between income from land and outgoings devoted to debt repayment. This was, however, an effective strategy. Furthermore, it did not involve the permanent alienation of land.[50] Page, observing that some of the other regular lessors at Oakington, Cottenham and Drayton ultimately abandoned their holdings, believed that Geoffrey King 'outwitted Fate' by avoiding this eventuality.[51] From the creditor's perspective also the relationship between indebtedness and leasing was far from straightforward. Land was let to John Noteman, one of the most frequent creditors at Oakington before 1350, on only one occasion, and in 1344 Noteman himself made a lease to John Sebely, a man who appeared twice as a debtor of Noteman.[52] This emphasizes that leasing and lending were not invariable signs of a tie of dependency, but were often part of a more complex, and hidden, individual economic strategy.

Finally, it may be observed that the case of the recurrent debtor who was probably borrowing to finance the acquisition of new resources was not limited to the period before 1320. In 1339, Andrew Noteman registered in the court an exchange of land that provided him with a vacant plot, on which, it is stated, he was to build.[53] Page considered Noteman's removal to have been a response to an ongoing feud;[54] whatever the case, this building programme would have required a considerable amount of cash, which probably goes some way towards explaining the series of cash debts recorded against Noteman in the succeeding years.[55] Just as importantly, the fact that quite large loans were made to Noteman, and to Geoffrey King and William Kyle, indicates that they were considered creditworthy.[56] In both periods of debt litigation activity, this awareness of creditworthiness was perhaps gained through personal familiarity between neighbours. It is significant, if not surprising, that all the litigants under consideration who had contact with each other were resident in the same village. Further research may confirm the impression, as yet poorly substantiated, that the tendency to lend and borrow was most pronounced where contacts between neighbours were most numerous.[57]

Conclusion

This preliminary examination of the Oakington evidence has made it fairly clear that, perhaps unsurprisingly, early fourteenth-century Oakington was much more like thirteenth-century Hinderclay than fifteenth-century Writtle in terms of the relationship between socio-economic status and involvement in lending and borrowing. Dearth and the other economic 'shocks' experienced by the peasantry between 1291 and 1350 clearly affected creditor-debtor ties in Oakington and Hinderclay in broadly the same ways. It seems incorrect, however, to conclude that pre-Black Death credit relations at Oakington consisted simply of a group of richer peasants lending to a poorer group, thereby creating and intensifying ties of dependence.[58] There were certainly a few lenders, such as John Wyot and Geoffrey, *serviens* of John Rous, who were clearly free from the kind of economic pressures experienced by the majority of those to whom they lent, but although such creditors were important, they were exceptional. Instead, in spite of the fact that the limited analysis carried out so far permits only rather speculative conclusions to be drawn, it may be argued that most credit transactions involved a sizeable group of middling peasants sharing common characteristics, and that even the most frequent debtors belonged to this group, albeit perhaps to its poorest strata. Within this group as a whole, most households must from time to time have been in a position to make surplus income available for lending, although in bad years or in less advantageous phases of their 'life-cycles' the same households could just as well find themselves faced with a need to borrow. This is reflected in the fact that even the most significant creditors such as John Noteman and John Gerard also borrowed on numerous occasions, while four of the six most frequent debtors also lent. The most vulnerable members of the middling group, such as William Fraunce and Geoffrey King, undeniably drew more frequently than others on the resources of their neighbours; however, they were still the 'equals' of their creditors in the sense that they had sufficient property and status with which to secure credit.

As already intimated, such conclusions must remain tentative until an exhaustive analysis of all the debt litigants has been carried out. They also raise further questions, such as the extent of the involvement of the very poorest villagers in the market for credit. To find such persons, it may be necessary to look at some of those who appeared least frequently rather than most frequently as debtors. Those who were only rarely in a position to offer security for a loan and only borrowed through need rather than for productive reasons would perhaps have been less likely to enter into the kind of credit agreement that found its way into court. Further research on the identity of those making single appearances in debt cases might therefore provide more evidence of the small 'survival' loans that were not always the prime concern of the debtors discussed in detail here, but must frequently have been sought by wage-earners and the landless.

Finally, while recognizing the burden that a lengthy tally of debts must have represented to the recurrent borrower, it is also necessary to ask what benefits such people might have enjoyed by being able to secure credit on a repeat basis. It seems that as long as credit was available, and as long as they were able to display enough creditworthiness to secure it, men like Geoffrey King could go into debt and maintain a precarious income fairly successfully, thereby avoiding total destitution.[59] Not only this, but in some cases, as has been shown, credit was the key not only to survival but to securing the landed resources that provided a much sounder basis for balancing future incomes.[60] Of course, such arrangements could not continue for long if the supply of credit dried up, and the early fourteenth century was precisely the sort of environment in which the risks facing potential creditors were regularly substantial enough to cause credit to be withdrawn, particularly if, as has been suggested, most lenders and borrowers were from the same socio-economic group and therefore equally vulnerable to dearth or disaster.[61] Yet these hints in the Oakington evidence of credit's potential to allow peasants to cope with uncertainty and shortage provide an incentive to look more closely in the course of future research at Mark Bailey's suggestion that 'if short- to medium- term loanable funds were locally and readily available to cover short- to medium-term financial difficulties, then the ability of ordinary people to weather the economic shocks of the period would have been significantly increased'.[62] They also force us to give greater attention to the reasons why lenders lent, and the terms they offered; in particular, they require us to gather more systematically the available scraps of information concerning the charging of interest. If rural credit was more widely and cheaply available and routinely relied upon than has perhaps been thought, then this may serve to resolve the apparent contradiction between pessimistic models of the household economy of the pre-plague peasantry and empirical evidence of the ability of such peasants to build houses and pay large entry fines with relative ease.[63]

Notes

1 I wish to thank Richard Smith and Phillipp Schofield for comments on earlier versions of this paper and Ros Davies for assistance with the tables.

2 As Mark Bailey writes, 'the scope for research into local money markets is considerable, since manorial court rolls contain numerous references to inter-peasant debt litigation, but hardly any such work has been undertaken': M. Bailey, 'Peasant welfare in England, 1290–1348', *Economic History Review* 51 (1998), 243. For a review of the small body of existing literature on credit and debt in the English countryside, and an indication of important research topics, see Schofield, 'L'endettement et le crédit', pp. 69–97.

3 *The Victoria History of the County of Cambridgeshire and the Isle of Ely* (Nine vols. to date, 1938–) (hereafter *V.C.H. Cambs*), ix, pp. 48–63, 71–84, 192–204. On Cottenham, J. R. Ravensdale, *Liable to Floods. Village Landscape on the Edge of the Fens, A.D. 450–1850* (Cambridge, 1974).

4 Cambridge University Library (hereafter CUL), Queens' College Muniments, Boxes 3 and 4 (Oakington court rolls). Hereafter all manuscript references to these rolls are given by number of court roll and membrane and by date of court session, e.g. 1/m.1r (12 Mar 1291). These records were an important source for F. M. Page's book on the Crowland estates, and in an appendix to that work she published an edition of the rolls relating to 23 of the 274 court sessions of the period 1291–1350 for which records survive: F.M Page, *The Estates of Crowland Abbey. A Study in Manorial Organisation* (Cambridge, 1934), pp. 333–91.

5 Figure 6.1 includes all actions in which money or goods were claimed by the plaintiff, most of which are explicitly described as 'plea of debt'. (The terms 'action', 'case' and 'plaint' are used interchangeably in this essay and simply mean 'civil lawsuit'.) The task of dividing the Oakington personal plaints into different categories is complicated by the presence of 'unspecified' plaints, in which the cause of the dispute was stated, but no definitive 'label' (such as 'plea of debt') was given to the action, and 'unknown' plaints, which simply provide evidence that a plaint was brought, but reveal nothing of its cause. As well as the debt plaints and 413 plaints of trespass and covenant, the Oakington court heard 127 'unspecified' plaints and 131 'unknown' plaints between 1291 and 1350. The 'unknown' category of plaints may conceal some additional debt plaints. However, even if half of the 'unknown' plaints are treated as if they were actually debt plaints, the increase in the number of new plaints per court session is still evident, moving from a mean 1.5 new plaints per session in 1311–20 (which was the maximum in any decade before 1330) to a mean 2.1 new plaints in 1331–40 and 2.3 in 1341–50.

6 This study presents preliminary findings from a doctoral research project in which court roll evidence concerning all the parties involved in debt plaints in this and one other manor court is considered.

7 For stimulating discussions of peasants as suitors in different legal jurisdictions, see P. R. Hyams, 'What did Edwardian villagers understand by law?', in Z. Razi and R. M. Smith, eds, *Medieval Society and the Manor Court* (Oxford, 1996), pp. 69–102, and Schofield, 'Peasants and the manor court', 3–42. Where the debt was in excess of 40 shillings the choice of jurisdiction was more limited, as cases involving sums above this limit required a writ: Beckerman, 'Forty-shilling jurisdictional limit', pp. 110–117; Palmer, *County courts of medieval England*, pp. 235–8.

8 Manors of Lisles, Burdeleys, Pelhams, Sames and the rectory, all held as part of Ely abbey's Cottenham estate: *V.C.H. Cambs*, ix, pp. 54–58; Page, *Estates*, pp. 18–28. Court rolls of the rectory manor survive from the 1420s: Cambridgeshire Record Office, L 1/57–65. Mention in the Oakington court rolls of presentments made in John de Lisle's court concerning illegal pasturing provides evidence that this Cottenham lord held a court baron at this period: 4/m.2d (10 Mar 1345).

9 For Swavesey Priory's manor in Dry Drayton, see W. M. Palmer and C. Parsons, 'Swavesey Priory', *Transactions of the Cambridgeshire and Huntingdonshire Archaeological Society* 1 (1904), 29–48. For the

Drayton properties of Barnwell Priory, see J. W. Clark, ed, *Liber Memorandum Ecclesie de Bernewelle* (Cambridge, 1907), pp. 136–7, 243, 310–12. The third manor was Chambres: *V.C.H. Cambs*, ix, pp. 76–7.

10 *Rotuli Hundredorum* (2 vols., Record Commission, 1812–18), ii, pp. 448–50. C.f. the comments in *V.C.H. Cambs*, ix, p. 199.

11 Hyams, *King, lords and peasants*, p. 20.

12 There were 22 reports of illicit court use in the period 1291–1380, appearing in 1294, 1295, 1296, 1297, 1300, 1301, 1306, 1307, 1315, 1330, 1331–2, 1335, 1338, 1339–43, 1340, 1344 (two), 1346, 1348, 1355, 1367 and 1373. Thirteen of the 22 instances record the use of ecclesiastical jurisdictions, as indicated by the mention of the 'official' in two cases, 'the chapter' in three cases, 'courts Christian' in seven cases and the court of the bishop of Ely in one other. Other jurisdictions used by the Crowland tenants included the county court at Cambridge, the sheriff's tourn, the hundred court (two instances, in one called 'le wapentak'), the justices of trailbaston in two cases and three unspecified prohibited courts. In only eleven cases is the cause of the lawsuit given: two involved debt, while seven cases involved adultery, and two defamation. It is interesting that other seigneurial courts do not feature among the jurisdictions allegedly used. However, the court rolls of nearby Landbeach show that residents of fourteenth-century Oakington and Cottenham did litigate in the courts of other lords. A licence to agree was recorded in 1371 in a debt case involving Robert Tue of Oakington, apparently as plaintiff. It is likely that this was the Robert Tue of Oakington regularly recorded in the Crowland rolls in trespass and debt cases between 1372 and 1375. There was also a debt case in 1380 at Landbeach involving John Shepherd and Richard Herd, both of Cottenham. Cambridge, Corpus Christi College Archives, XXXV/121 (court session of 23 Oct 1371); XXXV/122 (court session of 2 Oct 1380).

13 There were various scenarios involving litigation outside the home manor court which most likely did not generate a court amercement, simply because the rights of the lord were not infringed. Tenants both free and unfree almost certainly impleaded residents or tenants of other localities or manors in courts other than that of the plaintiff's home manor with relative impunity, for example. On the possibility that prohibitions on villeins suing in other courts were not in practice absolute, see Schofield, 'Peasants and the manor court', 21–2; Hyams, 'What did Edwardian villagers understand by law?', pp. 71–75.

14 L. R. Poos and R. M. Smith, '"Legal windows onto historical populations"? Recent research on demography and the manor court in medieval England', *Law and History Review* 2 (1984), reprinted as Part I of Poos, Razi and Smith, 'Population history of medieval English villages', in Razi and Smith, eds, *Medieval Society and the Manor Court*, pp. 305–308.

15 Clark, 'Debt litigation', pp. 247–79; see also E. Clark, 'Medieval debt litigation: Essex and Norfolk, 1270–1490' (unpublished Ph.D. thesis, University of Michigan, 1977), 104–92. Geertz's account of debt accumulation in a bazaar-type economy also emphasizes the mutuality of the advantages and obligations produced by debt accumulation rather than any exploitation of debtor by creditor: C. Geertz, *Peddlers and Princes. Social Change and Economic Modernization in Two Indonesian Towns* (Chicago and London, 1963), pp. 36–40.

16 Schofield, 'Dearth, debt and the local land market', 1–17.

17 *ibid.*, 14.

18 On the unusually wide jurisdiction of the Writtle court and its striking vitality throughout the fifteenth and sixteenth centuries, see K. C. Newton, *The Manor of Writtle. The Development of a Royal Manor in Essex, c.1086–c.1500* (Chichester, 1970), pp. 86–94.

19 For further comments on the differences between Writtle and Hinderclay, see Schofield, 'L'endettement et le crédit', pp. 88–91.

20 On these problems see Razi, *Life, Marriage and Death*, pp. 11–26; Bennett, *Women in the Medieval English Countryside*, pp. 199–205.

21 King v. Noteman: 4/m.7d (1 July 1346); Noteman v. King: 3/m.43d (11 July 1341), 4/m.6r (20 May 1346).

22 There is an extensive literature on English peasant economy and standards of living in the late thirteenth and early fourteenth centuries. An introduction is provided by C. Dyer, *Standards of Living in the Later Middle Ages* (Revised edn., Cambridge, 1998), chapters 5 and 6; this edition also provides a survey of the most recent contributions to the debate (pp. 287–96). Other important discussions of

the period and the issues involved include B. F. Harvey, 'Introduction: the "crisis" of the early fourteenth century', in Campbell, ed, *Before the Black Death*, pp. 1–24, and Bailey, 'Peasant welfare'. On conditions in the three decades singled out here, I. Kershaw, 'The Great Famine and agrarian crisis in England 1315–1322', *Past and Present* 59 (1973), 3–50, reprinted in R. H. Hilton, ed, *Peasants, Knights and Heretics* (Cambridge, 1976), pp. 85–132; Jordan, *The Great Famine*. On the effects of high taxation and recession in the late 1330s and early 1340s, M. C. Prestwich, 'Currency and the economy of early fourteenth-century England', in N. J. Mayhew, ed, *Edwardian Monetary Affairs 1279–1344* (British Archaeological Reports 36, 1977), pp. 45–58, and Maddicott, 'English peasantry and the demands of the Crown', pp. 285–359.

23 However, if this argument is correct, it is puzzling that the evidence in Table 6.2 for the 1290s – a generally difficult decade – is not more like that of the 1310s, 1330s and 1340s.

24 The wider issue of the nature of manor courts as legal institutions and their influence on the development and character of local credit markets is considered in my unpublished doctoral research: C. Briggs, 'Rural credit, debt litigation and the manor court in fourteenth-century England' (unpublished Research Fellowship dissertation, Trinity College, Cambridge, 2000).

25 Schofield, 'L'endettement et le crédit', pp. 85–96.

26 John Noteman as defendant: 3/m.8d (30 Apr 1328) (two plaints), 3/m.9d (29 Oct 1328), 3/m.11d (9 Oct 1329), 3/m.44r (8 Dec 1341), 3/m.49r (17 Oct 1342), 3/m.54r (2 Oct 1343), 4/m.7d (1 July 1346); Gerard as defendant: 3/m.31d (1 July 1339), 3/m.50d (16 Nov 1342) (two plaints), 4/m.8r (29 Nov 1345). Cousin as plaintiff: 2/m.26d (12 July 1323); King as plaintiff: 12/m.1d (10 Mar 1339), 3/m.32r (19 Oct 1339) (two plaints), 4/m.7d (1 July 1346); Andrew Noteman as plaintiff: 3/m.28r (16 Mar 1338) (two plaints); Kyle senior as plaintiff: 3/m. 28r (16 Mar 1338) (two plaints). Cases continuing over more than one court session are cited by the date of first mention. That an action was brought does not of course prove that a debt was owed, and not all of the actions cited in this note resulted in success for the plaintiff.

27 Schofield, 'Dearth, debt and the local land market', 13.

28 Public Record Office E 179/81/7 (county roll for Cambridgeshire and the Isle of Ely for twentieth of 1315). On this subsidy, see J. F. Willard, *Parliamentary Taxes on Personal Property, 1290 to 1334* (Cambridge, Mass., 1934), p. 21; M. Jurkowski, C. L. Smith and D. Crook, *Lay Taxes in England and Wales 1188–1688* (Public Record Office Handbook No. 31, 1998), pp. 32–3.

29 On exemptions, C. Dyer, 'Taxation and communities in late medieval England', in R. Britnell and J. Hatcher, eds, *Progress and Problems in Medieval England* (Cambridge, 1996), pp. 171–2; Jurkowski, Smith and Crook, *Lay Taxes*, pp. xxix–xxx; Willard, *Parliamentary Taxes*, pp. 87–92. It is unclear whether a minimum threshold of liability was specified in the instructions to the chief taxers for the twentieth of 1315. In his summary of the thresholds and exempted movables in the lay subsidies of 1275 to 1334, Jenks indicates that a 10*s* threshold applied to the 1315 subsidy but his omission of a reference to lower rate of tax (a twentieth) makes it unclear whether the threshold applied to both rates of tax or to the higher rate of tax only (a fiftieth): S. Jenks, 'The lay subsidies and the state of the English economy (1275–1334)', *Vierteljahrschrift für Sozial- und Wirtschaftsgeschichte* 85 (1998), 29–30. However, the minimum Drayton tax charge of 6*d* in 1315 suggests the taxers worked to a threshold of 10*s*.

30 2/m.8d (7 Dec 1311).

31 C. H. Evelyn-White, ed, *Cambridgeshire and the Isle of Ely: Lay Subsidy for the Year 1327* (reprinted from *East Anglian*, new series, x–xii, 1903–8), p. 74.

32 Debt to Carter: 1/m.4d (3 Feb 1294), 1/m.5r (24 Mar 1294); debt to Chaplain: 1/m.12r (25 Oct 1297); debt to Wyot: 2/m.8d (7 Dec 1311), 2/m.10d (15 Oct 1313). The assumption that these debts represent straightforward cash loans is based on the fact that the relevant entries simply record the sum owed and do not mention the circumstances of the original transaction. Other, fuller entries demonstrate that Fraunce also contracted debts that arose in the context of sales. In addition and apparently unconnected to the debt already referred to, Wyot also claimed from Fraunce three sums resulting from deferred payments, being 15*s* for one ox, and 23*s* and 13*s* 4*d* respectively for two horses; see 2/m.10d (15 Oct 1313), 2/m.11d (26 May 1314 and 6 Aug 1314), 2/m.12d (13 Dec 1314). Total debts expressed in cash terms claimed from Fraunce by all creditors in the period 1294–1313 totalled £9 0*s* 6*d*.

33 J. R. Ravensdale, 'Population changes and the transfer of customary land on a Cambridgeshire manor in the fourteenth century', in Smith, ed, *Land, kinship and life-Cycle*, pp. 202, 210.
34 1/m.10d (5 Mar 1296).
35 1/m.17d (4 May 1303). The only details given regarding this tenement at the time of the transfer were that it was previously held by Stephen Everard, and that Fraunce was to receive it 'excepting the messuage and croft'. We may infer the size of the property from later references to a holding formerly held by Fraunce, describing it respectively as a messuage and virgate, and a messuage and 30 acres, though it is not certain that these references are to a tenement which included the land granted in 1303: 2/m.22r (9 Mar 1321), 3/m.16r (16 May 1332).
36 John Cousin received the property surrendered by Agnes Saleman, entry fine four marks: 2/m.4d (28 Oct 1307). This transfer involved a retirement arrangement for Agnes. Also, John son of William Cousin entered the tenement formerly held by William Brown, fine five marks: 2/m.5d (22 Oct 1308). However, it is not clear that it was the same man in both cases.
37 Debt to Wyot: 2/m.2d (22 Jan 1306); debt to Carter: 2/m.9d (11 Nov 1312).
38 1/m.14r (22 Dec 1298).
39 Postan, 'Medieval agrarian society in its prime: England', pp. 627–8.
40 Page, *Estates*, pp. 108–112; *idem*, 'The customary poor-law of three Cambridgeshire manors', *Cambridge Historical Journal* 3 (1930), 125–133.
41 The compulsory grant by an heir to his siblings of a small portion of the holding: Page, *Estates*, p. 111.
42 2/m.12d (13/12/1314): *Johannes Wyot et Willelmus Fraunce concordant per licenciam de omnibus contractibus querelis et demandis a principio mundi usque in hunc diem et Willelmus ponit se. Et idem Willelmus cognovit se teneri predicto Johanni in viii.s. viii.d. soluendis ad pascham proximam futuram. . . .* But this evidently did not mark the end of their creditor-debtor relationship. An entry of October 1316 records the lord's grant of all Fraunce's lands in Drayton to Wyot for four years. The wording of the entry (*Dominus dimisit Johanni Wyot vicario de Cumberton totam illam terram in Drayton' quam fuit Willelmi Fraunce. . .*) makes it almost certain that Fraunce had died by the time of this transaction, and one may guess that his outstanding obligations to Wyot at the point of death accounted for the latter's claim on his property: 2/m.15d (23 Oct 1316). Fraunce probably died in the middle of 1316, as the last reference in the court roll to him whilst alive (located 2/m.14d) is as a personal pledge on 26 April 1316, but it should not be assumed that he died in the famine of that year. The entry of 16 May 1332 which refers to the debtor's former holding (n. 35 above) refers to Fraunce's properties taken into the lord's hand *per feloniam quam predictus Willelmus fecit pro qua suspensus fuit*. Yet if Fraunce really was hanged in 1316, the connections (if any) between his offence and his indebtedness can at present only be guessed at. It is well attested, however, that the economic hardships of these years encouraged crime, especially theft: B. A. Hanawalt, *Crime and Conflict in English Communities 1300–1348* (Cambridge, Mass. and London, 1979), pp. 238–60.
43 For Fraunce's four exchanges of land without licence, see 2/m.3d (22/2/1307), 2/m.10r (28 Sept 1314); for his two leases, one of which involved six selions leased jointly with John Cousin for one cropping, see 2/m.10d (15 Oct 1313). John Cousin's one exchange is recorded 2/m.8d (11 Oct 1311).
44 CUL, Queens' College Muniments Box 8 (Oakington and Drayton rentals, Crowland manors); for this interpretation of 'full-landed men', see Page, *Estates*, pp. 84–5, 89.
45 Located court roll no. 4, between membranes 6 and 7; c.f. Page, *Estates*, p. 40.
46 Presentment juror: 4/m.11d (25 Apr 1347), 4/m.16d (8 Oct 1347), 4/m.14r (2 May 1348), 4/m.13d (15 Oct 1348); traversing jury: 3/m.46d (17 Apr 1342). It is possible that Gerard was personally free despite holding a customary tenement, or he may simply have served on the traversing jury due to a shortage of free tenants; for traversing jury see Page, *Estates*, p. 34. Acting as collector: 3/m.22r (12 Oct 1336), 3/m.50r (16 Nov 1342); as hayward: 4/m.4d (28 July 1345).
47 *V.C.H. Cambs*, ix, p.197.
48 For leasing and indebtedness at Hinderclay see Schofield, 'Dearth, debt and the local land market', 14–15; for peasant leasing on the Crowland estates, see Page, *Estates*, pp. 112–114, and Ravensdale, 'Population changes', pp. 205–7.
49 Postan, 'Agrarian society in its prime', p. 626.
50 The longest term of any of King's leases was six years. The largest piece of land leased was a parcel of three acres.

51 Page, *Estates*, p. 113 ; see also Postan, 'The charters of the villeins', pp. 112–17.

52 Lease, Noteman to Sebely: 3/m.55r (26 Jan 1344). For Sebely as defendant in a debt case with two co-defendants, see 3/m.28r (16 Mar 1338); and with wife Amicia, see 4/m.5d (14 Jan 1346).

53 3/m.32r (19/10/1339): *Willelmus le Wryghte reddidit in manum domini unam placeam terre vacuam in hok' iuxta cimiterium et continentem in longitudine centum et viginti pedes et in latitudine centum et xx. pedes ad opus Andree Noteman quam quidem placeam idem Andreas edificabit. . . .* In return, Andrew demised to William two selions of customary land in Oakington.

54 Page, *Estates*, pp. 142–3.

55 For estimates of building costs, C. Dyer, 'English peasant buildings in the later middle ages (1200–1500)', *Medieval Archaeology*, 30 (1986), reprinted in Dyer, *Everyday Life in Medieval England*, pp. 133–165.

56 Andrew Noteman: owed 29*s* 5*d* in six debts, 1337–1348; Geoffrey King: owed 31*s* 1¼*d* in nine debts, 1338–1350; William Kyle senior: owed 58*s* 4*d* in five debts, 1327–47. These figures include only those debts expressed in cash terms. The median value of all 245 debts expressed in cash terms successfully claimed in the period 1291–1380 was 27*d*.

57 This is not to deny that the individuals discussed here occasionally became involved in credit transactions with persons not resident in their villages. As suggested in Schofield's essay in this volume, in particular circumstances outsiders could be important as sources of village credit. Hence it is interesting to find that in four of the six Oakington debt cases of this period in which the plaintiff is explicitly described as a non-resident, the defendant came from the group of 12 prominent creditors and debtors listed in Table 6.4. In 1338 Thomas Wych of Cambridge claimed four quarters of barley from Geoffrey King, and in 1346 a man of the same name and place of residence sought two quarters and one bushel of wheat and one and a half quarters of barley from William Kyle senior. In 1338 John le Clerk of Over claimed 11*d* from Andrew Noteman, while in 1341 William Waryn of Graveley jointly with Margaret widow of William Baroun claimed 4*s* from John Noteman. Schofield interprets such loans from outsiders as frequently involving richer villagers as borrowers. Such people turned to external sources because supplies within the village could not meet their need for credit for productive purposes. If that is what was happening in these Oakington cases, the fact that both a 'prominent creditor' and three 'frequent debtors' were involved might reinforce the suggestion that all the post-1320 litigants studied employed credit on a generally similar basis and belonged to broadly the same socio-economic group, with the possible exception of Geoffrey, *serviens* of John Rous. For first mentions of the four debt cases cited above, see respectively 3/m.28r (16 Mar 1338), 4/m.9r (11 Oct 1346), 3/m.30d (2 Nov 1338) and 3/m.44r (8 Dec 1341).

58 That credit may never have been extended to the poorest villagers is made clear in Schofield's article: 'Dearth, debt and the local land market', 13, 16 n. 67.

59 Geoffrey King appears to have been the only frequent debtor to survive the Black Death, appearing for the first time as a presentment juror in November 1349. Unsurprisingly, given the scale of the calamity of the Great Famine, the picture for the pre-1320 debtors is less optimistic. In particular, John Osborn is known to have become unable to maintain his tenement. In 1326, he surrendered ten customary acres 'through impotence', though this may have been as much a result of old age as loss of economic resources. That John was perhaps relatively old by 1326 is suggested by his regular appearances in the court rolls from 1291, the first full year of their survival, and by references to his son from 1309. For his surrender, see 3/m.4d (13 Jan 1326).

60 Peter Spufford's work on credit using probate accounts suggests that heavy borrowing was frequently a characteristic of seventeenth-century yeomen of relatively high inventoried wealth. His evidence provides support for the proposition that many recurrent rural debtors were in fact borrowing to expand their farming enterprises and maintain a relatively high standard of living, rather than to secure subsistence: P. Spufford, 'Credit in rural England before the advent of country banks', in *Banchi Pubblici, Banchi Privati e Monti di Pietà nell'Europa Preindustriale* (Atti della Societa Ligure di Storia Patria Nuova Serie Vol. 31, 1991), pp. 904–8; also P. Spufford, 'Long-term rural credit in sixteenth- and seventeenth-century England: the evidence of probate accounts', in T. Arkell, N. Evans and N. Goose, eds, *When Death Us Do Part. Understanding and Interpreting the Probate Records of Early Modern England* (Local Population Society, 2000), pp. 222–3.

61 On such problems of 'covariate risk' for the operation of credit as an effective form of insurance, see

J-P. Platteau, 'Traditional systems of social security and hunger insurance: past achievements and modern challenges', in E. Ahmad, J. Drèze, J. Hills and A. Sen, eds, *Social Security in Developing Countries* (Oxford, 1991), pp. 139–49.

62 Bailey, 'Peasant welfare', 243.

63 Dyer, *Standards of Living*, pp. 184–7.

Consolidated Bibliography

Published Primary Sources

A Lincolnshire Assize Roll for 1298 (P.R.O. Assize Roll No. 505), ed. W. S. Thomson (Lincolnshire Record Society, 36, 1944)

A Short Calendar of Deeds relating to Norwich enrolled in the Court Rolls of that City, ed. W. Rye (Norwich, 2 vols.: 1285–1306 (1903); 1307–41 (1915))

A Suffolk hundred in the year 1283, ed. E. Powell (Cambridge, 1910)

Abstracts of Feet of Fines relating to Wiltshire for the reigns of Edward I and Edward II, ed. R. B. Pugh (Devizes, 1939)

Aspin, I. S. T., *Anglo-Norman Political Songs* (Anglo-Norman Text Society, 1953)

Bateson, M. , *Borough customs* (Selden Society, 21, 1906)

Bond, E. A.,'Extracts from the Liberate Rolls relative to loans', *Archaeologia* 1st ser., xxviii (1840)

Bracton, ed. G. E. Woodbine and revised and translated by S. E. Thorne (four vols, Cambridge, Mass., 1968–77)

Bracton's Note-Book, ed. F. W. Maitland (three vols, London, 1877)

Brevia Placitata, ed. G. J. Turner and T. F. T. Plucknett (Selden Society, 66, 1947)

Calendar of Early Mayor's Court Rolls preserved among the archives of the Corporation of the City of London 1298–1307, ed. A. H. Thomas (Cambridge, 1924)

Calendar of letter-books, preserved among the archives of the corporation of the City of London at the Guildhall: Letter-books 'A' (c.1275–98), and 'B' (c.1275–1312), ed. R. R. Sharpe (London, 1899, 1900)

Calendar of plea and memoranda rolls, 1381–1412, ed. A. H. Thomas (London, 1926)

Calendar of plea and memoranda rolls, 1413–1437, ed. A. H. Thomas (London, 1943)

Calendar of wills proved and enrolled in the court of Husting, London. Part I. A.D. 1258–A.D. 1358, ed. R. R. Sharpe (London, 1889)

Cambridgeshire and the Isle of Ely: Lay Subsidy for the Year 1327, ed. C. H. Evelyn-White (reprinted from *East Anglian*, new series, x–xii, 1903–8)

Casus Placitorum, ed. W. H. Dunham jr. (Selden Society, 69, 1950)

Chronica Johannis de Oxenedes, ed. H. Ellis (London, Rolls Series, 39,1859)

Chronica monasterii de Melsa, ed. E. A. Bond (Rolls series, 3 vols., 1866–68)

Court roll of the manor of Downham, 1310–1327, ed. M. C. Coleman (Cambridgeshire Records Society, ii, 1996)

Court rolls of Walsham-le-Willows, 1303–1350, ed. R. Lock (Suffolk Records Society, xli, 1998)

Crime in East Anglia in the Fourteenth Century: Norfolk Gaol Delivery Rolls, 1307–1316, ed. B. Hanawalt (Norfolk Record Society, vol. 2, 1976)

De Antiquis Legibus Liber Cronica maiorum et vicomitum Londoniarum, ed. T. Stapleton (Camden Society, 34, 1846)

Earliest English Law Reports, vol. II, ed. Paul Brand (Selden Society, 112, 1996)

Early Registers of Writs, ed. E. de Haas and G. D. G. Hall (Selden Society, 87, 1970)

Early taxation returns. Taxation of personal property in 1332 and later (Buckinghamshire Record Society, 14, 1966)

'Eggington court rolls (1297–1572)', in *Hundreds, manors, parishes and the church. A selection of early documents for Bedfordshire*, ed. J. S. Thompson (Bedfordshire Historical Record Society, 69, 1990)

English Historical Documents, 1189–1327, ed. H. Rothwell (London, 1975)

Fleta, ed. H. G. Richardson and G. O. Sayles (Selden Society, vols. 72 (1953), 89 (1972), 99 (1983))

Glanvill, ed. G. D. G. Hall (London, 1965)

Glasscock, R. E., *The Lay Subsidy of 1334* (British Academy, Records of Social and Economic History, New Series, vol. 2, 1975)

'Ipswich borough records. No. 3 (Part 2, the borough). Reign of Edward III, 1327–1377', *East Anglian Daily Times*, Feb. 17th, 1927

Jacobs, J., *The Jews of Angevin England: Documents and records from Latin and Hebrew sources...... for the first time collected and translated* (London, 1893)

Leet Jurisdiction in the City of Norwich during the 13th and 14th Centuries, ed. W. Hudson (Selden Society, vol. 5, 1891)

Levy, S., 'The Norwich Day-Book', *Transactions of the Jewish Historical Society of England* 5 (1902)

Liber Memorandum Ecclesie de Bernewelle, ed. J. W. Clark (Cambridge, 1907)

Manorial records of Cuxham, c.1200–1349, ed. P. D. A. Harvey (Oxfordshire Record Society, 50, 1976)

Oschinsky, D., *Walter of Henley and other treatises on estate management and accounting* (Oxford, 1971)

Rokéah, Z. E., *Medieval English Jews and Royal Officials: Entries of Jewish Interest in the English Memoranda Rolls, 1266–93* (Jerusalem, 2000)

Rolls from the Office of the Sheriff of Bedfordshire and Buckinghamshire, 1332–1334, ed. G. H. Fowler (Bedfordshire Historical Record Society, 4to, 1929)

Rotuli Hundredorum (2 vols., Record Commission, 1812–18)

Select cases concerning the law merchant. Volume iii. Statute recognizances and special assizes, ed. H. Hall (Selden Society, 49, 1932)

Select cases from the ecclesiastical courts of the province of Canterbury c.1200–1301, eds, N. Adams and C. Donahue jr (Selden Society, London, 1981)

Select cases in the court of King's Bench under Edward I, ed. G. O. Sayles (Selden Society, 55, 1939)

Select pleas in manorial and other seignorial courts, ed. F. W. Maitland (Selden Society, 2, 1888)

Select pleas, starrs and other records from the rolls of the Exchequer of the Jews A.D. 1220–1284, ed. J. M. Rigg (Selden Society, London, 1902)

Skeat, W. W., *The vision of William concerning Piers the Plowman in three parallel texts together with Richard the Redeless by William Langland* (Oxford, 2 vols., 1886)

Starrs and Jewish Charters in the British Museum, vol 1, eds, H. Loewe, H. P. Stokes, I. Abrahams (London, 1930)

Statutes of the Realm (11 vols., Record Commission, London, 1810–1828)

Taxatio Ecclesiastica Angliæ et Walliæ, Auctoritate Papæ Nicholai IV, circa A.D. 1291, eds, T. Astle, S. Ayscough, and J. Caley (Record Commission, London, 1802)

The court rolls of Ramsey, Hepmansgrove and Bury, 1268–1600, ed. E. B. DeWindt (Toronto, 1990)

The Ipswich recognizance rolls, 1294–1327. A calendar, ed. G. H. Martin (Suffolk Record Society, 1973)

The Libelle of Englyshe Polcyce. A poem on the use of sea-power, 1436, ed. Sir G. Warner (Oxford, 1926)

The staple court book of Bristol, ed. E. E. Rich (Bristol Record Society, 5, 1934)

The statute merchant roll of Coventry, 1392–1416, ed. A. Beardwood (Dugdale Society, 17, 1939)

Two Bedfordshire Subsidy Lists. 1309 and 1332 (Suffolk Green Books, xviii, 1925)

Suffolk in 1327 being a subsidy return (Suffolk Green Books, ix, 1906)

Wilson, T., *A discourse upon usury by way of dialogue and orations, for the better variety and more delight of all those that shall read this treatise [1572]* (with an historical introduction by R. H. Tawney, London, 1925)
Wiltshire Inquisitions Post Mortem, ed. E. A. Fry (London, 1908)
Year Books 20 & 21 Edward I, ed. A. J. Horwood (Rolls Series, 1866)
Year Books 21 & 22 Edward I, ed. A. J. Horwood (Rolls Series, 1873)
Year Books 32 & 33 Edward I, ed. A. J. Horwood (Rolls Series, 1864)

Secondary Works

Allen, M., 'The volume of the English currency, 1158–1470', *Economic History Review*, 54 (2001)
Allen, M., 'The volume and composition of the English silver currency, 1279–1351', *British Numismatic Journal*, 2000, forthcoming
Bailey, M., *A marginal economy? East Anglian Breckland in the later middle ages* (Cambridge, 1989)
Bailey, M., 'Peasant welfare in England, 1290–1348', *Economic History Review* 51 (1998)
Bailey, M., 'The commercialisation of the English economy, 1086–1500', *Journal of Medieval History*, 24 (1998)
Bailey, S., 'Assignment of debts in England from the twelfth to the twentieth century. II', *Law Quarterly Review* 48 (1932)
Baldwin, J. W., *Masters, Princes and Merchants – the social views of Peter the Chanter and his circle* (Princeton, New Jersey, 1970)
Bartlett, R., *England under the Norman and Angevin Kings* (Oxford, 2000)
Bassett, M., *Knights of the shire for Bedfordshire during the middle ages* (Bedfordshire Historical Record Society, xxix, 1947)
Bean, J. M. W., *The estates of the Percy family, 1416–1537* (Oxford, 1958)
Beardwood, A., *Alien merchants in England, 1350 to 1377* (Cambridge, Mass., 1931)
Beardwood, A., 'Bishop Langton's use of statute merchant recognisances', *Medievalia et Humanistica* 9 (1955)
Beardwood, A., 'The Trial of Walter Langton, Bishop of Lichfield, 1307 – 1312', *Transactions of the American Philosophical Society* New series, 54 (1964)
Beardwood, A., 'Records of the trial of Walter Langeton Bishop of Coventry and Lichfield 1307–1312', *Camden Society* 4th ser., 6 (1969)
Beckerman, J. S., 'The forty-shilling jurisdictional limit in medieval English personal actions', in D. Jenkins, ed., *Legal History Studies* (Cardiff, 1975)
Beckerman, J. S., 'Procedural innovation and institutional change in medieval English manorial courts', *Law and History Review*, 10 (1992).
Bennet, E. K., 'The College of St John Evangelist of Rushworth', *Norfolk Archæology*, vol. 10 (1888)
Bennett, J. M., *Women in the Medieval English Countryside. Gender and Household in Brigstock Before the Plague* (Oxford, 1987)
Biddick, K., 'Medieval English peasants and market involvement', *Journal of Economic History*, xlv (1985)
Biddick, K., 'Missing links: taxable wealth, markets and stratification among medieval English peasants', *Journal of Interdisciplinary History*, xviii (1987).
Bill, P. A., *The Warwickshire Parish Clergy in the later Middle Ages* (Dugdale Society, Occasional Papers, no. 17, Oxford, 1967)
Bolton, J. L., *The medieval English economy, 1150–1500* (London, 1980)

Bowers, R. H., 'From rolls to riches: kings clerks and moneylending in thirteenth-century England', *Speculum*, 58 (1983)

Brand, P., 'Jews and the Law in England, 1275–1290', *English Historical Review* 115 (2000)

Britnell, R. H., '*Advantagium mercatoris*: a custom in medieval English trade', *Nottingham Medieval Studies* 24 (1980)

Britnell, R. H., *Growth and decline in Colchester, 1300–1525* (Cambridge, 1986)

Britnell, R. H., 'Sedentary long-distance trade and the English merchant class in thirteenth century England', in P. R. Coss and S. D. Lloyd, ed., *Thirteenth Century England. Volume 5. Proceedings of the Newcastle-upon-Tyne Conference, 1993* (Woodbridge, 1995)

Britnell, R. H., 'Urban demand in the English economy, 1300–1600', in J. A. Galloway, ed., *Trade, urban hinterlands and market integration,* c. *1300–1600* (London, 2000)

Britton, E., *The community of the vill: a study in the history of the family and village life in fourteenth century England* (Toronto, 1977)

Butler, L. H., 'Archbishop Melton, his Neighbours, and his Kinsmen, 1317–1340', *Journal of Ecclesiastical History* 2 (1951)

Carus Wilson, E. M., 'The first half-century of Stratford upon Avon' *Economic History Review* 8 (1965)

Chayanov, A. V., *The theory of peasant economy*, eds, D. Thorner, B. Kerblay, and R. E. F. Smith (Homewood, 1966)

Clanchy, M. T., *From memory to written record: England 1066–1307* (Oxford, 1993)

Clapham, J., *A Concise Economic History of Britain From the Earliest Times to 1750* (Cambridge, 1957)

Clark, E., 'Debt litigation in a late medieval English vill' in J.A. Raftis, ed., *Pathways to medieval peasants* (Toronto, 1981)

Cook, G. H., *Medieval Chantries and Chantry Chapels* (London, 1947)

Cramer, A. C., 'The origins and functions of the Jewish Exchequer', *Speculum* 16 (1941)

Cunningham, W., *The growth of English industry and commerce during the early and middle ages* (Cambridge, 5th ed., 1910)

Davies, J. C., *The baronial opposition to Edward II, its character and policy* (Cambridge, 1918)

Davis, M. D., 'The Mediaeval Jews of Lincoln', *Archaeological Journal*, 38 (1881)

Denholm-Young, N., *Seignorial administration in England* (London, 1937)

Dewindt, E. B., *Land and people in Holywell-cum-Needingworth. Structures of tenure and patterns of social organization in an east midlands village, 1252–1457* (Toronto, 1971)

Dobson, R. B., *The Jews of Medieval York and the massacre of March 1190* (Borthwick Papers, 1974)

Dyer, C., 'Changes in the size of peasant holdings in some west midland villages, 1400–1540', in R. M. Smith ed., *Land, kinship and life-cycle* (Cambridge, 1984)

Dyer, C., 'The consumer and the market in the later middle ages', *Economic History Review*, 2nd ser., 43 (1990), reprinted in *idem, Everyday life in medieval England* (London, 1994)

Dyer, C., 'The hidden trade of the middle ages: evidence from the west midlands', *Journal of Historical Geography*, 18 (1992), repr. in *idem*, *Everyday life in medieval England* (London, 1994)

Dyer, C., 'English peasant buildings in the later middle ages (1200–1500)', *Medieval Archaeology*, 30 (1986), reprinted in Dyer, *Everyday Life in Medieval England* (London, 1994)

Dyer, C., 'Taxation and communities in late medieval England', in R. Britnell and J. Hatcher, eds, *Progress and Problems in Medieval England* (Cambridge, 1996)

Dyer, C., *Standards of living in the later middle ages. Social change in England,* c.*1200–1520* (Cambridge, 1989; revised edn., Cambridge, 1998)

Elman, P., 'Jewish finance in thirteenth century England with special reference to royal taxation', *Bulletin of Institute of Historical Research* 15 (1938)

Elman, P., 'Jewish trade in thirteenth century England', *Historia Judaica* 1 (1939)

Faith, R. J., 'Berkshire: fourteenth and fifteenth centuries', in P. D. A. Harvey, ed., *The peasant land market in medieval England* (Oxford, 1984)

Farmer, D. C., 'Some grain price movements in thirteenth century England, *Economic History Review* 2nd ser., x, (1957–58)

Farmer, D., 'Marketing the produce of the medieval countryside, 1200–1500', in E. Miller, ed., *The agrarian history of England and Wales. Volume iii. 1348–1500* (Cambridge, 1991)

Firth, R., 'Capital, saving and credit in peasant societies: a viewpoint from economic anthropology' in R. Firth and B. S. Yamey, eds, *Capital, saving and credit in peasant societies. Studies from Asia, Oceania, the Caribbean and Middle America* (London, 1964)

Fontaine, L., 'Introduction', in M. Berthe, ed., *Endettement paysan et crédit rural dans l'Europe médiévale et moderne. Actes des XVII*[es] *journées internationales d'histoire de l'abbaye de Flaran, Septembre 1995* (Toulouse, 1998)

Fryde, E. B., 'Materials for the study of Edward III's credit operations, 1327–48', *Bull. Inst. Hist. Res.* xii (1949)

Fryde, E. B., 'The deposits of Hugh Despenser the younger with Italian bankers', *Economic History Review* second ser., iii (1951), reprinted in idem, *Studies in medieval trade and finance* (London, 1983)

Fryde, E. B., 'Loans to the English crown, 1328–31', *English Historical Review* lxx (1955), reprinted in idem, *Studies in medieval trade and finance* (London, 1983)

Fryde, E. B. , *Studies in medieval trade and finance* (London, 1983)

Fryde, E. B., *William de la Pole, merchant and king's banker* (London, 1988)

Fryde, E. B., *Peasants and landlords in later medieval England* (Stroud, 1996)

Fryde, E. B., and M. M., 'Public credit, with special reference to North-western Europe', in M. M. Postan, E. E. Rich and E. Miller, eds, *The Cambridge Economic History of Europe. iii. Economic organization and policies in the middle ages* (Cambridge, 1963)

Fryde, N., 'Antonio Pessagno of Genoa, king's merchant of Edward II of England', *Studi in memoria di Frederigo Melis*, ii (1978)

Fuss, A. M., 'Inter-Jewish loans in Pre-Expulsion England', *Jewish Quarterly Review* 65 (1975)

Geddes, P., *Inside the Bank of England* (Frome and London, 1987)

Geertz, C., *Peddlers and Princes. Social Change and Economic Modernization in Two Indonesian Towns* (Chicago and London, 1963)

Gilchrist, J., *The Church and Economic Activity in the Middle Ages* (London, 1969)

Giuseppi, J., *The Bank of England: a history from its foundation in 1694* (London, 1966)

Graham, R., 'The taxation of Pope Nicholas IV', *English Historical Review*, 23 (1908)

Hamilton Thompson, A., *The English Clergy and their Organisation in the Later Middle Ages* (Oxford, 1947)

Hanawalt, B. A., *Crime and Conflict in English Communities 1300–1348* (Cambridge, Mass. and London, 1979)

Harding, A., *The law courts of medieval England* (London, 1973).

Harris, G. L., 'Aids, loans and benevolences', *Historical Journal* vi (1963)

Harris, G. L., *King, parliament and public finance in medieval England to 1369* (Oxford, 1975)

Harvey, B. F., *Westminster Abbey and its estates in the middle ages* (Oxford, 1977)

Harvey, B. F., 'Introduction: the "crisis" of the early fourteenth century', in B. M. S. Campbell, ed., *Before the Black Death: Essays in the Crisis of the Early Fourteenth Century* (Manchester, 1991)

Harvey, P. D. A., 'Conclusion' in *idem*, ed., *The peasant land market in medieval England* (Oxford, 1984)

Harvey, P. D. A., and A. McGuinness, *A Guide to British Medieval Seals* (London 1996)

Hatcher, J., *The English tin industry and trade before 1550* (Oxford, 1973)

Heath, P., *The English Parish Clergy on the Eve of the Reformation* (London and Toronto, 1969)

Helmholz, R. H., 'Assumpsit and *fidei laesio*', *Law Quarterly Review* 91 (1976), reprinted in idem, *Canon law and the law of England* (London, 1987)
Helmholz, R. H., 'Debt claims and probate jurisdiction in historical perspective', *American Journal of Legal History* 23 (1979), reprinted in idem, *Canon law and the law of England* (London, 1987)
Helmholz, R. H., 'Usury and the medieval English church courts', *Speculum* 61 (1986), reprinted in idem, *Canon law and the law of England* (London, 1987)
Henry, R. L., *Contracts in the local courts of medieval England* (London, 1926)
Hettinger, M. J., 'Defining the servant: legal and extra-legal terms of employment in fifteenth-century England', in A. J. Frantzen and D. Moffat, *The work of work. Servitude, slavery, and labor in medieval England* (Skelmorlie, 1994)
Hillaby, J., 'Hereford Gold: Irish Welsh and English land – the Jewish community at Hereford and its clients 1179–125. Part 1', *Transactions of the Woolhope Naturalists Field Club*, 44, 3 (1984)
Hillaby, J., 'Hereford Gold: Irish Welsh and English land – the Jewish community at Hereford and its clients 1179–1253: Four Case studies', *Transactions of the Woolhope Naturalists Field Club* 45, (1985)
Hillaby, J., 'A magnate among the marchers: Hamo of Hereford, his family and clients, 1218–1253', *Jewish Historical Studies* 31 (1990)
Hillaby, J., 'The Hereford Jewry 1179–1290 – Aaron le Blund and the last decades of Hereford Jewry 1253–1290', *Transactions of the Woolhope Naturalists Field Club* 46 (1990)
Hilton, R. H., *The English peasantry in the later middle ages* (Oxford, 1975)
Hilton, R. H., 'Introduction', in *The transition from feudalism to capitalism* (London, 1978)
Hilton, R. H., 'Small town society in England before the Black Death', *Past and Present*, 109 (1984)
Holderness, B. A., 'The clergy as money-lenders in England, 1550–1700', in Rosemary O'Day and Felicity Heal, eds., *Princes and Paupers* (Leicester, 1981)
Holderness, B. A., 'Widows in pre-industrial society: an essay upon their economic functions', in R. M. Smith, ed., *Land, kinship and life-cycle* (Cambridge, 1984)
Holmes, G. A., 'The "Libel of English policy"', *English Historical Reviewo:*, ccxcix (1961)
Hook, M., and A. Macgregor, *Medieval England Archaeological Collections in the Ashmolean Museum from Alfred the Great to Richard III*, (Oxford, 1997)
Hunt, E. S., and J. M. Murray, *A History of Business in Medieval Europe 1200–1550* (Cambridge, 1999)
Hyams, P. R., 'The origins of a peasant land market in England', *Economic History Review*, xxiii (1970)
Hyams, P. R., 'The Jewish minority in medieval England 1066–1290', *Journal of Jewish Studies* 26 (1974)
Hyams, P. R., *Kings, lords and peasants. The common law of villeinage in the twelfth and thirteenth centuries* (Oxford, 1980)
Hyams, P. R., 'Deans and their doings: the Norwich inquiry of 1286', *Proceedings of the Berkeley Congress of Medieval Canon Law, 1980* (Monumenta Iuris Canonici, Series C, Subsidia, 7, Vatican City, 1985)
Hyams, P. R., 'What did Edwardian villagers understand by law?', in Z. Razi and R. M. Smith, eds, *Medieval Society and the Manor Court* (Oxford, 1996)
Jacobs, J., 'Aaron of Lincoln', *Transactions of the Jewish Historical Society of England* 3 (1899)
Jenkinson, H., 'Exchequer tallies' *Archaeologia* lxii (1911)
Jenkinson, H., 'William Cade a financier of the twelfth century', *English Historical Review* 26 (1913)
Jenkinson, H., 'Medieval tallies, public and private', *Archaeologia* lxxiv (1925)

Jenkinson, H., *A guide to seals in the Public Record Office* (London, 1968)
Jenkinson, H., and M. H. Mills, 'Rolls from a sheriff's office of the fourteenth century', *English Historical Review*, 43 (1928)
Jones, A. C., 'Bedfordshire: fifteenth century', in P. D. A. Harvey, ed., *The peasant land market in medieval England* (Oxford, 1984)
Jones, N., *God and the Moneylenders: Usury and Law in Early Modern England* (Oxford, 1989)
Jordan, W. C., *The great famine. Northern Europe in the early fourteenth century* (Princeton, 1996)
Jurkowski, M., C. L. Smith and D. Crook, *Lay Taxes in England and Wales 1188–1688* (Public Record Office Handbook No. 31, 1998)
Kaeuper, R. W., 'The Frescobaldi of Florence and the English crown', *Studies in medieval and renaissance history* 1 (1973)
Kaeuper, R. W., *Bankers to the crown* (Princeton, N. J., 1973)
Keene, D., 'Changes in London's economic hinterland as indicated by debt cases in the Court of Common Pleas', in J. A. Galloway, ed., *Trade, urban hinterlands and market integration, c.1300–1600* (London, 2000)
Kermode, J. I., 'Money and credit in the fiftenth century: some lessons form Yorkshire', *Business History Review* 65 (1991)
Kermode, J. I., 'Medieval indebtedness: the regions versus London', in N. Rogers, ed., *England in the fifteenth century* (Stamford, 1994)
Kermode, J. I., *Medieval merchants. York, Beverley and Hull in the later middle ages* (Cambridge, 1998)
Kershaw, I., 'The Great Famine and agrarian crisis in England 1315–1322', *Past and Present* 59 (1973), reprinted in R. H. Hilton, ed, *Peasants, Knights and Heretics* (Cambridge, 1976)
Kershaw, I., *Bolton Priory. The economy of a northen monastery, 1286–1325* (Oxford, 1973)
King, E., *Peterborough Abbey 1086–1310 – a study in the land market*, (Cambridge, 1973)
Kingsford, H. S., *Seals* (London, 1920)
Knowles, D. D., *The religious orders in England. 3 vols* (Cambridge, 1956–9)
Kowaleski, M., *Local markets and regional trade in medieval Exeter* (Cambridge, 1995)
Kuchenbuch, L., 'Kerbhõlzer in Alteuropa – Zwischen dorfschmiede und schatzamt' in B. Nagy and M. Sebõk, eds, *...The man of many devices who wandered full many ways.... Festschrift in Honor of János M. Bak* (Budapest, 1999)
Lacaita, P., *Comentum super Dantis Comoedium* (Florence, 1887)
Latimer, P., 'The English Inflation of 1180–1220 Reconsidered', *Past and Present*, 171 (2001)
Leconfield, Lord, *Petworth manor in the seventeenth century* (Oxford, 1954)
Levy, S., 'Aaron's debts sixteen years after his death', *Transactions of the Jewish Historical Society of England* 3 (1899)
Lipman, V. D., *The Jews of Medieval Norwich* (London, 1967)
Lipson, E., *An introduction to the economic history of England. I. The middle ages* (London, 1915)
Little, L. K., 'Pride goes before avarice: social change and the vices in Latin Christendom', *American Historical Review* lxxvi (1971)
Lloyd, T. H., *The movement of wool prices in medieval England*, (Economic History Review Supplement, 6, Cambridge, 1973)
Lloyd, T. H., *The English wool trade in the middle ages* (Cambridge, 1977)
Lloyd, T. H., *Alien merchants in England in the high middle ages* (Brighton, 1982)
Lomas, T., 'Durham: late fourteenth and fifteenth centuries', in P. D. A. Harvey, ed., *The peasant land market in medieval England* (Oxford, 1984)
Maddicott, J. R., *The English peasantry and the demands of the crown, 1294–1341, Past and Present Supplement 1* (1975), repr. in T. H. Aston, ed., *Landlords, peasants and politics in medieval England* (Cambridge, 1987)

Maitland, F. W. , *Collected Papers* (three volumes, Cambridge, 1911)
Mate, M., 'Monetary policies in England, 1272–1307', *British Numismatic Journal* 41 (1979)
Mate, M., 'The East Sussex land market and the agrarian class structure in the late middle ages', *Past and Present* 139 (1993)
Mayhew, N. J., 'Population, money supply, and the velocity of circulation in England, 1300–1700', *Economic History Review*, 2nd ser., xlviii (1995)
Mayhew, N. J., *Sterling: The Rise and Fall of a Currency* (1999)
Mayhew, N. J., unpublished paper on Gussage All Saints, Dorset
McFarlane, K. B., 'Loans to the Lancastrian kings: the problem of inducement', *Cambridge Historical Journal* ix (1947), reprinted in idem, *England in the fifteenth century. Collected essays* (London, 1981)
McIntosh, M. K., 'Money Lending on the Periphery of London, 1300–1600' *Albion* 20 (1988)
McIntosh, M. K., *Autonomy and community. The royal manor of Havering, 1200–1500* (Cambridge, 1986)
McIntosh, M. K., *Controlling misbehavior in England, 1370–1600* (Cambridge, 1998)
McLaughlin, T. P., 'The teaching of the canonists on usury (XII, XIII, and XIV centuries)', *Medieval Studies* 1 (1939)
Menache, S., 'Matthew Paris's attitude toward Anglo-Jewry', *Journal of Medieval History* 23 (1997)
Miller, E., and J. Hatcher, *Medieval England: towns, commerce and crafts, 1086–1348* (Harlow, 1995)
Moorman, J. R. H., *Church life in England in the thirteenth century* (Cambridge, 1946)
Morris, C., 'A consistory court in the middle ages', *Journal of Ecclesiastical History* 14 (1963)
Morris, R. K., 'The Church in the Countryside: Two Lines of Inquiry', in, Della Hooke, ed., *Medieval Villages: A Review of Current Work* (Oxford University Committee for Archæology, Monograph No. 5, Oxford, 1985)
Muldrew, C., 'Credit and the courts: debt litigation in a seventeenth-century urban community', *Economic History Review*, xlvi (1993)
Muldrew, C., 'The culture of reconciliation: community and the settlement of economic disputes in early moderrn England', *The Historical Journal* 39 (1996)
Muldrew, C., *The economy of obligation* (Basingstoke, 1998).
Mundill, R. R., 'Anglo-Jewry under Edward I – credit agents and their clients', *Jewish Historical Studies* 31 (1990)
Mundill, R. R., 'Lumbard and son: the business and debtors of two Jewish moneylenders in late thirteenth-century England', *The Jewish Quarterly Review* lxxxii (1991)
Mundill, R. R., 'Rabbi Elias Menahem: a late-thirteenth-century English entrepreneur', *Transactions of the Jewish Historical Society of England* xxxiv (1994–6)
Mundill, R. R., *England's Jewish Solution: Experiment and Expulsion, 1262–1290* (Cambridge, 1998)
Mundill, R. R., 'Medieval Anglo-Jewry: Expulsion and Exodus' in F. Burgard, A. Haverkamp, G. Mentgen (Hrsg.) *Judenvertreibungen in Mittelalter und Früher Neuzeit* (Hannover, 1999)
Naughton, K. S., *The gentry of Bedfordshire in the thirteenth and fourteenth centuries* (Department of English Local History Occasional Papers, Leicester, 3rd ser., 2, 1976)
Newton, K. C., *The Manor of Writtle. The Development of a Royal Manor in Essex, c.1086–c.1500* (Chichester, 1970)
Nightingale, P., 'Monetary contraction and mercantile credit in later medieval England', *Economic History Review*, 2nd ser., xliii (1990)
Nightingale, P., *A Medieval Mercantile Community: the Grocers' Company and the politics and trade of London 1000 – 1485* (Yale UP, 1995).
Nightingale, P., 'Norwich, London, and the Regional Integration of Norfolk's Economy in the

First Half of the Fourteenth Century', in J. A. Galloway, ed., *Trade, urban hinterlands and market integration, c.1300–1600* (London, 2000)
Ormrod, W. M., *The Reign of Edward III* (New Haven and London, 1990)
Ormrod, W. M., 'The Crown and the English economy, 1290–1348', in B. M. S. Campbell, ed., *Before the Black Death: Essays in the Crisis of the Early Fourteenth Century* (Manchester, 1991)
Owst, G. R., *Literature and the pulpit in medieval England* (Oxford, 1961)
Page, F. M., 'The customary poor-law of three Cambridgeshire manors', *Cambridge Historical Journal* 3 (1930)
Page, F. M., *The estates of Crowland Abbey. A study in manorial organisation* (Cambridge, 1934)
Palmer, R. C., *The county courts of medieval England, 1150–1350* (Princeton, 1982)
Palmer, W. M., and C. Parsons, 'Swavesey Priory', *Transactions of the Cambridgeshire and Huntingdonshire Archaeological Society* 1 (1904)
Pantin, W. A., *The English church in the fourteenth century* (Cambridge, 1955)
Parkes, J., *The Jew in the Medieval Community* (London, 1938)
Parsons, J. C. , *Eleanor of Castile: Queen and Society in Thirteenth Century England* (London, 1995)
Phillips, J. R. S., *Aymer de Valence, earl of Pembroke, 1307–1324. Baronial politics in the reign of Edward II* (Oxford, 1972)
Platteau, J-P., 'Traditional systems of social security and hunger insurance: past achievements and modern challenges', in E. Ahmad, J. Drèze, J. Hills and A. Sen, eds, *Social Security in Developing Countries* (Oxford, 1991)
Plucknett, T. F. T, *Legislation of Edward I* (Oxford, 1949).
Pollock, Sir F., and F. W. Maitland, *The history of English law before the time of Edward I* (2 vols., Cambridge, 2nd ed., 1968)
Poos, L. R., Z. Razi, R.M. Smith, 'The population history of medieval English villages: a debate on the use of manor court records', in Z. Razi and R. M. Smith, eds, *Medieval society and the manor court* (Oxford, 1996)
Postan, M. M., 'Credit in medieval trade', *Economic history review* 1 (1928), reprinted in Postan, *Medieval trade and finance* (Cambridge, 1973)
Postan, M. M., 'Private financial instruments in medieval England', *Vierteljahrschrift fur Social- und Wirtschaftsgeschicte* xxiii (1930), reprinted in idem, *Medieval trade and finance* (Cambridge, 1973)
Postan, M. M., 'Medieval agrarian society in its prime: England', in M. M. Postan, ed., *The Cambridge Economic History of Europe, I, The Agrarian Life of the Middle Ages* (2nd ed., Cambridge, 1966)
Postan, M. M., *The medieval economy and society* (Harmondsworth, 1972)
Postan, M. M., 'The charters of the villeins', in *idem, Medieval Agriculture and General Problems of the Medieval Economy* (Cambridge, 1973)
Power, E. E.,'The wool trade in the fifteenth century', in E. E. Power and M. M. Postan, eds, *Studies in English trade in the fifteenth century* (London, 1933)
Power, E. E., *The wool trade in English medieval history* (Oxford, 1941), p. 45.
Prestwich, M. C., 'Currency and the economy of early fourteenth-century England', in N. J. Mayhew, ed, *Edwardian Monetary Affairs 1279–1344* (British Archaeological Reports 36, 1977)
Pugh, R. B., 'Some medieval moneylenders', *Speculum* 43 (1968)
Rabinowitz, J. J., *Jewish Law* (New York, 1956)
Raftis, J. A., *Peasant economic development within the English manorial system* (Stroud, 1997)
Ravensdale, J. R., *Liable to Floods. Village Landscape on the Edge of the Fens, A.D. 450–1850* (Cambridge, 1974)
Ravensdale, J. R., 'Population changes and the transfer of customary land on a Cambridgeshire manor in the fourteenth century', in Smith, ed, *Land, kinship and life-Cycle* (Cambridge, 1984)

Razi, Z., *Life, marriage and death in a medieval parish: economy, society and demography in Halesowen (1270–1400)* (Cambridge, 1980)
Re, E., 'La compagnia dei Riccardi in Inghilterra e il suo fallimento all fino del secolo XIII', *Archivio della Societa Romana di Storia Patria* 37 (1914)
Reynolds, S., *An introduction to the history of English medieval towns* (Oxford, 1977)
Richardson, H. G., *The English Jewry under Angevin kings* (London, 1960)
Rodes, Jr, R. E., *Ecclesiastical administration in medieval England* (Notre Dame, Indiana, 1977)
Roover, de, R. *Money, Banking and Credit in Medieval Bruges* (Cambridge, Mass., 1948)
Rosenwein, B. H., and L. K. Little, 'Social meaning in the monastic and mendicant spiritualities', *Past and Present* 63 (1974)
Roth, C., *England in Jewish History* (The Lucien Wolf Memorial Lecture, London 1949)
Roth, C., *A History of the Jews in England,* (Oxford, 1978)
Rubin, M., *Charity and Community in Medieval Cambridge* (Cambridge, 1987), pp. 224–5.
Russell, E., 'The societies of the Bardi and the Peruzzi and their dealings with Edward III, 1327–45', in G. Unwin, ed., *Finance and trade under Edward III* (Manchester, 1918)
Salzman, L. F., *English trade in the middle ages* (Oxford, 1931)
Schofield, P. R., 'Dearth, debt and the local land market in a late thirteenth century village community', *Agricultural History Review* 45 (1997)
Schofield, P. R., 'L'endettement et le crédit dans la campagne anglaise au moyen âge', in M. Berthe, ed., *Endettement paysan et crédit rural dans l'Europe médiévale et moderne. Actes des XVIIes journées internationales d'histoire de l'abbaye de Flaran, Septembre 1995* (Toulouse, 1998)
Schofield, P. R., 'Peasants and the manor court: gossip and litigation in a Suffolk village at the close of the thirteenth century', *Past and Present* 159 (1998)
Schofield, P. R., 'The social economy of the medieval village' (forthcoming)
Scott, K., 'The Jewish arcae', *Cambridge Law Journal* 10 (1950)
Simpson, A. W. B., *A History of the Common Law of Contract: The Rise of Assumpsit* (Oxford, 1975)
Smith, R. M., 'Some issues concerning families and their property in rural England 1250–1800', in *idem*, ed., *Land, kinship and life-cycle* (Cambridge, 1984)
Smith, R. M., 'A periodic market and its impact upon a manorial community: Botesdale, Suffolk, and the manor of Redgrave, 1280–1300', in Z. Razi and R. M. Smith, eds, *Medieval society and the manor court* (Oxford, 1996)
Spufford, M., 'Peasant inheritance customs and land distribution in Cambridgeshire from the sixteenth to the eighteenth centuries', in J. Goody, J. Thirsk and E. P. Thompson, eds, *Family and Inheritance. Rural society in Western Europe, 1200–1800,* (Cambridge, 1976)
Spufford, P., *Money and its uses in medieval Europe* (Cambridge, 1988)
Spufford, P., 'Credit in rural England before the advent of country banks', in *Banchi Pubblici, Banchi Privati e Monti di Pietà nell'Europa Preindustriale* (Atti della Societa Ligure di Storia Patria Nuova Serie Vol. 31, 1991)
Spufford, P., 'Long-term rural credit in sixteenth- and seventeenth-century England: the evidence of probate accounts', in T. Arkell, N. Evans and N. Goose, eds, *When Death Us Do Part. Understanding and Interpreting the Probate Records of Early Modern England* (Local Population Society, 2000)
Stacey, R. C., 'Jewish lending and the medieval English economy', in R. H. Britnell and B. M. S. Campbell, eds, *A Commercialising Economy: England 1086–c.1300* (Manchester, 1995)
Stow, K. R., 'The good of the church, the good of the State: Popes and Jewish money', in D. Wood, ed, *Christianity and Judaism* (Studies in Church History, 29, Oxford, 1992)
Swanson, R. N., 'Standards of Livings: parochial revenues in Pre-Reformation England', in C. Harper-Bill, ed., *Religious Belief and Ecclesiastical Careers in Late Medieval England* (Studies in the History of Medieval Religion, vol. 3, (Woodbridge, Suffolk, 1991)

Tanner, N. P., *The church in late medieval Norwich, 1370–1532* (Pontifical Institute of Medieval Studies, Toronto, 1984)
Thrupp, S. L., *The Merchant Class of Medieval London* (Chicago, 1948)
Vinogradoff, P., *Villainage in England* (Oxford, 1892)
Walter, J., 'The social economy of dearth in early modern England', in J. Walter and R. Schofield, eds, *Famine, disease and the social order in early modern society* (Cambridge, 1989)
Watt, J. A., , 'The English Episcopate, the State and the Jews: The evidence of the thirteenth century conciliar decrees', in P. R. Coss and S. D. Lloyd, eds, *Thirteenth Century England: Proceedings of the Newcastle upon Tyne Conference* (Woodbridge, 1987)
Wedemeyer Moore, E., *The Fairs of Medieval England – An Introductory Study* (Toronto, 1985)
Whitwell, R. J., 'Italian bankers and the English crown', *Transactions of the Royal Historical Society* New series, 17 (1903); T. F. Tout, *The political history of England from the accession of Henry III to the death of Edward III (1216–1377)* (London, 1905)
Willard, J. F., 'The crown and its creditors, 1327–33', *Eng. Hist. Rev.*, 42 (1927)
Willard, J. F., *Parliamentary Taxes on Personal Property, 1290 to 1334* (Cambridge, Mass., 1934)
Williams, G. A., *Medieval London: From Commune to Capital* (University of London Historical Studies, vol 11, 1963)
Williamson, J., 'Norfolk: thirteenth century', in P. D. A. Harvey, ed., *The peasant land market in medieval England* (Oxford, 1984)
Wolf Hemmeon, de, M., *Burgage Tenure in Medieval England,* (Cambridge, Mass., 1914)
Woodcock, B. L., *Medieval ecclesiastical courts in the diocese of Canterbury* (Oxford, 1952)
Wrightson, K., 'Medieval villagers in perspective', *Peasant Studies* 7 (1978)

Unpublished theses

Bischoff, J. P., 'Economic change in thirteenth century Lincoln – the decline of a cloth industry' (unpublished Ph.D. thesis, Yale University, 1975)
Briggs, C. D., 'Credit and debt in medieval Cambridgeshire: Oakington, Cottenham and Dry Drayton, 1291–1348' (unpublished M.Phil thesis, University of Cambridge, 1998)
Briggs, C., 'Rural credit, debt litigation and the manor court in fourteenth-century England' (unpublished Research Fellowship dissertation, Trinity College, Cambridge, 2000)
Clark, E., 'Medieval debt litigation: Essex and Norfolk, 1270–1490' (unpublished Ph.D. thesis, University of Michigan, 1977)
Cohen, S., 'Plea Roll of the Exchequer of the Jews Michaelmas 1277 – Hilary 1279' (unpublished Ph.D. thesis, University of London, 1951)
Elman, P., 'Jewish finance in thirteenth century England with special reference to royal taxation', (unpublished M.A. thesis, University of London, 1936)
Lieberman, S. T., 'English royal policy towards the Jews' debtors, 1227–1290' (unpublished Ph.D. thesis, University of London, 1983)
McNall, C., 'The recognition and enforcement of debts under the statutes of Acton Burnell (1283) and Merchants (1285), 1283–1307' (unpublished D.Phil. thesis, University of Oxford, 2000)
Mundill, R. R., 'The Jews in England 1272–1290' (unpublished Ph.D. thesis, University of St Andrews, 1987)
Zwanzig Bennett, E., 'Debt and credit in the urban economy: London 1380–1460' (unpublished Ph.D. thesis, Yale University, 1989)

Subject Index